Additional Praise for
Supply Chain as Strategic Asset: The Key to Reaching Business Goals

"*Supply Chain as Strategic Asset* serves as a great prequel to *Enterprise Supply Chain Management*. Sehgal's new book helps wrap the framework of strategic planning around the supply chain capabilities previously covered. The combination of business theory with practical case studies and examples help drive home valuable lessons that executives should take to heart."

—David Landau,
Vice President, Manhattan Associates

"Business processes are the source of competitive advantage in the 21st century. Vivek Sehgal expertly connects the dots between business strategy and supply chain strategy. He explains that supply chain strategy must be derived from business strategy, but also that competitive advantage through supply chain must be built into the processes by pro-active design. The time for pushing industry best practices is over. As Vivek explains, now is the time to pro-actively create superior processes that will result in the creation of competitive advantage."

—Dustin Mattison,
Founder, logipi.com

"It goes without saying that a lot has changed and continues to change in business today. For those businesses with significant working capital commitment and risk associated with a smoothly functioning and adaptable supply chain these are challenging times. There are very few people who can translate the importance of a value added supply chain to a business than Mr. Sehgal. Take the translation one step further and you have a manual that peels back the layers for understanding and actionable knowledge. Like Vivek's previous book this is a must have on the shelf for not only supply chain executives, but those executives who want their supply chain capabilities to be competitive differentiators."

—Craig LaFrance,
Director of Business Development, CDC Software

Supply Chain as Strategic Asset

Supply Chain as Strategic Asset

The Key to Reaching Business Goals

VIVEK SEHGAL

WILEY

John Wiley & Sons, Inc.

Published by John Wiley & Sons, Inc., Hoboken, New Jersey.
Published simultaneously in Canada.

For general information on our other products and services or for technical support, please contact our Customer Care Department within the United States at (800) 762-2974, outside the United States at (317) 572-3993 or fax (317) 572-4002.

Wiley also publishes its books in a variety of electronic formats. Some content that appears in print may not be available in electronic books. For more information about Wiley products, visit our web site at www.wiley.com.

Library of Congress Cataloging-in-Publication Data:

Sehgal, Vivek.
  Supply chain as strategic asset : the key to reaching business goals / Vivek Sehgal.
    p. cm. — (Wiley corporate f&a ; 22)
  Includes index.
  ISBN 978-0-470-87477-6 (hardback); ISBN 978-0-470-93966-6 (ebk);
ISBN 978-0-470-93967-3 (ebk); ISBN 978-1-118-00287-2 (ebk)
  1. Business logistics. 2. Strategic management. I. Title.
  HD38.5.S444 2011
  658.7—dc22   2010031878

10 9 8 7 6 5 4 3 2 1

To Devyani, Parth, and Richa

Contents

Preface

CREATING AN EFFECTIVE SUPPLY chain is essential for a business to compete. But the scope of supply chains is so great that it is a tough task simply to *describe* what an effective supply chain is, let alone *create* one. This book provides a valuable road map for defining and creating a supply chain strategy that will help you build an effective supply chain that supports your business strategy. It begins by providing an overview of the development of the strategic management discipline to its current state and then proceeds to define supply chain strategies, reviewing the strengths and weaknesses along with the reasoning behind the selection of one specific strategy over others. It also investigates the relationship between some well-known business strategies and how they may affect the selection of the supply chain strategy.

While there is an abundance of literature on corporate strategy, there is not nearly enough thought given to the area of how the supply chain can support strategy and help achieve business goals. It is hoped that the reader will gain a fresh perspective on thinking strategically about the supply chain. Throughout the book you will also find sidebars with examples from the industry to illustrate a concept or to highlight a point made in the main text. Also covered in the book is the role of technology in this process and how technology, along with the supply chain, is a valuable tool to realize business goals.

The book concludes by showing how the three strategies—business, functional, and technology—need to work together in order to maximize performance. It shows how misalignment among the three creates friction and inefficiencies that prevent organizations from reaching their full potential. As part of the discussion, it explores the organizational structures that may help in establishing the culture for the alignment of the three strategies.

I hope that business and technology managers find this book to be particularly useful, and that it helps clarify how corporate strategies affect their supply chain and technology selections, why this relationship needs to be clearly understood, and how to create and maintain a nurturing organizational environment that values the convergence of the three strategies.

In my experience, most businesses currently fail to see this relationship. There are several reasons for this: the executive leadership generally grasps the concept of business strategy very well, but very few of them realize how supply chain strategy (as well as other functional strategies) provides them with the tools to realize the goals of their business strategy. The current thinking on supply chain strategy typifies supply chains as lean, agile, speculative, and so on. This is an inherently flawed view, because most supply chains will have to be all of the above to successfully support the complex business models of most modern corporations. This book presents a new way of thinking about supply chain strategy by first establishing the core process of balancing demand and supply and managing the inherent variations in both.

HOW IS THIS BOOK ORGANIZED?

Chapter 1

In this chapter, we provide an overview of the underlying precept of the book, which is the belief that the business strategy of a firm must define and drive the competitive advantages sought by it. In turn, these competitive advantages sustain the development and growth of the business of the firm. The process of the creation of superior business capabilities from the corporate strategy consists of the strategy development, strategy planning, and strategy execution. This chapter provides an overview of the process and describes these steps, and introduces the concepts of functional and deployment strategies and their relationships with the business strategy. In doing so, it lays the foundation for the rest of the book and the flow of the discussion on the subject of strategic alignment among the business, functional, and deployment strategies.

Chapters 2 and 3

In these two chapters, we will review the basic concepts of business strategy. This will be done by reviewing the existing literature and concepts on strategy development and management. We will review the fundamental strategies as first suggested by Porter and how these strategies affect the supply chain management functions in an organization. We will also review the resource-based view of strategy and the concept of competing on capabilities.

With real-life examples from the industry, we will see how the basic concepts of strategy have evolved and what that means to the strategy development and implementation processes for the companies today. The scope of recent changes in the global environment makes the process of strategy development more complex, as the number of factors and the amount of available information that must be considered has expanded. The amount of economic and demographic data that is currently generated and made available by various government agencies across the globe provides much greater visibility into our changing world, but also makes the task of strategy development very complex. The rapid rate of changes also affects the process of strategy development by requiring that business strategies are reviewed more frequently than ever before.

The major changes in the business environment in the past couple of decades have been driven by social, political, technology, and cost considerations. Examples of such changes are widespread: outsourcing, subcontracting of business functions, commoditization, telecommunications, megacorporations, regulations, and huge advances in companies' abilities to leverage IT systems in their pursuit for efficiency. These factors have considerably changed the business background and affected the way the underlying strategies should be formulated and deployed. Another consequence of the faster rate of change is that it requires companies to be more nimble to react, review, and adjust their strategies to remain competitive.

All these factors have changed the way that corporations have traditionally looked at the relationship between their corporate strategy formulation and realization. More than ever, it is important that corporations develop a clear and transparent process to translate their business strategy into business capabilities and the ability to deploy them using technology so that the cycle from strategy development to creation of capabilities can be shortened and the business strategy itself can be updated more frequently.

Since there is abundant literature available on corporate strategy formulation and development, we will keep that part of the discussion limited to a review of the main concepts on the subject, but spend more time on relating these concepts with the functional and deployment strategies as well as the impact of a changing business environment on the conventional concepts of business strategy as summarized earlier.

Chapters 4, 5, and 6

These three chapters of the book will focus on functional strategy: the definition of functional strategy, its concepts, and its role in supporting and realizing the strategic objectives. Functional strategy has not been included as an explicit part of strategy development in most companies and therefore provides an excellent opportunity for corporations to distinguish themselves by aligning their operations with their strategies through the development of a functional strategy. Functional strategy development is the part of strategic planning in which corporations must analyze their functional capabilities, understand the gaps that will cause strategic failure, understand the enhancements that will not only allow a short-term win but also provide a competitive advantage that can be sustained in the medium to longer term, and, finally, help them prioritize their investments into building the capabilities that are required for strategy realization.

Businesses need many different functions to operate effectively. Examples of such functions are human resources, marketing, product development, supply chain, merchandising, accounting, and so on. Any of these functional areas can become a strategic focus for the corporation, if the capabilities enabled by that function can help the company achieve the goals of its corporate strategy. However, we will focus primarily on the supply chain functions. We will review the fundamental strategies that can be pursued for designing supply chains, understand what these are and when to use them, and relate these supply chain strategies back to the business strategies to show how they can support the corporate strategies and help realize the goals set by these strategies. We will also review how these functional strategies not only depend on the business strategies, but also affect them in turn, setting up not a one-sided but an active two-sided relationship between the two.

Chapter 7

In this chapter, we will review the role of technology in today's corporations, with a specific focus on its ability to create and maintain capabilities that are central to the competitive advantages sought by their strategies. We will see why technology management should be viewed as one of the primary competencies of the business rather than as a supporting activity.

We will review enterprise architecture and its role in defining and implementing a technology strategy. We will also evaluate the current state of enterprise architecture in the corporations, its organizational limitations as well as the opportunities and potential evolution. We will identify factors that inhibit the enterprise architecture from successfully driving technological change that can lead the corporations from viewing the technology as a necessary evil to viewing it as an evolutionary enabler.

We use the technology strategy interchangeably with the term deployment strategy, because we see the technology strategy as the core component of the larger deployment strategy that may also include other aspects for successful deployment, such as organizational structure and change management. This interchangeability of the two terms is based in the belief that technology remains the most direct and tangible component of deployment strategy as an enabler for creation of strategic capabilities. In this context, the core objective of a deployment strategy consists of aligning the technology strategy with the business and functional strategies, so that capital investments can be prioritized toward the creation of coherent and sustainable solutions that create long-term competitive advantages for the corporation. Finally, we will see how achieving such an alignment provides an agile, flexible, and cost-effective process for the creation and maintenance of competitive advantages in an ever-changing business environment.

Chapter 8

In this concluding part of the book, we will review how the three strategies—business, functional, and technology—come together and enable a corporation to create and maintain competitive advantages that are sustainable in the long term. We will review what types of organizational structures support such an alignment and others that may inhibit it. We will review other organizational factors that affect successful strategy alignment and suggest how to manage them better to achieve the holy grail of functional capabilities that can keep a corporation at the edge of the value creation frontier.

A NOTE ON TERMS USED TO DENOTE STRATEGIES

Since we use many similar terms interchangeably, we would like to mention them up front.

Corporate strategy is used interchangeably with *business strategy*. In the context of this discussion, both of these refer to the output of strategic management exercises that establish the long-term direction for a corporation. Both these terms will generally refer to the strategy formulation or development aspect of business strategy. Some companies develop business strategies at several levels of the organization, such as their business units or regional organizations. This aspect of developing the business strategy at different organizational levels is not quite relevant in our context and, therefore, will be largely ignored in the discussion. The same is true for different types of strategies: for example, a strategy for growth, a strategy for market penetration, a strategy for customer service, and so on. While companies may pursue specific strategic directions for achieving different business goals, we will refer to the organizational strategies simply as *corporate* or *business strategy*.

Functional strategy primarily refers to the long-term direction selected by the corporation for developing functional capabilities. To achieve a specific goal set by the corporate strategy, corporations will generally have many options. These options will belong to different business functions and the corporation will have to select one or more of these functional groups to create the functional capabilities that would help the company move towards its strategic goals. Since this book is primarily about *supply chain strategy*, these two terms are used interchangeably depending on the specific context of the sentence. *Functional strategy* is used when the statement makes sense across functions and *supply chain strategy* when it is specific to the supply chain function.

Deployment strategy and *technology strategy* have also been used interchangeably. The *deployment strategy* refers to the larger context to manage the deployments of specific projects/programs. In this larger context, the *deployment strategy* may have components addressing technology, change management, organizational incentives, success metrics, and so on. *Technology strategy* refers specifically to the long-term direction established to manage technology. When seen in the context of capital investment layouts, technology remains the largest and most important part of a deployment strategy through its ability to enable business processes, constrain the scope and impact of business processes, and its effect on long-term costs for sustaining the competitive advantages. Therefore, *deployment strategy* and *technology strategy* have been used interchangeably throughout this book.

We refer to a *business function* as a collection of *business processes* that together enable a logical function. For example, demand forecasting will be a *business function* that provides the ability to produce demand forecasts. However, the individual *processes* that enable this function consist of processes for collecting historical demand data, processes of cleansing this data, processes of creating statistical forecasts, and so on. While that is the general usage of the terms *business function* and *business process*, they are also sometimes used as equivalent to each other. *Business function* is sometimes simply called *function* and is also used as a synonym for *functionality* or *functional capability* or *functional competence*, based on the context.

Acknowledgments

I AM THANKFUL TO Manhattan Associates for their support throughout the project and for creating an environment where thought-provoking discussions encourage learning every day. Thanks to our CEO, Pete Sinisgalli, for his encouragement, and to our EVP, Eddie Capel, for always being open to explore new ideas and concepts and for making time for stimulating discussions on how supply chains can provide the strategic edge to pioneering firms, big and small. I also wish to thank my friend Randy Hill, who was kind enough to review some of the initial drafts to validate concepts and provide feedback.

Introduction

WHILE THE SUPPLY CHAINS of today extend through most of the value chain activities of a business as originally described by Porter, they are essentially a set of capabilities that organizations build to operate, survive, and grow. *Harvard Business Review*'s capability-based view of business strategies contends that it is essentially the organizational capabilities that create competitive advantages. Organizations that have more superior capabilities than their peers in their industry will normally have a competitive advantage over them. Conversely, a competitive advantage can be created by carefully building the organizational capabilities. Organizational capabilities may belong to one of the many functions that businesses must master to compete effectively. Supply chain management happens to be one such function. Building superior supply chain capabilities then becomes a tool in the hands of business leaders to not only support efficient operations, but to wield as a competitive asset that can be leveraged to create competitive advantages.

If you had to decide what supply chain capabilities your company should build to create advantage, what would they be? Supply chains have a wide variety of functions affecting the whole value chain of a business from the inbound raw materials through production and distribution of finished goods to the customers. Given this large scope, what should an ideal supply chain enable, how should it support the business, and how can one decide what capabilities should be created making the best use of capital investments to create competitive advantages that not only support today's requirements, but also position the company for future growth and profitability?

We are all familiar with constantly juggling the conflicting goals of minimizing inventory while establishing the highest service levels, reducing labor while increasing throughput, and reducing supply costs while maintaining stable supplies. We know that a supply chain that is integrated with the rest of the business functions, that senses changes, adapts, optimizes, and works within the larger business context, without any conflicts would be great. What we grapple with is how this vision can be translated into specific capabilities, prioritized, deployed, and measured. This is not a theoretical discussion: Pioneering companies must continuously define their best supply chain practices, determine what are their peers doing, and decide which capabilities they must build to leverage their supply chains as a competitive asset.

The supply chain's wide footprint does not help. Its equally wide impact on everything from day-to-day operations to return on assets (ROA) also makes it complex to size it up. Even defining what comprises an effective supply chain is no easy task. Is it the ability to quickly react to volatile demand? Is it the ability to maintain the highest inventory turnover in the industry? Does it mean having the lowest days of accounts receivable? What about accounts payable? Shortest cash-to-cash cycle? Highest ROA? Agility? Lean manufacturing? Optimal product mix? Highest resource utilization?

In fact, an effective supply chain may do all of the above or none of them. What makes up an effective supply chain is unique to each business and its context must be constrained by the business goals of the company. The current supply chain strategy literature talks about a supply chain being either lean or agile or speculative, or having another type of attribute, as if there is a singular type of supply chain that you can design and create that will address all your business needs. The reality is more complex. Any real supply chain must be agile but also lean, it should be demand-driven but also supply-aware, it should help lower costs but also raise efficiency. The fact is that a lot of the success metrics that we relate with supply chains are opposites, and so are the demands placed on the supply chains. That is why there is no *right* supply chain prescription—it is only *right* for you if it *works* for you. In this context there really are no templates for creating the *right* supply chain; rather, it is a private affair, a customized plan, a personal destination that every company must define and pursue for itself.

Therefore, creating a supply chain that is an organizational asset becomes a corporate quest that may draw from research, innovation, partnership, and solutions, but must define for each company the goals of that company, in terms of how supply chain capabilities should be aligned with the larger corporate strategy. The organization must also define a deployment strategy to create these supply chain capabilities that lead to competitive advantage for the corporation that can be sustained and evolved continuously in tandem with corporate strategy. A supply chain that is a competitive advantage can only be created through thoughtful design that follows the diktats of the business strategy. Without such an explicit alignment, there would always be conflicts between what the business seeks and what the supply chain can deliver.

An organically grown supply chain is reactive by design and therefore cannot become an asset to be leveraged for growth or competitive advantage. This means that for a supply chain to become a strategic asset, capabilities must be analyzed and business requirements explicitly stated that align to business goals. Once the capabilities are known, they must be enabled, which increasingly happens through the tools of new technology. Technology has become the de facto enabler of business capabilities. It is great for creating cost-effective, streamlined, and standard processes that are largely skill independent. Technology has been the single largest contributor for increasing productivity over the past few decades, as the figures for productivity in the nonfarm businesses of the United States show. However, technology brings additional complexity that needs to be managed and that is where the deployment strategy comes in. Just as the supply chain strategy needs to be explicitly aligned with the business strategy, a deployment strategy must align with the goal of enabling the supply chain capabilities. This deployment strategy must ensure that the technology complexity remains manageable, but cost-effective and capable of enabling the desired business capabilities. (See Figure I.1.)

Let us dwell a little more on these concepts:

1. Corporate strategy must drive the supply chain capabilities. This is essential for various reasons, some of which we will touch upon here. A supply chain cannot realistically evolve in a vacuum; if it does, then the likelihood

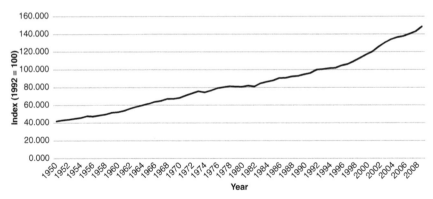

FIGURE I.1 U.S. Productivity for Nonfarm Business Sector, Index (Output per Hour)

Source: Bureau of Labor Statistics (Series Id PRS85006093).

of its being able to support the strategic goals is slim. A supply chain designed in a vacuum will idealize theoretical capabilities that may not create any competitive advantages. Supply chains can also not be a result of reacting to organic growth. These supply chains are reactive by design and therefore, do not create any competitive advantage: they simply bring a company up to its peers in that industry segment. This leaves the obvious choice: The supply chains must be diligently designed to create capabilities that will allow companies to achieve the goals of their business strategy by explicitly creating the desired competitive advantages.

Supply chains are fundamental to create capabilities that, in turn, create competitive advantages supporting the corporate strategy. If the *right* capabilities are created, then the corporation enhances its likelihood of having day-to-day operations that are aligned with its larger goals and therefore move the corporation towards its stated objectives. If the *right* supply chain capabilities are not created, then the operations will not be able to support the strategic goals of the corporation, creating inherent internal frictions and inefficiencies. Therefore, misalignment between the corporate strategy and its supply chain strategy will definitely result in poor, inefficient operations and a low return on assets, and also directly affect the corporation's ability to realize its business strategy.

Supply chain initiatives are expensive and require capital investments. For the supply chain initiatives to be successful contenders for the capital investments, they must be aligned with the corporate strategy and support the strategic goals of the firm. In turn, the capabilities they create have the potential to become long-term *process assets* for the corporation.

Supply chain systems do not operate in isolation. They operate in larger system landscapes interacting with many other corporate systems, exchanging data and information, affecting other processes, accepting inputs, and providing outputs to support multifunctional processes that cut across departmental and organizational boundaries. This means that the supply chains cannot be developed in isolation, but must be thought of and planned as an integral part of other corporate systems. This requires that the supply chain development align itself with the corporate strategy so that it is also aligned with the larger corporate landscape, supported by and supporting the other systems that it interacts with.

2. A deployment strategy must exist that supports both, the corporate and the supply chain strategies. A well-developed deployment strategy can help in creating a viable ecosystem of processes to create strategic capabilities allowing for *flexibility*, *efficiency*, and *sustainability*. Since technology has

been the single biggest enabler of such capabilities, our discussion of deployment strategy will be primarily limited to technology strategy. To that extent, this book uses the two terms interchangeably.

Technology strategy then becomes critical in the quest for creating supply chain capabilities that are not only aligned with the corporate strategy but have been implemented in such a way that allows them to evolve and keeps them sustainable over the long term. These are two of the most critical aspects of any capability, if it is to provide a competitive advantage to the corporation. Evolution is the capacity to *extend* and *enhance* a capability, once it has been put in place. For example, after a statistical forecasting capability has been created, it can be extended by adopting this for new merchandise, by an extended forecast horizon, or by other downstream processes such as price-optimization. It can also be enhanced by adding the ability to consider price as a demand-influencing factor, in addition to the historical sales that are typically the input, to the statistical forecasting. The extension primarily refers to the extension of scope where a capability can be used, and enhancement refers to the enrichment of the capability by its ability to model more parameters to closely model real-life scenarios. Generally speaking, the ability to extend and enhance any capability that is enabled through technology depends heavily on technology itself. Hence, the technology strategy needs to provide such *flexibility*.

The second attribute of the technology strategy is *efficiency*. This refers to how quickly it allows the corporation to create new capabilities or enhance existing ones. The current focus on service-oriented architecture (SOA) is an example of a technology strategy that allows efficiency of capability creation and enhancement. Efficiency affects the cost of creating or enhancing a capability and the speed with which it is created. The extent of competitive advantage created by a capability is directly proportional to the cost and speed of creating it. With time, all competitive advantages may perish and the speed of creating them faster allows the pioneers to leverage them longer than their peers in the industry.

The third attribute of the technology strategy mentioned here is *sustainability*. This refers to the cost of maintaining the capability over the long term: in technology parlance, total cost of ownership (TCO). Any technology strategy that is not sustainable over time will eventually fail to support the supply chain and corporate strategies.

3. A supply chain strategy must exist for it to become a competitive asset. This is another way of saying that supply chain capabilities must be explicitly

designed and pursued for deployment in a proactive manner to create competitive advantages. A reactive supply chain enabled through organic growth of business capabilities cannot deliver competitive benefits. The supply chain strategy directs the evolution of supply chain capabilities that the corporate strategy requires. However, the supply chain capabilities build on themselves and are integrated with other corporate systems. This creates a logical evolutionary sequence that should be followed for the optimal development of the supply chain processes.

A well-designed supply chain strategy process should allow the corporation to assemble a larger picture of the desired supply chain capabilities and to evaluate their dependencies among themselves and with other functions. Such a planning process allows for evaluating the feasibility of success for creating these capabilities through the technology strategy. This enables the corporations to create an optimal and logical sequence for the development of supply chain capabilities that support the corporate strategy, can be implemented within the constraints of the technology strategy, and are harmoniously integrated with other corporate systems.

Supply chain strategy is derived from the corporate strategy but, in turn, it also affects the evolution of the corporate strategy. For example, if a company creates a comprehensive demand management capability that allows it to accurately forecast demand and manage its inventories, then the resulting growth in revenues (by reducing lost sales) and profitability (by reducing the need for scheduled clearance events) may prompt a focus on a cost-based corporate strategy where the corporation pursues the goal of being a price leader. In an alternative scenario, if the supply chain capabilities were to produce a close to 100 percent perfect order fulfillment rate, the focus of corporate strategy may move to customer differentiation through guaranteed order fulfillment.

A similar relationship exists between the supply chain strategy and technology strategy. Functional strategies (such as the supply chain strategy) affect technology strategies and, in turn, are shaped by them. If a supply chain strategy mandated real-time inventory updates from its stores and warehouses to the corporate offices and a technology strategy responded by creating a reliable network with distributed applications, then the supply chain strategy becomes free to leverage the newly created technology infrastructure for creating other functional capabilities, such as collaborating with stores on their replenishment plans or real-time price changes.

When all three strategies discussed here are aligned and integrated in a symbiotic, *mutually beneficial* relationship, the corporation can truly create a competitive asset through its supply chain. In this state, the supply chain capabilities are aligned with the corporate strategy and directly support its goals. The technology strategy is aligned with the requirements of functional strategies and provides a flexible and sustainable way to create and maintain the process capabilities mandated by the business strategy. The business strategy, in turn, leverages all the deployed functional capabilities and evolves with the knowledge that these capabilities can be continuously enhanced in a sustainable fashion so that the corporation always remains at the edge of the *value creation* frontier.[1]

Supply Chain as Strategic Asset

CHAPTER ONE

Planning and Realizing the Goals of a Business Strategy

T HE OBJECTIVE OF THIS chapter is to familiarize the reader with the subject of this book as well as set the expectations for how this will be discussed. The basic premise of the book is the concept that a strategy can be realized by creating business capabilities. To that extent, the role of the strategy is to establish the goals and the role of capabilities is to provide a way to realize those goals by creating competitive advantages embedded within regular business operations. This is the precept that we will follow throughout this book.

The capabilities we will be focusing on are specifically the supply chain capabilities of an organization. In recent years, the functional footprints of supply chains have grown to include most of the original value-chain functions envisaged by Michael Porter in his groundbreaking work on business strategy and the creation of competitive advantages. Therefore, the supply chain remains the key to realizing the business goals of a company. While supply chain capabilities include processes and the supply chain network, consisting of facilities for manufacturing, sourcing, stocking, and selling, the warehouse, transport equipment, and labor, it is the process capabilities that tie these resources together and create the ability to leverage these resources in the most effective manner. *To that extent, the focus of our discussion implicitly remains on the supply chain processes, even though it is assumed that the physical resources that a process would need are present as required.*

Technology is heavily used in enabling the process capabilities and this dependence brings the technology strategy into the equation. We will progressively cover all these topics as we build our case for aligning the strategies.

STRATEGY

Strategic management has become a mainstay of the corporate world in the past few decades. It started as a balancing act between the external and internal forces in a corporation where the firm matched its (internal) strengths and weaknesses against the (external) opportunities and threats.[1] Porter then provided a more detailed framework to conceive of the corporate strategy through his Five Forces (see Figure 2.2) and three fundamental strategies based on cost, differentiation, and focus. Since then, corporate strategy has evolved in many ways and researchers have enriched the basic concept in several different ways. Business strategy that leads to competitive advantages has many facets: it can be viewed through the lens of the three fundamental types of strategies as Porter suggested, as a balance between the internal and external forces, or as competitive advantage gained through resources, products, technology, and other specific organizational skills that may be difficult for the competition to imitate. As the business environment changes, firms may have to rethink strategy and realign their efforts to leverage the changes in the external business environment.

For example, consider the strategy now being adopted by the big music labels as the Web-based digital downloads become the mainstay for an industry that had traditionally relied on selling CDs through a retail distribution system. After the initial failed attempts to resist the change and throwing legal challenges to the fundamental shifts in the environment, the industry finally had to transform itself and change their strategy from a retail/distribution model to a digital download model. Along the way, they have to redefine their processes, throw away capabilities they had developed over time and create new capabilities that did not exist. Think of the distribution model for music in the 1980s and 1990s compared to the distribution model prevalent today. The physical distribution channels and all related processes of manufacturing, distribution, logistics, and store-based selling are no longer important in the new landscape. The management of inventories as the music charts changed the demand for specific artists/songs, the process for determining what to sell, what to stock and how much, and when to start the clearance sales have ceased to be relevant in an industry that is going digital. The new distribution processes need skills that are very different from the previous ones. The new model concerns itself more with the bandwidth for downloads and electronic copyrights protection algorithms rather than worrying about safety stocks and shipping costs.

Such change is constant. While the pace of change will be different in different industries, change itself remains a constant. Since change is a constant, all corporations must continually move to adapt to such change. Those who have explicitly invested in strategy will continue to move toward their stated objectives in spite of the changes in their environment, while others may just move involuntarily in response to external and internal forces. Most large corporations have a strategy, though the extent of formal discipline applied to the strategy varies from one company to the next. Accordingly, corporate strategy in a company may either be formally structured with a lot of thought put into it or more informal. It can be well articulated or not so well expressed. It may be well accepted and appreciated or not. It is both attractive and effective, however, to have a strategy that is publicly articulated and that can be elaborated in various analyst calls to provide justification for a corporation's actions, investments, direction, and plans.

For now, let us leave the subject of strategy here with the assumption that the basic concepts of strategic management are well understood and a well-established part of corporate management mind-set today. We will revisit the subject in detail later in the book.

STRATEGY REALIZATION THROUGH FUNCTIONAL CAPABILITIES

What comes next is the main concern of this book. To be effective, a strategy must be implemented. This means that the strategy that establishes the corporate intent, through which competitive advantage will be created, must then be expanded to articulate actions that will take the business toward its strategic goals. As shown in Figure 1.1, the whole process can be thought of as consisting of three basic steps:

1. Strategy *development*, that is, the process of evaluating the internal and external imperatives, analyzing the industry, products, and customers, and defining an overriding principle of how the company will try to grow. This is equivalent to defining the "what" and "why" of the problem.

Strategy Development	Strategy Planning	Strategy Implementation
Process of establishing the central principle of business growth by careful analysis of external and internal environments, industry, products, and customers.	Process of assessing current state of business capabilities and determining gaps to be filled to support the direction set by the business strategy for business growth.	Process of defining, starting, and managing individual projects to create business capabilities aligned with the stated business strategy and prioritized through planning.

FIGURE 1.1 Strategy Life Cycle

2. Strategy *planning* is the process of assessing the current state of the corporation and evaluating various alternatives that can be potentially considered to achieve the stated imperatives of the business strategy. This step consists of analysis, evaluation, articulation, and prioritization of these alternatives, in effect defining the "how" of the problem.

3. Strategy *implementation* is the process of starting and managing the individual projects to implement the favored alternative from step two.

Let us refer to the combined steps 2 and 3, the process of analysis, evaluation, prioritization, articulation, and implementation of the components of strategy as the process of strategy *realization*. This is depicted in Figure 1.2.

Why use the term strategy realization? Strategy realization provides the broader context than is provided by a weaker term like strategy execution. It emphasizes the distinction between strategy planning and strategy execution, both of which must be addressed to successfully realize a corporate strategy.

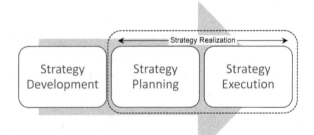

FIGURE 1.2 Scope of Strategy Realization

Firms cannot jump from strategy development to strategy execution, and strategy planning must connect the two. Therefore, strategy realization is an explicit choice to denote that the realization is much more than execution.

Before any strategy can be executed, it must be analyzed to understand the answers to the following questions. What goals does it establish for the corporation? What capabilities are required to achieve these goals? Which ones of these capabilities are new? Which ones exist but must be enhanced or extended? What is the cost of developing these capabilities? What is the sustainability cost of these capabilities? What kind of competitive advantage do these capabilities create? Can this competitive advantage be sustained? How long can such an advantage be sustained? What are the constraints to such capability development? These and similar questions are what are addressed by the strategy planning step. They help the organization translate strategy into goals and required capabilities. They also help in prioritizing the development of such capabilities, thereby driving capital investment to support the strategy.

STRATEGY PLANNING: THE MISSING LINK

While most companies have some level of formally defined business strategy and an ongoing slew of projects creating new capabilities and enhancing existing ones, most do not have a formal process for the activities identified in the strategy planning step. This void is also reflected in the existing literature on corporate strategy: there are plenty of books on strategy development, a few on strategy execution, but practically none on strategy planning that connects development to execution. Strategy execution emphasizes the actual execution activities: program management, project management, change management, communication, training, and all other organizational aspects for successful execution. While that is important, the intermediate analysis provided by strategy planning is the missing link in most modern corporations in any recognizable formal fashion. In absence of this planning step, corporations fail to establish and prioritize the execution efforts that are aligned with the goals of the business strategy, and fail to identify and prioritize the filling of specific capability gaps. Throughout the book, this will become clear as we describe real-life corporate examples, analyze their strategic successes and failures, and relate them to their financial performance and goals.

Consider a corporation that wants to follow a cost leadership strategy. To realize this strategy, the corporation must develop capabilities that would establish cost leadership for its products that are similar to those offered by its competition and provide comparable value to the consumers. The cost advantage can be derived by gaining efficiency in many functions. It may be derived from creative sourcing practices, cheaper manufacturing methods, or reduction in the cost of operations and logistics. Each one of these options will result in providing the corporation with some amount of cost leadership. Each one of these options will also require a definite amount of capital to develop, adopt, and maintain that capability. These options will result into changes: organizational, process, and cultural, that must be managed for successful adoption. Finally, each of these options will provide a strategic advantage with a limited amount of sustainability as other companies race to develop similar capabilities and the advantage is lost. These are the questions that are answered in the strategy planning step. It helps to define these options, analyze them, evaluate their costs and sustainability, and help the corporation eliminate options that are not right for them. The analysis must also identify any process, technology, and organizational constraints that must be addressed for successfully developing the selected capabilities for cost leadership. If the firm decides to derive the cost advantage through investing in new manufacturing technology, then it will need to evaluate and decide, in addition to the capital costs, whether it has trained personnel who are ready to execute the new technology, whether the new technology will impact any downstream or upstream processes, how this will affect their throughput and efficiency, depreciation, operating cash flow, and so on. Any gaps that this analysis may reveal must be addressed or they may threaten successful execution and negatively affect the overall results further on in the execution cycle.

Therefore, developing the right set of capabilities is the primary key to strategy realization, as shown in Figure 1.3. Strategy planning helps in

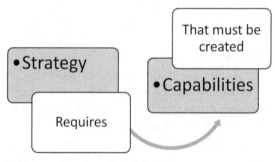

FIGURE 1.3   A Strategy Requires Capabilities

identifying and prioritizing these capabilities before strategy execution can take over the implementation of individual programs and projects to make them a reality. These capabilities create or enhance functional competencies in a corporation. *Functional competencies are a set of related business processes that are unique to the corporation in providing a specific capability and hence creating the competitive advantage.* Wal-Mart's capabilities in inventory management and distribution are examples of such functional competencies. While the individual pieces of inventory management at Wal-Mart may be standardized (such as using a predetermined ordering level with continuous inventory review), their integration with other Wal-Mart processes provides the related set of business processes creating a unique functional competency that creates the competitive advantage. As long as other firms are unable to replicate similar process integration, Wal-Mart will have a sustained advantage through this capability. Figure 1.4 shows this relationship, in which the strategy requires capabilities that are created through building functional competencies, which is a set of related business processes *unique* to a corporation.

To create long-term sustainable competitive advantage, firms must evaluate their functional competencies to decide where the best opportunities exist that are aligned with their functional strengths and will allow the firm to realize their strategy. We will call this the firm's functional strategy. The functional strategy is derived from the business strategy by analyzing the capabilities that must be created to realize the business strategy. Functional strategy is aligned with and supports the business strategy. Functional strategy provides the first step toward strategy realization by establishing and prioritizing the capabilities that must be created.

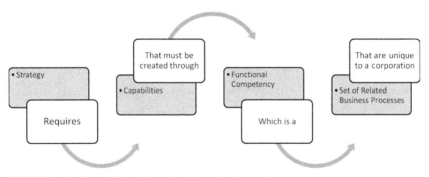

FIGURE 1.4 Capabilities Required by a Business Strategy

TECHNOLOGY AS THE ENABLER

Now, let us turn our attention to how these capabilities are created and supported in the modern context. Let us review our definition of capabilities: they are functional competencies that are sets of related business processes (remember the implicit focus on process capabilities and the assumption that physical resources required by these processes will be created and made available as part of creating the process capability). This brings the current discussion to technology because technology is the main support for all business processes across modern corporations. Technology has become the all-pervasive, omnipresent, underlying foundation that creates, supports, and constrains the business processes in all major corporations. *Technology, therefore, can be the beneficent enabler for the business to create competitive advantage or the wretched constraint that becomes an anchor stuck in the sands of time to prevent progress.* Since technology provides the foundation for all business processes and enables or constrains the creation of new capabilities, this is the next logical step in strategy planning and realization. This concept is shown in Figure 1.5, which extends the concept presented in Figure 1.4 by adding technology as the enabler of the business processes.

While Porter and others grouped technology in the secondary or supporting activities for a corporation, the technology has finally moved to the forefront and must be looked at as one of the primary capabilities for any firm. Today, it is almost inconceivable to think of a firm existing without some amount of technology supporting its processes, which, in turn, create and support the capabilities of the firm. Therefore, the ability to manage technology has moved from a

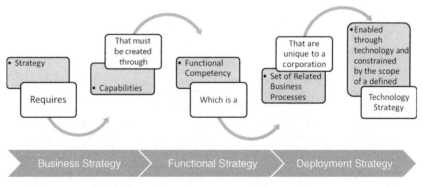

FIGURE 1.5 From Business Strategy to Functional Strategy to Deployment Strategy

KMART **VERSUS WAL-MART**

A great example of this appears in the study of Kmart versus Wal-Mart. While Kmart held a position of advantage in the early 1980s, Wal-Mart quickly overtook it in only a decade by developing superior supply chain capabilities enabled by technology. While Wal-Mart's supply chain capabilities have received wide recognition, the fact remains that Wal-Mart could not have been successful if it had not also developed a significant capability to leverage technology at the same time. It is unthinkable that a company the size of Wal-Mart (in 1991 when Wal-Mart's revenues surpassed Kmart's, it reported over $30 billion in sales; it now has revenues over $400 billion) would have been successful in creating key supply chain capabilities without technology. It is also unthinkable that Kmart, which was comparable to Wal-Mart in sales (and larger in fact, by store count) did not have the capital to invest in similar efforts. In fact, in the early 1990s, Wal-Mart and Kmart were both credited with having the "most sophisticated distribution systems among all of the retailers in the world."[2] Both followed a "low price" strategy coupled with large discount stores and sophisticated distribution systems. However, Kmart was unable to manage technology to consistently align its capabilities with its strategies for growth and survival. Kmart tried to grow through acquisitions but never developed the capability to successfully leverage technology to integrate and operate these acquired assets profitably. In contrast, Wal-Mart primarily grew organically (with some exceptions, such as Philips Food Centers, MacLane Company, and The Wholesale Club) and consistently improved its supply chain capabilities through investments in technology. The expanded example is provided at the end of Chapter 7.

former, secondary position to primary prominence, and firms that are unable or unwilling to see this shift will perish.

A well-thought-out technology strategy can go a long way in providing the flexibility that a business will inevitably need. Technology involves substantial capital investments to procure, install, and maintain, and therefore must become part of the strategic planning process to provide a long-term foundation that supports the current operations and does not hinder the evolution of a business strategy as the environment changes and the firm adapts. In fact, there is no dearth of examples to show where absence of technology strategy has resulted in substantial loss of corporate performance, as well as examples where technology strategy has provided the foundation for building and maintaining competitive advantage.

We will refer to this alternately as the deployment strategy throughout this book. Deployment strategy provides a larger context for the deployment of technology as well as the deployment of business processes enabled by such technology. Deployment strategy must also be aligned with the business and functional strategies of the firm and must support both. Since a lack of proper technology can constrain the business capabilities that can be effectively deployed, therefore, the deployment strategy constrains the scope of such capabilities for the realization of business strategy.

CREATING COMPETITIVE ADVANTAGE THROUGH FUNCTIONAL CAPABILITIES

The focus of this book is to evaluate how the functional capabilities create competitive advantage and why it is imperative that the firms understand the correlation among the business, functional, and deployment strategies to achieve sustained competitive advantage. A 1995 article[3] in *Harvard Business Review* on corporate strategy talked about a *resource-based view* (RBV) of the firm. In this view, companies are seen as "different collections of physical and intangible assets and capabilities." The authors further argue that "competitive advantage ultimately can be attributed to the ownership of a valuable resource that enables the company to perform activities better." The "valuable resource" in this definition is a tangible or intangible resource or a capability. In contrast, the argument that we are going to follow is that capabilities are the core driver for creating and maintaining the competitive advantages while the tangible or intangible assets are merely the by-products of such capabilities. For example, owning proven oil fields can be a big tangible asset for an oil company, however, unless they also possess the capability to harness the fields (technology, processes, capital, and labor), those oil fields (the tangible asset) by themselves are only an advantage in theory. Conversely, creating an effective process capability can sometimes result in tangible assets. A successfully created capability to reduce inventories may result in free operating cash flow that can then be used for any other purpose, such as to acquire a tangible asset in the form of a warehouse or store. Similarly, the capability to have perfect order fulfillment may enhance a corporation's reputation for being customer-centric, which then becomes an intangible strategic asset that can be leveraged in a differentiation strategy.

Therefore, while this RBV view is somewhat aligned with the capability view presented here, the authors fail to emphasize the strong connection between the corporate strategy and functional capabilities that becomes the core driver for the firms to realize their strategy.

While capabilities to gain competitive advantage can be developed in diverse business functions, our primary focus will be the supply chain capabilities and the competitive advantages that can be created through such capabilities. The examples provided throughout this book will use the supply chain as the key functional area to create competitive capabilities. Supply chain process capabilities primarily help in reducing costs or increasing the efficiency of capital used, while simultaneously supporting operational flexibility and agility, all of which can be directly leveraged to support most basic business strategies based on price leadership, differentiation, or focus.

Reducing costs as a strategy has become a primary strategy for many businesses in recent years. There are several reasons for this, but the most important reason is that the increasing globalization results in more and more commoditization of products that deteriorate the brand premiums and indirectly deal a blow to product differentiation as a strategy. The face of this commoditization in America is Wal-Mart and its assortment of cheap functional products that address the utilitarian functions without the brand premium. But this process is not limited to America: it is widespread across the globe, with the growth of the middle class in China and India and their aspirations to match the lifestyles of developed countries at a fraction of the cost. Both of these phenomena, that of Wal-Mart driving down costs to expand its market share and of developing countries providing new markets for cheaper utilitarian products, have propelled cost as a strategy to the forefront of the three fundamental strategies suggested by Porter. If cost is the core strategy of choice, then supply chain becomes the core business function that can help corporations realize that strategy. Examples of creating and maintaining competitive advantage through supply chain capabilities abound, with Wal-Mart being the most obvious and visible. However, these supply chain capabilities must be aligned with the strategic goals of the corporation to successfully create the competitive advantages that the corporation seeks.

When companies pursue differentiation or focus as their primary strategies, the focus of the corporate supply chain capabilities must be to produce process agility and flexibility, rather than reducing the cost of operations. Customer-focused capabilities such as having the visibility of inventory across the chain and the ability to accurately predict the status of orders and delivery can lead to create the differentiation that is sought by businesses. Product-focused capabilities can provide similar differentiation through the ability to personalize individual orders or products based on customer preferences. Companies like Nike and Land Rover have successfully developed supply chain capabilities to support their differentiating strategies that allow customers to personalize their products, with accurate projections of when those products will be manufactured and delivered. This requires that their supply chains must have visibility into inventory and labor across the entire supply chain, to be able to promise the final delivery of product personalized to their customer's tastes.

Finally, no strategy can guarantee a sustained competitive advantage unless it evolves, reacts, predicts, and even preempts the changes in the environment. Such evolution will almost always result in the changes required in the capabilities developed. As most such capabilities are closely tied to the business processes and depend on technology, the ability to develop these capabilities to support the evolving and shifting strategic push requires that firms develop equally agile functional and technology strategies that not only allows the initial creation of these capabilities, but continuously support their evolution, as well.

THE ALIGNMENT OF BUSINESS, FUNCTIONAL, AND TECHNOLOGY STRATEGIES

So far, we have established the outlines of the three strategies—business, functional, and technology—and a general idea of why they should be aligned. The objective of this book is to describe a clear line of dependence among these three strategies, their relationships with one another, and therefore their ability to affect and support each other.

Business strategies tend to be generic and we will review the three basic strategies suggested by Porter as well as some other concepts, such as the resource- and capability-based views of competitive strategies. In an enterprise, adopting any of these strategies requires many diverse initiatives that are spread across a wide spectrum of business functions. All these initiatives together are designed to support the goals of the strategy. For example, a customer differentiation strategy may trigger several developments in various business functions: enhancing the ability to fulfill orders faster by reducing lead time, providing inventory visibility, increasing perfect order fulfillment rates, providing customization opportunities, self-service for tracking order status, setting up help lines, investing in training associates, providing help in using the product, creating customer credit options, and so on. While the initiatives in the examples are not exhaustive by any means, they already cover several business functions within the enterprise: supply chain, merchandising, customer service, and finance. This is quite true for almost any strategy at the enterprise level due to their generic nature and higher-level goals. While this book uses such examples to demonstrate how these different functions support the basic business strategies, we will continue to use supply chain examples when discussing details and in order to explain the underlying concepts and relationships between the business strategy and functional strategy.

The functional strategy section of the book will explain the general foundation of the concept of functional strategies and establish how these strategies help define the process capabilities required to support the business goals. We will then use the discussion to develop and define supply chain strategies and establish the relationship between the supply chain strategies and the three basic business strategies based on cost, product differentiation, and customer focus. We will see how successful corporations ensure that these strategies are aligned and leverage the synergies produced through such an alignment, as well as how they have created competitive advantage and sustained such advantage in the face of inevitable changes in the environment. Finally, we discuss how your company can do the same by following a formal process to align and realign these strategies as the marketplace changes and new realities emerge.

The discussion on technology strategy is designed to be open and equally applicable to all functional strategies, although we will continue to derive our examples from the supply chain functions to further build and support the functional focus.

Aligning the three strategies is the shortest, fastest, and least expensive way for a firm to achieve its desired competitive position. It prevents waste and experimentation, forces analysis and thoughtful decision-making, creates awareness of the firm's needs, and provides an objective criterion to make capital investments. Achieving such an alignment is equivalent to "achieving lean" in the strategy process itself, from development through planning to execution.

2

Understanding Strategy

ORPORATIONS ARE PRIMARILY FINANCIAL entities whose main objective is to create wealth for their shareholders. This is a passive definition, because it fails to communicate the complexities of all the functions that must be managed and aligned on a daily basis to achieve the goals of the corporation. Of course, for best results, the company's daily operations and functional capabilities must support their business strategy for survival and growth. The objective of business strategy is to ensure the continued economic growth of the corporate entity and to increase its market value through competitive positioning of the company and a close alignment between the business strategy and operational capabilities of the company ensures that the company makes a little progress every day in moving toward its stated business goals. Hill and Jones's value creation frontier, shown in Figure 2.1, captures the concept that corporations must continuously strive to be somewhere on this value creation frontier to be competitive.

 WHAT IS STRATEGY?

Strategy is fundamental to business strategy, but what is strategy? Defining strategy is not easy; the word has varied connotations and often requires a

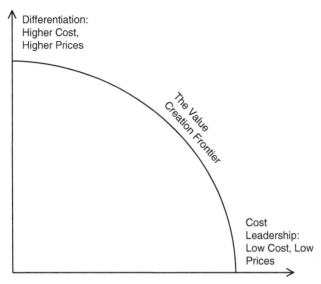

FIGURE 2.1   Value Creation Frontier

Source: Adapted from Hill and Jones, *Strategic Management Theory* (Houghton Mifflin Company, 2006).

specific context to be understood. For this discussion, that context is business. But even when strategy is viewed within the context of business, the multitude of dimensions, the wide scope of business functions, long-term planning horizons, somewhat subjective forecasts of the business environment—all make the concept of strategy so abstract that it is difficult to nail down a single definition. However, most of us innately understand what strategy is; we know what it is when we talk about it or think about it. Therefore, instead of addressing the question directly and trying to find the words to define *strategy*, let us look at some analogies in order to establish a few facts about it.

If you are a skier, you would likely be familiar with the ski maps of your favorite resort. These maps lay out the ski paths, clearly identifying dangerous slopes and other obstructions that a skier should avoid. However, the ski maps don't necessarily show each and every tree stump and boulder, other skiers, or cliffs along the route. The intention of the ski map is simply to establish the overall direction and provide landmarks along the way to help the skier keep on the track. The skier is ultimately responsible for coming down the mountain without running into other skiers, trees, boulders, and other visible or perceived obstructions. And as long as the skier aligns his action of descending the route shown in the map, he can be reasonably sure of making it down safely. Along the path, the skier is bound to come across some of the obstructions noted on the map, static as they are in nature, such as trees and cliffs. But they would also encounter an ever-changing trail opening in front of them as other skiers cross their path, appearing and disappearing as they too traverse the same terrain. It is the objective of our skier to use the map to their advantage, but also to ensure that they successfully dodge other skiers while negotiating the terrain.

Compare the skiing scenario with a business. It must establish a destination, chart out a course to negotiate the industry landscape, avoid head-on collisions with competitors, and simultaneously make progress in moving toward its goal.

Of course, if there were no ski maps, most skiers would either stay away from the slopes or do their own homework to establish the safest trails. They might speak to others who have successfully skied down those slopes, try to get an aerial view of the mountains, or choose to trek downhill to establish a ski path to safely negotiate the mountains. In each case, the skier is trying to establish his *strategy* to ensure a safe and enjoyable trip. This analogy of our pioneer skier applies to corporations that pioneer a new industry, segment, or product.

In both examples, it is important for the skier to have all of the following information: their current position, the desired landing position, an overall view of the surrounding mountains, specific identified slope, markers along the way, and finally a good understanding of the selected route marked on the map, to safely arrive at the bottom.

A business strategy is similar to creating a map of a ski trail, to understand the obstructions, have a destination, and chart a route to reach the desired destination in the business environment. Of course, the analogy ends there, because there are two main exceptions to this analogy: There are no satellite views available for the business landscape and the landscape is continuously changing. Businesses have to establish their strategy while considering a plethora of variables that define the landscape of the industry they are competing in, including external and internal constraints and opportunities, organizational strengths and weaknesses, competition, business goals, the regulatory environment, and so on. Furthermore, businesses have to continuously monitor for changes to ensure that their strategy remains viable.

Porter identifies the five forces for competitive positioning and strategy assessment as follows: existing rivalry between corporations, threat of new market entrants, bargaining power of buyers, power of suppliers, and the threat of substitute products. Considered together, this information produces the

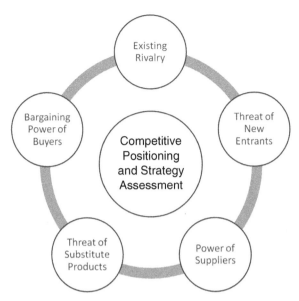

FIGURE 2.2 Porter's Five Forces Framework for Strategy

Source: Adapted from Michael E. Porter, *Competitive Advantage: Creating and Sustaining Superior Performance* (The Free Press, 1985).

equivalent of the aerial view of the competitive landscape and helps the business understand the obstacles and establish a clear direction for survival and growth.

From this view, the business strategist needs to discriminate between the obstacles that should be avoided and others that must be overcome. For obstacles to be avoided, the strategy must establish alternative paths around them; for those to be overcome, an analysis must be done to establish the feasibility for prevailing over these business obstacles, and understand the resources and the skills required to do so. *Strategy is about knowing the lay of the land in business terms.* A strategist needs to clearly understand the business of the corporation and its competition, obstacles to business survival and its growth, strengths, weaknesses, compatibilities, opportunities, and the objectives of the business.

However, having a strategic direction is only the beginning of the journey and not an end in itself. *No strategy, however brilliant, produces results unless executed.* Therefore a strategy needs a *plan* of execution for realization. Let us take another analogy to understand the need for an execution plan to achieve the goals set by the strategy.

If one were to plan an expedition to climb K2, the second-highest summit in the Himalayas, one would need much more than a map of the terrain. From the map, a mountain climber would select a specific route using his or her own experience and understanding of the terrain and alternative routes. This route will then largely determine everything else that is needed for the expedition, including the weather in which to launch the expedition, duration of expedition, equipment, base camps, and so on. Think of the process for the selection of the base route as the *strategy development*, and using it to plan the entire expedition. The execution plan will necessarily deal with the details of the actual schedule, individual responsibilities, and the resources that must be available for the realization of the plan. With this plan, one would need a team of committed members who share the common objective, believe in the plan, and are ready to try it. They also must have the right resources and the right skills for the job, as well as the will to execute. The plan will likely set up specific goals with clear time lines, consume specific resources, and have alternatives to consider when the unexpected weather conditions foil the primary plan. It will have to identify roles of the individual team members and the jobs they must complete for the whole team to be successful.

Based on the route, one will plan to set up their base camps. During the expedition, one will need to determine the exact position of the team to establish that the team is on track with the plan, that progress is being made on time and on the selected route, and that the base camps are reached at or in the vicinity of the originally selected spots. If the plan is not being closely followed and the team gets lost, it will affect the expedition through unexpected delays or higher costs, and the consequences can even be fatal. There are other considerations as well: if the selected equipment is not appropriate for the job, if the food and oxygen supplies are not sufficient, if team members are unable to work together, or if the communication system breaks down between the scouting and main parties, it can lead to inefficient execution, or outright failure. In addition to the factors that can be planned, there are always factors that cannot be precisely predicted or controlled. Think of the weather, landslides, injuries, and sickness. These elements add uncertainty and risk beyond what can be planned and executed in a controlled fashion. Think of all these steps in the context of *strategy planning*.

In spite of all the planning, the final conquest will depend on the cumulative results of all the actions taken by the individual team members, planned or unplanned, to respond to the expected and unexpected events, and each individual goal achieved along the way. Any actions that are not aligned with the common objective of the team may render the expedition a failure.

Of course, such actions may also result in wasted resources and time, both of which may contribute toward the failure of the team to achieve their goal or may even prove fatal. All these actions align with the concept of *strategy execution* in our discussion.

There are a lot of parallels to be drawn from this analogy. Businesses need a high-level strategy to establish their desired destination and the direction. To execute on the strategy, they need a plan that must be credible to the team who will be executing it. They need resources, skills, and the will to execute. They need to measure their progress every now and then and make sure they are on track. Just like the expedition party on K2 in this analogy, they are bound to encounter unexpected situations and must have the ability and agility to adapt to them before these changes derail their plans. But the biggest lesson to take from this analogy is that, to be successful, businesses need all aspects of *strategy development, strategy planning,* and *strategy execution* to be aligned.

ATTRIBUTES OF STRATEGY

The analogies presented here will help us in defining some of the key attributes of strategy. It will also help in understanding what constitutes the development of strategy and the planning that is required to realize the goals of the strategy. Together, they will help us clearly visualize and understand the subject of business strategy and its implications.

Strategy Must Establish the Destination

Business strategy must establish the destination for the business. Within the competitive landscape, where does the firm see itself? With time, industries mature and the industrial landscape changes. These changes affect everything from profitability to customer expectations. In the younger days of an industry, as the product evolves, the size of the market is limited, entry barriers are generally high, manufacturing capacities are limited, costs are high, the customer expectations are low, but healthy margins generally exist. As the industry matures and the product becomes a commodity, the size of the market expands, but increased competition, high customer expectations, and excessive manufacturing capacity increase price pressures and reduce margins. As firms move through this life cycle, they must continuously evaluate their position in the evolving business environment and decide how they must

IBM: **FOCUSING ON STRENGTHS**

IBM introduced its personal computer (PC) on August 12, 1982.[1] During the 1980s and early 1990s the IBM personal computer dominated the personal computers market, overcoming the competition posed by Commodore, Atari, and Apple. In the mid-1990s Compaq and IBM dominated the PC market, with IBM having the second largest market share (8.6 percent) in 1996, just behind Compaq (10 percent). Dell and Hewlett Packard eventually pushed IBM to fourth position by 2001 and IBM began losing money on the PC business. In the quickly commoditizing PC market, IBM had a choice to make: to stay in the PC market and fight the price wars or move out of the low-value business and focus on their other strengths. In 2004, with a declining market share of just over 5 percent, IBM decided to sell its PC business to Lenovo in December. (In 2009, HP led the PC market with almost a 20 percent market share with Lenovo in fourth place, with a market share of 8.1 percent.)

respond to the changes. They must establish where they want to be, in advance of the expected changes, to be successful and adopt tactics that will enable them to do so.

Business strategy must drive the firm to evaluate the changing competitive landscape and continuously establish where the firm needs to be in future—so that the company can start building new capabilities and shed old ones to be successful as the business environment around them changes and evolves.

The question of establishing a goal or destination needs to be reviewed along many dimensions:

- **Time dimension.** Where is the firm today and where does it plan to be at the end of its strategic planning horizon? How long is the strategic planning horizon? What constitutes a long-term horizon for one company may not be so for another. It depends heavily on the industry and the products, and their current position in their life cycles.
- **Industry dimension.** How is the firm positioned within the segment it operates in and where does it want to be strategically? Is the firm in the right industry? Is the industry right? Is it a growth industry or a mature industry or still in its infancy? What prospects does the industry face as a whole?

- **Products and services dimension.** How is the firm positioned versus its competition? Where would the firm desire to be positioned versus the competition?
- **Customer dimension.** What market share does the firm command? What segment do their customers belong in? Is this the right segment for the firm to service? What is the trend in the market share? Where does the firm want to be in terms of market share?
- **Financial dimension.** Finally, what are the financial goals that the firm wants to achieve? All businesses are financial entities and their individual financial goals affect the strategy just as much as the other factors mentioned here.

Strategy Must Establish the Direction

Having a destination may not be enough. Strategy must further define a preferred direction that the firm must pursue to reach the established destination. Answering the destination question requires evaluation of the current position of the firm as well as the desired position within the industry landscape considering the time to get there and expected changes within the industry, products, and customers. Answering the direction question establishes the preferred route to get the firm from their current situation to the desired future position.

As in the analogy of the mountain climbers, there will be several possible paths for a corporation to move from its existing position to the desired position in its competitive landscape. The business strategy must establish which one of these several possible paths the firm wants to follow. In determining the best option, the strategist will evaluate each transition path in terms of its opportunities and obstructions. Obstructions need to be overcome or avoided: If it can be overcome, does the company have the resources and the skills to overcome it, and if it must be avoided, can the company identify a solution to bypass the obstacle? Opportunities need to be leveraged and extended.

As strategy, each of the alternate paths that a firm may decide to pursue to fulfill their business goals will have different strengths and weaknesses. Considering the obstacles, opportunities, costs, and the time lines, the firms can select their preferred direction in pursuit of their strategic goals.

Strategy Drives Cross-Functional Capabilities

Strategy must drive a firm's business capabilities. Since strategic business decisions are made for the entire business, they impact all business functions supporting the firm. Therefore, business strategy not only drives the business

DELL's **STRATEGIC DECISION**

In May 2007 Dell decided to start offering their desktops and laptops through the retail channel. Until that time, Dell had successfully followed the direct-sales model that had made it the number-one PC seller by market-share. However, the PC market had changed and Hewlett Packard, with its focus on quality and cost, was fast growing to become the number-one PC manufacturer. Having decided to sell through the retail channel, Dell had a decision to make: Should they continue to manufacture their own machines as they had been doing in the past, or should they follow the larger industry practice of subcontracting the manufacturing? Their own manufacturing facilities had served them well in the past, allowing them to configure each machine to their customer's specific design, as well as maintaining the industry's best cash-conversion cycle through their build-to-order model. Contract-based manufacturing, on the other hand, had been the established business model in the industry and had propelled firms like HP to the top position in the personal computers market in 2007. Each of these options would have their own obstacles, opportunities, costs, and time line, and it would be the job of the business strategists at Dell to decide what would work best. Dell is slowly changing their manufacturing model to leverage more outsourced manufacturers, while incorporating the new distribution channel.

capabilities, but also has cross-functional impact. However, during the strategy development phase, the focus lies more on the desired destination and the preferred direction, rather than how it will be achieved. To that extent, the strategy during development stage may not explore its functional impact, though it will later drive the evolution of many business functions. For now, it evolves largely unconstrained, with the constraints coming up during the analysis and planning phases, in which the "how" is answered.

This is generally true for most of the decisions made at a business strategy level. Because business strategy affects the fundamental business models for the firm, it mandates changes in business capabilities that go across functions and must be enabled to realize the goals of the strategy.

Strategy Must Drive a Feasible Plan

Business strategy can neither be created nor deployed in a contextual vacuum. Strategy must establish reasonable goals and, therefore, must drive

IMPACT **OF DELL's DECISION**

Continuing the example of Dell, their decision to sell through the retail channel would eventually force Dell to rethink many functions of their business. Dell's strategic business decision can potentially affect all their functions of manufacturing, demand planning, inventory management, warehousing, and distribution. Till 2007, when Dell decided to sell through the retail channel, it had employed a direct-sale model for demand management, an assemble-to-order model for manufacturing, and shipped directly to their customers, with little need for stocking/warehousing for most of their inventory. However, the business decision to sell through retail stores would require Dell to rethink almost all of the functions mentioned here. Dell must forecast demand, manufacture to stock, and distribute in bulk to retail stores. One single business decision for Dell impacts business functions across the firm and requires new or enhanced capabilities for these business functions.

a feasible plan to achieve those goals. Since business strategy can impact a large number of business capabilities, the realization of its goals can only be achieved through a long-term plan consisting of several initiatives that incrementally build the desired capabilities. If the desired capabilities or the deployment plans are not feasible, the strategic goals of the firm cannot be achieved.

To be feasible, each of the incremental plans must be reconciled within the constraints of cost, time, logical sequence, resources, risks, and skills that the firm can expend in pursuit of its business goals. As these plans are essentially incremental in building new capabilities over time, the business strategy must identify practical metrics to track and monitor the success of these initiatives. These metrics should also consistently validate the direction of the evolution of the business to ensure that it is still aligned to the original goals of the strategy and that the goals of the business strategy are still relevant.

In plain terms, the plan establishes measurable goals and timelines, so that progress can be tracked and success can be measured. The plans must also define the risks and an action plan to manage the potential risks. Most risks can be mitigated or eliminated through alternate courses of action. Finally, the strategic plans must also identify what constitutes catastrophic failure and an exit strategy to minimize the harm done to the business, if such a situation arises.

Strategy Must Be Articulated

To be successful, strategy must be clearly articulated. It must be presented as simple enough to be understood by the large majority of the corporate stakeholders, its employees, shareholders, and customers. Any strategy that is not well understood fails to build the credibility that is necessary to its success. People need to believe in the strategy before they will align themselves and their actions to it.

Strategy Must Be Adaptable

Finally, strategy must be adaptable in response to expected and real changes in the business and competitive environment of the firm. As the environment changes, firms need to review and reevaluate their strategy to ensure that it stays relevant for their survival and growth. As discussed earlier, Porter identifies five forces that should trigger firms to review their business strategy: existing rivalry, threat of new entrants, power of suppliers, threat of substitute products, and bargaining power of buyers (see Figure 2.2). This means that strategy is not static, and since business strategy drives all other strategic planning in corporations, therefore, it follows that all strategy must be adaptable. We will review this concept again in the context of functional and technology strategies later in the book.

Other Attributes

The following list addresses some other attributes of strategy that don't necessarily fit in any of the characteristics presented so far but, nonetheless, often appear in discussions on strategy:

- Strategy causes as well as enables change management.
- Strategy is a combination of objective and subjective analyses.
- Strategy affects organizational policies.
- Strategy drives and is driven by the organizational structure.
- Strategy affects and is affected by the organizational culture.
- Strategy needs a team who believes in it and will drive the strategy through projects, plans, operations, and events. To be effective, the core team must *own* the strategy and associate their success with the success of the strategy.
- The strategy needs resources and skills to be realized. These resources can be financial, human, mechanical, information, or other types of assets.

LEVELS OF STRATEGY PLANNING

The business strategy can be created and articulated at many levels. A commonly encountered approach for a large conglomerate, for example, is to define business strategy at the corporate level and then adapt the strategy for business units or divisions. For global companies, it may sometimes make sense to have regional strategies that are aligned with their local aspirations and industry landscapes. This is an example where the business strategy is being developed along the organizational axis.

However, business strategy can also exist at multiple levels along the axes of time and business functions. It is not uncommon to have both a long- and mid-term strategy for merchandising and customer service. In fact, almost any annual report for a company these days will mention of the firm's mid-term and long-term strategies, or their strategies to improve specific business functions that are considered core strengths for the business.

Therefore, strategy can be seen along the organizational dimension, time dimension, and business function dimension (see Figure 2.3). The organizational dimension gives rise to the traditional levels of strategy reflecting the corporate structure. The time dimension provides the horizon-based strategy hierarchy, and the functional dimension allows the strategy to be expended into terms of the impacted business functions.

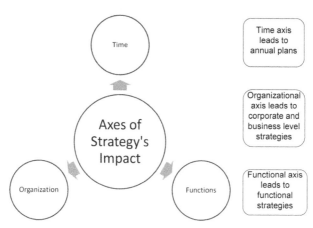

FIGURE 2.3 Axes of Strategy's Impact

Organizational Hierarchy of Strategy

Business strategy along the organizational groups in business has been the most common way to think about the strategy hierarchy as it is naturally aligned with the corporate organizational structures. It is a clean way to differentiate the roles between the corporate offices and operating business units, or between the holding companies and their constituent businesses. The strategy at the corporate level is generally thought to deal with larger issues of portfolio, growth, and corporate resource allocations. The strategy at the business level is generally supposed to drive product and customer strategies and positioning of the business within the industry. See Figure 2.4 for a representative organization hierarchy for the business strategy defined at three levels.

This kind of differentiation works quite well for conglomerates consisting of a large number of businesses or business units (BUs), possibly in different industries, controlled through some kind of a corporate structure. Such a structure will require a corporate strategy to continuously evaluate the portfolio of businesses it owns and the allocation of corporate resources across these businesses. The corporate strategy in this case will evaluate what businesses to get into, what businesses to get out of, and allocate financial and human resources to align the businesses with the corporate direction and strategy. Then, within the context set up by the corporate strategy, individual businesses can decide how to formulate their own strategies to grow, maintain, or dilute their market-share and reposition themselves to align with the corporate priorities. The individual businesses may further have operating units that may also formulate their own strategy within the parameters set up by the business strategy at the BU level.

FIGURE 2.4 Organizational Hierarchy of Business Strategy

This kind of distinction by level is merely an organizational reflection on the concept of strategy. The levels simply help in propagating the relevant strategy goals and constraints along the organizational structure of the corporation. While the business strategy at different hierarchical levels of the organization focuses on different aspects, an all-encompassing business strategy needs to consider and address all of these aspects from portfolio management to product positioning that are mentioned here as part of corporate and business level strategies. Therefore, devoid of the organizational context, these levels of strategy lose their scope definitions. As a result, while these levels are mentioned here as part of reviewing the prevailing concepts in strategy, this book does not distinguish between corporate- and business-level strategies and uses both these terms interchangeably to refer collectively to all the aspects of a business strategy.

Time Hierarchy of Strategy

Strategies can also be expanded using time of impact. It is not uncommon to hear managers speaking of the *long-term* strategies or *short-term* strategies. These strategies merely reflect the time horizon that a strategy is supposed to impact. It is important to understand that the context of time is just as unique to a corporation as the structure that may be used in defining the organization-based hierarchy levels. While three to five years may be considered long term in one industry, it may be medium for another, and short for yet another industry. The time horizons are a result of several industry attributes including maturity, level of ongoing innovation, and potential for disruption through technology changes or alternate business models, as well as changes in the regulatory environment.

Functional Hierarchy of Strategy

Another way to expand the corporate strategy is by breaking it down to identify its impact on specific business functions. The goals of the business strategy drive the capabilities needed by the firm to achieve them. These capabilities may originate through competency in several business functions creating a hierarchical relationship between the business strategy and the selected business functions it drives. The process will involve taking the business strategy and expanding it to identify its potential impact on relevant business functions to drive the business capabilities which must be developed or enhanced to support the goals of the business strategy. This concept is reviewed in Chapter 1, where we argue that strategies drive the creation of

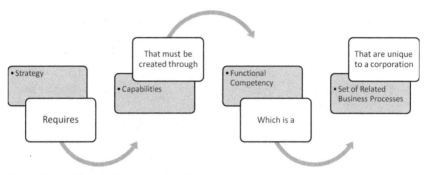

FIGURE 2.5 Capabilities Required by Business Strategy

functional capabilities that ultimately create and sustain competitive advantages for the business (see Figure 2.5).

The functional hierarchy of strategy is the basic concept that we will explore in the rest of the book as we continue down the path of defining how business strategy should drive supply chain capabilities.

THE STRATEGIC HORIZON OF IMPACT

Before moving forward with other strategic management concepts, we will mention the concept of the *horizon of impact* for any strategy. Any business strategy, when executed, will affect the business functions as well as the organization. The business functions must evolve to support the desired goals of the strategy and the organization must adapt to the changes caused by such an evolution. Understanding the impact of a strategy provides the right structure for an objective analysis of the resources, skills, and time lines required to realize the strategy and is important when evaluating the potential success of the strategy itself. A visual representation enables a quick understanding of changes that must be managed as part of realizing the strategy.

Imagine a three-dimensional model representing time, business functions, and organization along the three axes and then marking the relative impact of change on each axis due to the new strategy. Then, the relative volumes of matrices created using the three axes of organization, time, and business functions will represent the relative impact of the strategy and, therefore, the amount of change that must be managed (see Figure 2.6). Each of the blocks represent a business function, where the length denotes the time that this

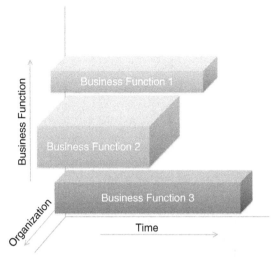

FIGURE 2.6 Strategic Horizon of Impact along Function, Organization, and Time

business function is expected to take to create the required capabilities, the depth shows the relative impact on people to learn and adapt to the changes in the capabilities, and the height represents the amount of changes within the business function starting from its current state. A proper analysis to produce a graphic of this kind provides a simple tool to grasp the impact of a strategic business decision, if the firm decides to pursue the strategy.

As strategy is propagated along its own hierarchies of time, organization, and business functions, its horizon of impact is shortened and it becomes more specific. In Dell's example, the initial analysis of impact may happen at the corporate level, where specific changes may not be discernible, but as one moves down, for example, to analyzing the impact on the PC business unit, the desired changes become more specific to predict and understand.

This multidimensional visualization of strategy's impact also makes clear how different organizational units of a corporation following a single strategic goal set by the corporate strategy may achieve it by developing different functional capabilities.

For example, if the corporate strategy is to be the cost leader, then the individual business units following this common goal may achieve it through different means. While one business unit may achieve this through innovation in manufacturing processes and reducing their costs, another may achieve the same through relocation of manufacturing facilities to be closer

THE **HORIZON OF IMPACT OF DELL's STRATEGY**

For example, let us go back to Dell's decision in 2007 to start selling its personal computers through the retail channel. As part of the analysis, one could construct a diagram showing the horizon of impact of this business decision on Dell. Let us focus on two business *functions* of supply planning and distribution for demonstrating this tool. Dell will have to rethink its supply planning function from an assemble-to-order to a combination of assemble-to-order and make-to-stock to address their new retail channel, while simultaneously supporting the direct-sales model. This would require major changes in the supply planning function, starting from demand forecasting, product mix planning, and production planning. These changes can be quantified using the number of business processes impacted. Creating these new supply planning capabilities will most likely require the implementation of new technology solutions, changes in processes for creating and communicating factory production schedules, and probably changes in standard operating procedures on the factory floor itself, driving the different quality checks for the two different types of manufacturing models. These changes can be quantified by estimating the cost and *time* to implement the new solutions. The changes in capabilities will also require corresponding *organizational* changes, in which Dell may decide to create separate teams to plan the two streams of demand.

Finally, all these changes will impact people, who will have to learn the new tools and processes and adapt to the new organizational structure. These changes can be quantified by the number of people affected through the organizational restructuring. A similar analysis can also be conducted by outlining how the distribution function will change and evolve in response to the business decision of selling through retailers. The visualization can then represent the relative amount of change in these two business functions driven by Dell's business strategy. This provides a quick visual tool to grasp the potential impact of a strategic decision.

to the source of raw materials and thus reducing transportation costs. Each of these business units may also establish their own targets for cost reduction, which together will help the corporation achieve its consolidated cost-reduction target.

In a retail business scenario targeting cost reduction, merchandising process capabilities may be enhanced to achieve cost reductions through better sourcing and better contract negotiations, or supply chain functions can be improved to achieve the same cost savings by optimizing inventory and distribution procedures. In each case, the functional strategy dictates the capabilities that must be developed to support the strategic goals. Each of these functional strategies can have a limited impact on costs and a firm may decide to follow either one or both, based on their own preferences and existing organization skills. Available budgets, the time frame to create the new capabilities, and the ability to adapt to the changes in processes and organization would be other relevant factors to consider.

In conclusion, understanding the horizon of impact of a strategy provides the structure for an objective analysis of required resources, skills, and time-lines to realize the strategy and is important to evaluate the potential success of a strategy.

In this chapter, the focus is on providing analogies for the concept of strategy, which is central to any successful business enterprise. This is done deliberately to bring out the importance of strategy and ensure that the readers connect strategy with real-life examples of any large, complex undertaking, whether commercial or not, rather than an abstract, theoretical concept. The definition of strategy has been difficult to pin down and, therefore, it has not offered much practical value for managers, having little to offer in specific guidance for a corporation. Then, there have been many obfuscations: many corporations believe their annual budgeting exercise is strategy, while others set up war-rooms to tackle pressing problems and believe that this is strategy. Of course, the objective of this chapter is to quell those notions and present strategy as something everyone can understand:

- ■ Strategy as a guiding, driving force that establishes a destination
- ■ Strategy as a continuum shifting from planning to execution, in which the planning end proposes a long-term direction moving toward the business goals and the execution end supports day-to-day existence of the corpo-rations through its routine operations—the continuum passing through functional strategy connecting the two ends and creating capabilities to support the strategic goals on one end and the operations on the other end.

Therefore, the focus of this chapter is to look at the concepts of strategy based on what it should do and what attributes should characterize it. While the characterization was generic, the impacts of strategy in an organizational context are real and specific. This was emphasized in the sections on the levels of strategy planning and the strategic horizon of impact that created the relationship between the generic nature of strategy and its very real, specific impact on business organizations when strategic planning is used as a means to run a business enterprise.

Moving beyond that, we present the current thinking on business strategy. A lot of work has been done on business strategy and its role in creating competitive advantages to create, sustain, and grow business opportunities. This is the subject of Chapter 3, where we review the existing concepts of business strategy and present several points of views on business strategy.

CHAPTER THREE

Concepts of Business Strategy

T FIRST, THERE WAS Adam Smith's "invisible hand," shaping companies, industries, and business environments. The invisible hand referred to market forces beyond any single corporation's control but affecting its fortunes, nevertheless. The business managers saw themselves passively as functional administrators having little control over the fate of their enterprises. Then came business leaders like Alfred Sloan (General Motors) and Chester Barnard (AT&T) who thought of business strategy in terms of the strengths and weaknesses of the competitive environment and strategic factors that depended on organizational action. Ken Andrews added the concept of balancing internal strengths with external threats, a strategy that eventually evolved into the famous SWOT (strengths, weaknesses, opportunities, and threats) analysis. Michael Porter gave us the generic business strategies and a way to think about the competitive advantages created by them. The thinking on business strategy continues to change, with new methods being introduced—the resource-based view, capabilities-based advantages, and so on.

The objective of this chapter is to review the current mainstream thinking on business strategy so that we can dwell on the concepts later and use them when discussing functional and technology strategies.

PORTER'S GENERIC STRATEGIES

Since Porter identified the three generic strategies for building competitive advantage, they have been a staple of all strategy discussions. We will review these three generic strategies as they provide the most basic context for thinking about strategy for business and also provide a useful framework for further discussion on functional strategies.

Porter's generic strategies represent a company's strength in the two basic areas of cost advantage and differentiation. In fact, Porter argues that all other corporate strengths originate in one of these two basic strengths and therefore, cost and differentiation advantages or disadvantages will determine how well a business can position itself versus its competition in a given industry. These strategies are called generic strategies because they are equally applicable across industries and businesses. All businesses offer some products or services that have a finite cost and must provide some value to the consumer for them to pay for these products or services. The cost advantage originates in the cost of producing these products and services and the differentiation advantage originates in the value provided by a product or service.

Cost Strategy

The generic cost strategy is based on the ability of a firm to have the lowest cost of producing the goods or services it sells. As long as the firm can maintain this position within its industry segment, it will continue to be most profitable within that segment. The cost comparison must be based on a comparable product or service that consumers perceive as providing equal utility value or equal satisfaction. Creating cost leadership means that the firm must evaluate its value chain and identify areas for cost savings. Achieving these cost savings may drive the company to invest in better processes through automation, technology, and optimization. Therefore, creating cost advantages needs investments. To successfully pursue a cost strategy, the company must achieve a price performance that is greater than the cost of creating that advantage (see Figure 3.1).

Once this cost leadership position has been achieved, the firm has two options. It can either translate this position into higher profitability by selling at prices comparable to its competition or it can increase its market share by selling at a price lower than the average industry price for comparable products or services (see Figure 3.2).

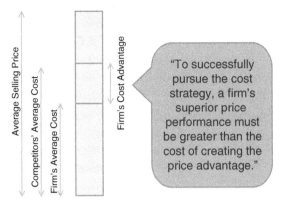

FIGURE 3.1 Cost Strategy Showing a Firm's Cost Advantage

Cost advantages can be created by a corporation in several ways, all of which must lead to labor, material, or time efficiencies. Innovations in product design and manufacturing, better technology to automate manufacturing processes and reduce waste, process innovations to reduce process lead time for manufacturing as well as distribution, and automation to make resources more efficient can each contribute toward creating cost advantages. Economies of scale can also tremendously help in reducing costs by reducing the unit manufacturing costs as well as by creating business and financial leverage with suppliers, distributors, and other partners.

A cost strategy requires that the firm understands the cost drivers and the cost behavior. This mandates an extensive framework that must allow the

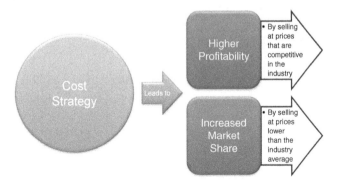

FIGURE 3.2 Cost Strategy May Lead to Higher Profitability and/or Increased Market Share

WAL-MART: **COST ADVANTAGES**

Consider Wal-Mart and its consistent pursuit of lower costs. While it now is the largest retailer of the world, which definitely enables it to take advantage of the *economies of scale*, Wal-Mart began as a small business. However, low cost has always been its strategy for growth. In its early days, Wal-Mart created cost advantage by following unconventional buying, distribution, and pricing strategies. Rather than buying through wholesalers, Wal-Mart started buying directly from the manufacturers. This also forced Wal-Mart to establish their own distribution centers for deliveries to the stores rather than depending on the wholesalers' distribution infrastructure. Wal-Mart also pursued a pricing strategy that was very different at the time: instead of charging higher prices and then organizing promotions and clearance events, Wal-Mart emphasized *everyday low prices*. Certainly, it would have taken consumers of the era a little time to realize that *everyday low prices* was not a temporary gimmick, but a promise that Wal-Mart kept day after day. Of course, as Wal-Mart grew to be the largest retailer in the world, it not only has enviable capital resources to sustain these advantages by continuously improving its operations, but also enjoys unparalleled economies of scale.

firm to capture and analyze costs associated with its value chain processes. Capturing all relevant cost elements is a difficult proposition and something that needs a consistent focus to create in spite of the widespread deployment of digitized processes through enterprise resource planning (ERP) systems and analytic capabilities created through data-warehouses.

Another important factor is that an effective cost strategy must be pursued across the board, across all processes, and a fierce focus on cost reduction must be maintained at all times.

Once the cost advantage has been created, the firm's focus shifts to sustaining that cost advantage to avoid losing to the competition, who will try to play catch up. Sustaining the cost advantage involves a consistent evaluation of the cost drivers and cost-saving opportunities, and relentless pursuit of continuous improvements in all value chain processes. This focus will eventually lead to integrated business processes and collaboration capabilities with partners that allow continuous reduction in the cost of operations through automated process integration, shared plans, management by exceptions, and the capacity to quickly react to plan volatility across the value chain. While individual processes and solutions for obtaining cost advantages will continue to become more commonplace, the integrated ecosystems connecting these processes will always remain unique to an organization. This uniqueness is what creates a sustainable cost advantage that is hard for competitors to mimic or reproduce. The tools that Wal-Mart uses for cost reduction, like demand forecasting and inventory optimization, are not unique to them. These solutions have been available for over two decades for any company to deploy and leverage. What makes Wal-Mart unique is its ability to integrate these processes with the rest of their value chain so that they can quickly react to changes in demand and sometimes proactively manage demand and inventories. This integration and their unique process landscape is what makes Wal-Mart successful and is also what makes it hard for other retailers to mimic it, in spite of the parity at the level of individual solutions.

Differentiation Strategy

This strategy is based on creating the differentiation in the offered products or services by creating unique features that are not provided by any other competitor within the industry segment and that are valuable to the customer. For this strategy to be successful, the unique features of the products and services must be valuable to the customer *as perceived by her*. Customers pay a premium for products only when they perceive a distinct value in its unique features. Contrast this with the differentiation created through a cost leadership strategy where the difference of cost is directly measurable and objective in nature.

Porter also asserts that to establish unique features that may be valuable to its customers, firms should not restrict their search to their products, but rather should review their whole value chain. The differentiation that drives unique value proposition for the customer is not constrained to the products alone, but it can come from any part of its core or extended value chain involved in creating, distributing, or servicing its products or services.

While one company leverages their ability to resolve customer concerns by providing them with prompt service throughout their extended travel experience, another may achieve such differentiated service through a completely different route.

Like cost strategy, there are many ways to create differentiation to drive the customer value equation. The differentiation can come from superior design, manufacturing, raw materials, quality, performance, longevity, service,

TRAVELOCITY: **DIFFERENTIATION THROUGH CUSTOMER SERVICE**

Consider Travelocity's tagline, "You will never roam alone," along with their gnome who magically appears to help when their customers' trip doesn't go as planned. This message is specially targeted to create the perception of the additional value that the company is trying to create through its focus on customer service after the initial service of booking the travel has been completed. The company obviously hopes to extend its market reach through the emphasis on providing service throughout the travel experience rather than only in the act of booking travel.

total cost of ownership, and so on. For example, a firm may pursue better design for creating the differentiation. A well-known example is Lexus, which highlights its "pursuit of perfection" in designing cars that can park themselves, or can switch on wipers when it is raining. Design-based differentiation may be extended with better raw materials or better manufacturing methods. All of this may lead to a product that is more reliable with a rich set of features that the customers value and, therefore, are ready to pay a premium for.

Obviously, creating differentiating products or services has its own costs. Having better designers adds to the cost of payroll, better materials add to the cost of purchasing, better manufacturing may have higher overheads because of more expensive machinery, and so on. Therefore, it is important for the firms

TRACTOR **SUPPLY COMPANY: DIFFERENTIATION THROUGH LOCATION STRATEGY**

For the Tractor Supply Company, this differentiation comes simply from their location strategy. Being largely focused in the rural areas, their value proposition to the customer is simply understanding the needs of the rural lifestyle and addressing it in their own neighborhoods. Their advertisement campaigns highlight this uniqueness by using the tagline "The stuff you need *out here*."

pursuing this strategy that the cost of creating these differentiators is less than the price premiums that the firm is able to charge for them.

While discussing the differentiation strategy, Porter makes an important observation: that *differentiation cannot be understood by viewing the firm in aggregate*, but stems from specific activities a firm performs and how they affect the buyer. There are two components of this statement, the first one simply asserting that firms in an industry segment may look too much alike when seen in aggregate and, therefore, a casual observation may not reveal any differences at all. Their business models may be too similar and undistinguishable from one another. The second component states that the differentiation arises from specific activities that a firm performs and how they affect the firm's customer. This indicates that value creation can come from any activity as long as it creates value for the customer and that it is the specific processes supporting that activity that create such value. This concept is being highlighted here since this is strongly aligned with the core precept of this book that functional capabilities create competitive advantages.

Sometimes, the differentiation that creates the competitive advantages may even arise from the extended value chain rather than the core value chain of the firm. For example, consider Honda dealerships. Honda created a customer experience that was consistent across its dealerships by creating standards for merchandising, floor planning, and services. The company, in this case, is trying to create a differentiation in an extended part of its value chain rather than the core value chain activities of designing and manufacturing of the cars.

Product-based differentiation, of course, is easier to grasp as a concept. Superior design, better materials, above-par quality, durability, and reliability are common attributes that we think of when thinking of products and routinely associate these attributes strongly with the product of some firms rather than with others. This makes the firms able to charge a premium for the perceived value that customers derive from their products. Toyota's value of perceived *reliability* allows it to claim a premium on its most popular brand, Camry, year after year, even when there are equally good cars produced by the competition. Quality, in general, is the most pursued differentiator for products and services. In fact, Hill and Jones identify superior quality as the first building block for the competitive advantage. They have further qualified "superior quality" as *reliability* or *excellence*. When quality is viewed as reliability it is closely related to the product or service aspect of the corporation. In this sense, the quality reflects the dependability of the products and the consistency of the experience.

TOYOTA: **RELIABILITY AND EXCELLENCE**

Many examples can be thought of to describe this specific point: Toyota cars have long been defined in terms of their dependability or quality. That perception provides Toyota with a competitive edge that other manufacturers may not have. When quality is viewed as excellence, it may be related to the product or the process. Toyota shows this aspect of quality with their branding of Lexus. In this case, not only is the product supposed to be dependable (hence quality as reliability), but there is a greater emphasis on the whole customer experience of buying and owning a Lexus that is built on the process excellence. Excellence, in this case is the *whole* customer experience, from the product presentation through product quality, purchasing, servicing, leasing, and other customer interactions with Toyota during the ownership of the car. This perception of excellence provides Toyota with a competitive advantage in the luxury segment of cars. No matter how we look at the quality, as reliability or as excellence, it has the ability to create differentiation and provide a price premium driving the firm's differentiation strategy. (Also see a brief history of Toyota and their recent vehicle recalls in the section on *Understanding Advantage* later in this chapter.)

The last important point we touch on in this strategy is the perception of the buyer of the value provided by the differentiators. Any differentiation strategy will work only when the uniqueness is *perceived* to have enough value to the customer that they can be persuaded to pay more for that differentiator. Unless this is true, a differentiation strategy cannot succeed. To create this perception, the firms may engage not only in innovative product design but also in marketing campaigns that support the firm's strategy by highlighting these differences in their product or by attaching a wow factor or status with the firm's products. Apple has adopted this strategy a number of times, in which the innovative product design has been heavily supported through marketing that highlights the "cool" factor of owning an Apple product. Almost all the great brand successes share this aspect of the differentiation strategy to some extent.

Focus or Segmentation Strategy

This third generic strategy suggested by Porter is based on creating a market niche. This can be viewed as pursuing differentiation strategy on a combination of the product and customers. Focus is created when the firm creates a differentiated product or service for a targeted customer segment. Therefore, focus is the intersection of the product and customer segments that a firm may decide to leverage. This strategy may reduce the target market, but, by focusing on a well-defined segment, it is expected that the firm can better design and sell its products to a well-profiled and well-understood customer base, rather than trying to design something that will appeal to everyone. Once the focus segment has been established, the firm may actually decide to differentiate on cost, features, service, or on any number of factors that are most relevant to the targeted segment of the market.

This strategy can be realistically used for segments where substitution is hard or competition is low or nonexistent. Both of these situations can exist, if the targeted segment is too narrow or too small to interest the larger, well-entrenched competitors. Similar opportunities may also exist when the segment provides low profitability and hence creates a lack of interest on the part of competitors to seriously pursue it.

It is generally considered that the focus strategy is more suited to smaller players or smaller businesses within large conglomerates due to its inherent focus on specific segments of a broad market. Conventional strategy discussions mention this almost as a fact. As a result they also caution that the resulting low volume of business may likely have higher costs due to reduced ability to control costs due to low leverage with suppliers and manufacturers. This, however, is not entirely true as exceptions exist.

DIRECT **AIR's SEGMENTATION STRATEGY**

Direct Air recently opened its operations, offering flights between Toledo and two warm-weather spots, Myrtle Beach, South Carolina, and Punta Gorda, Florida, after Delta and Continental dropped service out of the Toledo airport in 2008.[1] The large airlines no longer found smaller airports worth the trouble, likely due to low passenger volumes. However, once these segments have been discovered, other firms can move in with a focus strategy to service the same market. These segments can exist at both ends of the cost spectrum, such as in commodities where low cost is imperative, as well as high-end luxury goods where cost is generally not a factor.

COMPUTER **ASSOCIATES: SENSING MARKET OPPORTUNITY**

Consider the case of Computer Associates[2] (CA): the company made a business model out of building products designed to improve the performance of IBM equipment. In 1976, CA started its business by selling software for IBM mainframes. Their focus throughout the 1980s continued to be products designed to improve the performance of IBM equipment. As IBM upgraded its computers, its software maintained backward compatibility so that IBM customers were able to run their older programs. The backward-compatible design meant that the IBM computers were not running as efficiently as possible. CA sensed this market opportunity and filled the niche by offering products to make IBM computers run more efficiently. As IBM was not interested in this market segment (since that would have required IBM to acknowledge deficient programs), CA did not have to worry about any competition from the much bigger IBM. CA saw huge growth in 1980s and its revenues crossed the $1 billion mark in 1989—just eight years after going public in 1981. Today, CA has grown to be a $4 billion company and their focus has broadened to providing enterprise management solutions and services for technology. Computer Associates saw a niche segment and addressed the market by providing support for otherwise obsolete technology. This turned out to be an extremely profitable business for CA and allowed the company to become a technology giant.

The niche segment in which the focus strategy may deliver results can arise from many sources. These can be a specific demographic, a geographic market, a product line, and so on. An example of demographic focus is Abercrombie & Fitch, which primarily focuses on casual-wear for the target consumer age of 18 through 22. Southwest Airlines started by focusing on a geographic niche by initially serving the Texas cities of Dallas, Houston, and San Antonio. It later expanded to include destinations in other neighboring states such as Nevada, New Mexico, and Oklahoma. It eventually gave up its geographically focused strategy to grow and became the sixth-largest U.S. airline in 2007.

The field of corporate strategy has continuously evolved since Porter first suggested the three generic strategies presented here. We will present some of the later concepts that have enriched the field since. The objective of presenting these concepts is simply to refresh the reader's views on strategic management and competitive advantages, and not to provide a comprehensive coverage of these concepts. As we progress through the thought process presented in this book, these concepts will be helpful in establishing the themes of creating and maintaining competitive advantages through process capabilities.

THE RESOURCE-BASED VIEW

The resource-based view (RBV) of strategy has been advanced in recent years. This concept is based on the central argument that a firm's competitive advantage originates from its unique resources, and the sustainability of these advantages comes from the difficulties for the competitor in attempting to duplicate them. These resources can be tangible or intangible. Examples of tangible resources are assets such as cash, real estate, and accounts receivables, and examples of intangible resources are brand, social image, and the culture of the company. To this, most researchers add the capabilities of a company as being the third category of resources, such as supply chain capabilities.

What makes these resources valuable? The answer lies in their *uniqueness*. While several other criteria have been conventionally applied to determine the value of resources in their ability to create competitive advantage, the core value of these resources remains in their uniqueness. A resource is unique when it is rare and therefore not abundantly available. A resource is unique when it cannot be imitated or copied very easily. A resource is unique when it cannot be replaced very easily. Therefore, all these attributes—namely rareness, inimitability, and nonsubstitution—add up to make a resource valuable. These and similar attributes have been mentioned repeatedly by various authors, most notably by Barney[3] in his VRIN (Valuable, Rare, Inimitable, and Nonsubstitutable) criteria.

However, the first characteristic of in the VRIN definition, *Valuable*, can be problematic to determine. What is valuable to one company may not be so to another. While resources like cash can be precisely measured, the exact value of some intangible resources, for example, may be difficult to determine. The inability to define what is valuable in an objective manner sometimes leads to criticism of this theory. Therefore, to be valuable, the resource must also be relevant in the current context of the firm. Having a lot of free cash flow can be a huge asset for a young company in an emerging industry, but not so important in a mature industry where there are no growth avenues left to invest that cash. In the latter case, then, the *value* of available cash as a resource is limited.

In another example, consider why most car companies have developed separate brands for their luxury vehicles. Why would a company want to spend a substantial amount of money rather than leveraging one of their existing strong brands? Toyota launched Lexus as a separate brand when they wanted to get into the luxury car segment rather than leveraging its original Toyota brand. In most cases, the underlying reason is that in the context of what the company is trying to do (that is, to create an image of luxury), the old brand was simply not relevant due to its close association with low-cost vehicles. Therefore, the old *brand* was just not the right *resource* in the new context, even though the original Toyota brand in its own right has considerable value for the firm.

The other attributes of resources in the RBV concept are less problematic to define and understand than the concept of *valuable*. If a resource is *rare* or a firm has a monopoly on its supply, then in the right context this can definitely create competitive advantage for the firm. For example, in 1902, De Beers controlled 90 percent of the world's diamond production, through a monopoly created by its vast holdings of a rare natural resource—the diamond mines.

When a resource cannot be easily imitated by the competition, it creates sustainability of the competitive advantage for the firm owning that resource. Brand reputation falls in this category. While other firms can create their own brands, this generally takes a long time and substantial amounts of investments. Advantage created through patents and other protected intellectual property also falls in this category, because it cannot be imitated. Corporate culture and employee loyalty are other examples that illustrate a resource that may be hard to duplicate by the competition. In fact, any resource that is created through the unique growth path and unique corporate experience is generally very hard to imitate by the competition. Consider some of the management techniques of Japanese manufacturers. While *kaizan* (continuous improvement), *muda* (waste reduction), *just-in-time,* and *quality circles* as techniques entered the vocabularies of Western companies in the 1980s and 1990s, the cultural context of the Japanese companies of those years was impossible to duplicate. Japanese companies thrived with these and other techniques in their corporate culture, which placed high value on loyalty, hierarchy, lifelong employment, and, above all, a cultural drive for perfection. In this case, the Japanese culture was an important part of the competitive advantage for the Japanese companies. In fact, the American companies' inability to recreate the cultural context is what made these advantages so sustainable for the Japanese manufactures at the time.

The last attribute relates to the inability or difficulty for the competition to *substitute* the resource that is driving the resource-based advantage. These advantages may arise through processes that are too complex to understand, too advanced for their time, too expensive, part of the intellectual property of a firm, or are integrated uniquely with other processes at the firm such that an isolated process has no intrinsic value unless it is combined with others in the unique ecosystem of the firm.

All resources will depreciate over time and their ability to create advantage will erode through imitation and substitution. Since it is almost impossible

HARD **TO IMITATE: UNIQUE STRENGTHS**

Consider Wal-Mart's supply chain. While each individual process is well understood and generally available as a solution offered by myriad supply chain vendors, it is the integrated *whole* that makes Wal-Mart's supply chain unique, hard to imitate, and hard to substitute for the competitors.

Another example: in May 2009, Chevron announced the crude oil production from its deep-water Tahiti fields. Tahiti is one of the largest oil fields in the Gulf of Mexico and the deepest oil-producing field till now. According to the company's press release,[4] "Tahiti is located at Green Canyon Blocks 596, 597, 640 and 641, approximately 190 miles (305 kilometers) south of New Orleans, and in approximately 4,100 feet (1,250 meters) of water. Primary pay sands are Lower to Middle Miocene from 23,000 to 28,000 feet and lie below a salt canopy ranging from 8,000 to 15,000 feet thick. The deepest producing well is more than 26,700 feet, a record for the Gulf of Mexico." The total cost of the first phase of the project was $2.7 billion. This is definitely an example of resources that are hard to substitute due to the very large capital required to do so and that therefore present a very high barrier to entry for smaller competitors.

As another example, consider the fuel-hedging practices of Southwest Airlines. Fuel cannot be substituted in an airline context and Southwest's practice of hedging actually allowed them to leverage lower fuel prices over the long run as well as to avoid the wild fluctuations of the last couple of years, thereby providing them with a smoother, more reliable cash flow for their operations. While fuel hedging as a practice is not unique, the unique process at Southwest was a resource that their competitors could not easily substitute.

to have a resource-based competitive advantage that is sustainable forever, what can a company do to extend the life of such advantages? Continuous evaluation of valuable resources and matching investments to upgrade them can extend and sustain the advantages over time. While Tahiti is the largest oil field in the Gulf of Mexico, that provides only a limited time-advantage to Chevron, which must continue to invest in similar fields to maintain its competitive advantage. In fact, Tahiti is simply one of 40 projects in which Chevron's share of the investment is over $1 billion. A similar situation exists at Wal-Mart: while Wal-Mart already has one of the retail industry's most efficient supply chains, it has continuously invested in supply chain innovations to sustain that advantage. In 2007, it reported a capital investment of $3.3 billion (or 21.5 percent of its total capital investments) on information systems and distribution initiatives. In 2008 and 2009, it continued investing similar amounts of capital in supply chain areas, with $3 billion in 2008 and $2.75 billion in 2009. This shows how Wal-Mart is consciously investing to maintain the competitive advantages that it has created over the years with the industry's best capabilities in supply chain planning and the distribution systems.

Therefore, for companies with a RBV for creating competitive advantages, they must continuously evaluate what resources are most valuable to them, assess the ability of the resource to sustain the advantage, find out ways to upgrade the resource to keep the competitive edge, and finally, invest in these upgrades to ensure that their resources' ability to provide a strategic edge does not erode as other companies in the segment catch up and find ways to imitate or substitute the same resources.

CAPABILITIES-BASED STRATEGIES

The early 1990s brought a new concept to the strategy planning. This concept was based on the fact that companies compete on their capabilities. Stalk, Evans, and Shulman[5] presented this concept with various examples from the industry, including Wal-Mart and Kmart.

Conceptually, this is the most important idea that we discuss throughout this book.

This concept provides a logical extension to the cost, differentiation, and focus-based strategies of Porter. To create any of the advantages, whether it is price leadership, superior product, or superior customer service, a firm needs to develop specific capabilities. Until such capabilities are developed, the strategy and its purported advantages remain theoretical. While the thought process behind the reasons for why some companies succeed better than others and the exploration of the underlying differences in their broad business strategies is important, it is the capabilities that actually deliver the advantages sought by these strategies. Therefore, development of capabilities provides the only tools for realizing the goals of the business strategy.

To that extent, it is quite distressing that this concept was floated relatively late in the strategy literature because that tends to show that researchers until that time had an overly theoretical inclination in pursuing the subject of business strategy. After all, the fact remains that companies need capabilities to do business and the company having superior capabilities will derive some advantage out of that. Whether a capability provides a *time advantage*, such as the ability to go-to-market faster than others, a *cost advantage*, such as the ability to either sell cheaper or have better profitability due to lower costs, or an *efficiency advantage*, such as having the ability to do something faster so that fewer resources are required to do the same amount of work—each or all of these advantages will eventually enhance the company's ability to maintain or improve its position within the industry segment.

Another reason for stating that a capability-based strategy is the most effective is that no matter what strategy a company establishes, these strategies eventually must drive day-to-day operations and activities in order to affect changes on the ground and make the firm realize the benefits of the strategy. Capabilities provide that link between the strategy and operations. Capabilities are process-based, but may demand the creation of assets as part of the process. A statistical process for demand forecasting may require a computing asset as part of the process. A manufacturing process for making steel efficiently will require a blast furnace as an asset as part of the manufacturing process.

Operations and activities are most efficiently performed when *standard* processes have been established to do so; further, if such processes have been *automated*, they make these operations and activities even more efficient and less error-prone. *Standardization* provides consistency and *automation* provides efficiency, the two key words in creating a reliable, repeatable process that is not dependent on individual skills, subjective whims, or individual levels of sophistication.

In summary, creating a business capability requires the creation of a process that may require leveraging physical assets that may exist or may need to be created as part of the new capability. We want to make this definition clear, though our main discussion of capabilities will primarily focus on creating the process side of supply chain capabilities, even as these processes will inevitably leverage existing assets and may require creating new ones.

A refresher on the three generic strategies is presented earlier in this chapter. The following section shows how each one of these strategies eventually requires that the firm develop capabilities in its selected functional areas that are better than those of the competition.

Cost Strategy as Capabilities Driver

The cost strategy requires the ability to reduce costs to establish the price leadership or enhanced profitability. This strategy will require that the firm relentlessly focuses on each activity and either eliminates it, merges that activity with another, or reduces the cost of performing that activity. Cost in the corporate structure comes from direct costs such as the purchases of raw material, products, and services, and indirect costs such as maintaining corporate offices, infrastructure costs for new technology, and product distribution. A cost strategy requires that the firm reviews all these costs, not only the direct costs related to the product, but also the cost of other activities in its entire value chain. For a typical retailer, for example, the actual cost of merchandise may only make up 40 to 60 percent of their total cost of goods sold. The other costs for a typical retailer will come from distribution expenses, inventory stocking expenses, store operations, technology, cost of capital, and other overheads. These other costs may easily add another 30 to 40 percent to the original cost of merchandise. Comparable ratios of material to sales exist for manufacturers. Therefore, creating a cost advantage requires that all activities contributing to the cost be evaluated. Then, the actual cost advantage may come from any of these activities based on a firm's capabilities in specific business functions that may be superior to the competition. For example, better sourcing decisions may directly reduce the cost of purchasing merchandise, or savings in any number of supporting activities, such as warehousing, transportation, inventory reduction, and purchasing automation, may provide the cost advantages. But to create the cost advantage through these capabilities, each of these functions will require that the firm creates the capability to conduct these activities *more efficiently, faster,* and *cheaper* than its competitors.

Differentiation Strategy as Capabilities Driver

The second generic strategy revolves around differentiation. Creating differentiation also requires the creation of capabilities that will allow the firm to drive

WAL-MART: **A PIONEER IN SUPPLY CHAIN INNOVATIONS**

Wal-Mart again provides a great example. Wal-Mart did not start as a retail behemoth and reduce its merchandise costs through its huge buying leverage. Rather, it reduced its costs through all the other value chain activities by focusing on building supply chain and merchandise planning functions that allowed it so that it can start leveraging its size for directly reducing the cost of merchandise through volume-based negotiations. Remember that Wal-Mart was the first large retailer to bypass the wholesalers and set up its own distribution network and, from then on, they have been pioneering supply chain innovations, whether they consist of cross-docking, demand collaboration with suppliers, vendor-managed inventory, or, more recently, radio frequency identification (RFID) technology. Each of these capabilities, in turn, allows them to continue sustaining their cost advantage.

the differentiation in the products and services it offers. This differentiation may come through innovation in product design or manufacturing, customer service, delivery, or any other activity in the value chain of the firm. Depending on the functions that the firm decides to pursue to create differentiation, relevant capabilities must be created that are better than the capabilities of their competitors to drive the competitive advantage.

Focus Strategy as Capabilities Driver

The third generic strategy of focus is also realized only through specific business capabilities that the firm decides to develop or enhance so that the firm can do some selected business functions better than its competition.

The objective of presenting these examples is to show that, irrespective of the business strategy pursued by the firm, the firm must create certain capabilities that would allow it to be better at selected business functions than its competitors. In turn, these capabilities become the source of the competitive advantage for the firm and position the firm to fully leverage its business strategy for profitable survival and growth. As every strategy goal can potentially be reached by pursuing several different functional capabilities or a combination of them, therefore each firm must determine which capabilities it wishes to focus on and develop to be better than its competitors.

KINDLE's **DIFFERENTIATION STRATEGY**

Amazon's introduction of Kindle exemplifies several of these differentiation aspects: it represents the product innovation since this is the first device of its kind and it also represents a delivery model for content that allows the users to get instantaneous access to books and newspapers that they have paid for. Compare the delivery models for the conventional books purchased on Amazon and those purchased on Kindle. In fact, Amazon has been in the forefront of using differentiation as a core business strategy, just as Wal-Mart has been using cost as their core business strategy. Amazon first introduced the Web-based bookstore, thus providing virtually an endless selection of books that no physical store can match, thus creating a differentiator that gave them the edge on competition as well as providing them the cost advantages coming from not having to maintain physical stores. Now, the introduction of Kindle is almost as big a disruption to the conventional model of selling content and provides another huge differentiator to Amazon that will be hard for its competitors to match. But both these differentiators have required that Amazon create unique capabilities that its competitors simply did not have the ability, inclination, or skills to create. While Amazon's competitors, Barnes & Noble and Borders, did eventually create their own Web stores, they could never replicate Amazon's cost and delivery models to erode its competitive advantages. Similarly, Amazon had to develop the capability of creating and managing digital content before it could leverage Kindle as a differentiator, which once again will continue to sustain Amazon's competitive advantages over its competitors until they can develop a similar capability.

E-TRADE's **FOCUS STRATEGY**

A great example of focus strategy is E-trade. When E-trade started its operations in the early 1990s, it created a niche for itself by pursuing the individual investors who were technically savvy and wanted a self-guided model for investing. However, pursuing this focused strategy meant developing new capabilities to attract and support this customer niche, and it did this by creating a brand-new way of letting customers trade in a self-service model through a hosted Web site that was easier to use and provided better information to make decisions and execute trades than any of their competitors at the time. Of course, most of these advantages for E-trade have been eroded in recent years as the online trading industry has matured and competitors have caught up with E-trade in providing similar services.

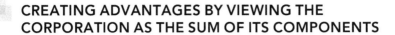

CREATING ADVANTAGES BY VIEWING THE CORPORATION AS THE SUM OF ITS COMPONENTS

Another way to think of strategy and competitive advantage is to think of corporations as the sum of their components. After all, a corporation is really a sum of its parts and is just as good as those parts would make it. Collis and Montgomery state that "most multibusiness companies are the sum of their parts and nothing more."[6] They continue by presenting their triangle of corporate strategy, with Resources, Organization, and Businesses as the three sides of the triangle, explaining that, "great corporate strategies come in the first instance from strength in each side of the triangle: high-quality rather than pedestrian resources, strong market positions in attractive industries, and an efficient administrative organization."

This is an internally focused view of the corporation, similar to the strategy view proposed by Kenneth Andrews and based on an analysis of a firm's internal strengths. There will always be external opportunities to be leveraged by a firm, but in most cases these opportunities are equally available to every participant in an industry segment, creating a competitive parity. Identifying such opportunities early can provide some temporary advantage to the firm, but a sustained advantage normally comes from a firm's own strengths.

Therefore, in this view, when it comes to sustained competitive advantage, a corporation can generally leverage only what it has. This is a logical way to think of how a corporation creates and maintains its competitive edge. Earlier in this chapter, we review the thinking on the resource-based view (RBV) and the capabilities-based competitive advantages for a corporation. Both of these views can actually fit very nicely with the view of the corporation as the sum of its components, since the components of the corporation consist of its resources and its capabilities. Leveraging these resources and capabilities is what allows a firm to create and sustain the competitive advantages that move the firm toward achieving its strategic goals.

Figure 3.3 shows the three major components that a corporation can leverage to create competitive advantage. These are products, processes, and people. These are what makes one corporation different from another and creates their unique identity as a corporation. The resources are shown in the center of the picture and represent resources like cash, assets, brand value, and so on. Think of these resources as a required condition for an enterprise to exist or create advantages: the corporation must have these resources to leverage the three core components of *products*, *processes*, and *people*.

In an alternate view, Hill and Jones refer to the four building blocks of competitive advantage as superior quality, superior customer service, superior

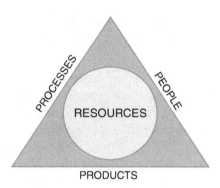

FIGURE 3.3 Components of a Corporation

innovation, and superior efficiency.[7] However, every one of these building blocks can be traced back to one of the components presented in Figure 3.3 that make up the corporation and create a competitive source of differentiation for it. Quality is primarily an attribute of *product*, customer service being an attribute of *process*, innovation is a result of *process* and *people*, and efficiency can be generally achieved through a good *process*.

Superior *quality* has been qualified as reliability or excellence. When quality is viewed as reliability, it is closely related to the *product* or service aspect of the corporation. In this sense, the quality reflects the dependability of the *products* and the consistency of the user experience with this *product*. Many examples can be thought of to describe this specific point: Toyota cars have long been known for their dependability or quality. That perception provides Toyota with a competitive edge that other manufacturers do not have. When quality is viewed as excellence, it may be related to the *product* or the *process*. Toyota shows this aspect of quality with their branding of Lexus. In this case, not only is the product supposed to be dependable (hence quality as reliability), but there is a greater emphasis on the whole customer experience of buying and owning a Lexus that is built on the *process* excellence. Excellence in this case is whole customer experience from the product presentation, product quality, buying, servicing, leasing, and every contact that a customer may make with Toyota. This perception of excellence is what provides Toyota with a competitive advantage for the luxury segment. No matter how we look at the quality, as reliability or excellence, it maps to the *product* or *process* constituencies in the view of the corporation presented earlier.

Superior *customer service* is generally a result of *process*. Customers interact with a corporation through its customer management *process*, which is sometimes delivered through its *people*. A self-help Web site that allows the customers to check the status of their order is a result of the *process* established by the firm for providing this aspect of customer service. Whether this self-help enables one to check the real-time status of the order or shows you a status that is only updated every other week, will determine whether this process is capable of providing any competitive advantage for the corporation or not. The richness of the underlying business function that a self-help customer service application provides will determine the customer satisfaction and therefore its superiority over similar capabilities provided by the firm's competitors. In a different scenario, customer service could be delivered through a call center or a store, where the customer interacts with the corporation's *people*, who, in turn, depend on its *processes* to serve the customer. In any case, the combination of *people* and *processes* enables customer service and the extent of its superiority over a competitor's capability determines whether it creates any advantage for the firm or not.

Innovation is the next identified building block of competitive advantage. Innovation that creates competitive advantage can happen both in *products* and *processes* that the customers interact with. But innovation is a result of *processes* and the *people* in the corporation. The people's skills, training, and competence play a definite part in the creation of innovation; however, the process must support a culture of innovation and provide the right opportunities for people to create and encourage innovation. Apple is generally thought of as a company with innovative products, and it must have processes that support such innovation. Supporting innovation takes a special kind of outlook, but also a risk-tolerant culture that promotes thinking out of the box and does not put an unacceptably high price on failures.

The last building block mentioned in the Hill and Jones model is *efficiency*. Efficiency is generally a direct result of the *process*. These processes can represent a wide spectrum of a firm's business and range from the manufacturing process to the customer support process, purchasing process, or demand planning process, but all processes can offer an efficiency advantage for the corporation. A good process provides a *repeatable* and *dependable* sequence of activities that can be done *efficiently* to produce *consistent* results. Let us dwell on this definition for a few seconds to absorb the key words: repeatability creates consistency of results, which is important for creating quality (as reliability or as excellence), dependability creates certainty of the outcome (think of this as being highly available), and efficiency means the rate of throughput (output of the process per unit of time). Efficiency is generally a result of well-automated *processes*. Most of the efficiency growth seen in the last few decades in America has been the result of technology-based processes that have automated the processes and reduced the dependence on human effort and skill to complete the job (see chart in the Introduction for the productivity growth in the United States). This is true for manufacturing processes with automation through computer-controlled machinery and industrial robots, as well as for back-office and other processes through large-scale adoption of solutions like ERP.

Finally, we will mention the corporate culture as the basic ecosystem in which the components of a corporation work together. While the effect of corporate culture is hard to measure in an objective fashion, organizational culture matters. Culture affects people and their behaviors directly; it affects how they think and react. It affects their risk-tolerance or risk-averseness and therefore their ability to create innovation in the corporate workplace. Culture affects customer service directly, but it also affects product quality indirectly by affecting the will to innovate. A culture of empowerment will produce a better customer service, while a culture of extreme control will almost always create issues in all areas of corporate functions. Kotter and Heskett presented an interesting study of corporate culture and its impact on their performance in 1992.[8] They analyzed the results of 207 American companies over an 11-year period to report that "firms with cultures that emphasized all the key managerial constituencies (customers, stockholders, and employees) and leadership from managers at all levels outperformed firms that did not have those cultural traits by a huge margin. Over an eleven-year period, the former increased revenues by an average of 682 percent versus 166 percent for the latter . . . and improved their net incomes by 756 percent versus 1 percent."

The culture is represented in Figure 3.4, showing the corporation as the sum of its components. Note that the corporate culture permeates all other aspects of the corporation.

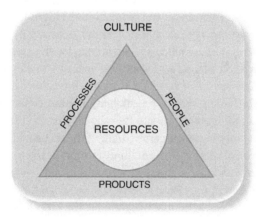

FIGURE 3.4 Components of a Corporation Immersed in Its Culture

CREATING ADVANTAGES THROUGH THE VALUE CHAIN

Porter mentioned the concept of *value chain* in his book on competitive advantage.[9] The value chain represents a sequence of activities conducted by a firm that add value to the inputs to create an output product or service that the firm's customers find valuable. The generic examples of such activities are product design, manufacturing, marketing, sales, distribution, and support. Porter presented the concept in the context that every firm has "primary" and "support" value chain activities and that these activities can create competitive advantages for the firm through careful analysis and assessment of these activities to determine their contribution to the fulfillment of buyer needs. Porter also mentions the concept of the value chain belonging to a single firm and existing within the larger ecosystem of the value chains of its partners, such as suppliers and customers. Porter calls this extended view the *value system*.

The idea of the value chain was proposed in the context of Porter's three generic strategies, in which Porter argued that competitive advantages can come from any part of a firm's value chain. He postulated that firms should carefully deconstruct their value chains to analyze their operations and tasks and evaluate each of them in the context of their ability to create cost or differentiation advantages for the firm. He emphasized two aspects of value chains:

1. The opportunity for creating advantages can come from any part of the value chain
2. Value chains for firms in a competitive segment look alike at a higher level, masking differences that can provide the opportunities to create competitive advantages.

Both of these approaches are quite valid even today. The opportunities to create advantages remain in improving individual processes, but they become obvious only after the high-level view has been deconstructed into its constituent processes. Once the process is deconstructed and each component of the process is well understood for its value within the whole process, the opportunity to leverage it for creating advantage may come from several possible changes, such as making these processes more efficient through automation or integrating the process with other functions (value chain linkages, as described by Porter) to make the whole chain more efficient. The advantages gained through superior processes may come from automation that increases the efficiency, reliability, and repeatability of the process; reduction in cost;

enhanced visibility across the chain; and better user efficiencies, allowing managers to instead focus on resolving process exceptions. The basic idea revolves around analyzing the processes of the value chain, identifying those that can be improved, and making the required improvements to create and sustain competitive advantage.

A large number of activities in Porter's value chain are part of today's supply chains: activities within the corporation that form the value chain and the extended supply chains through collaboration with the partners who form the value system. Porter's value chain included the functions of inbound logistics, operations, outbound logistics, marketing and sales, and service. The scope of supply chain activities in modern corporations includes all these functions, with the exception of sales and marketing, which is a separate business function outside the functional scope of supply chain. However, sales and marketing drives the demand planning functions of the supply chain and must be integrated with the supply chain functions for effective management of all these functions. In fact, this integration itself has great potential for becoming a competitive advantage when leveraged properly.

There are many other management concepts that share this idea of creating advantages through the value chain. One example can be found in Toyota's *lean manufacturing* philosophy. The concept is based on the core precept of elimination of waste (*muda*) from every activity that is conducted for the production of goods and services. This is similar to Porter's call to analyze and assess every activity in the *primary* value chain to determine its contribution toward the needs of the buyer and its cost compared to the competitors.

Porter considered the activities of inbound logistics, operations, outbound logistics, marketing and sales, and service as the *primary* activities in the corporate value chain. They are considered *primary* because these activities are essential to the production, sale, and delivery of the product to the buyer. The value chain is extended with the inclusion of the *support* activities consisting of procurement, technology development, human resource management, and firm infrastructure. These activities are considered to be the *support* activities, because they support the primary activities and each other by providing purchased inputs, technology, human resources, and any other infrastructural input. Finally, Porter concludes that any of these activities can be used to create competitive advantage for the firm, when they are contributing directly toward creation of value for the firm's buyer.

However, to identify how an activity can create advantage, these activities need to be broken down into subactivities and tasks. These tasks need to be analyzed to find those that align with the internal skills and strengths of the organization. These tasks are potential sources of creating advantage, if they directly contribute toward the value created by the parent process. By leveraging their unique organization skills to do these tasks better, firms can create the superior processes necessary for creating competitive advantages. The advantages primarily originate through reduced costs, increased efficiencies, better quality of products or services produced, faster time-to-market for introduction of new products, or extension of the product life cycles—any combination of these can be the result of an improved process.

Of course, such an analysis of processes and tasks assumes that the firm understands its value chain and has the ability to expand it to specific process tasks to be able to analyze and find the potential areas of improvement. This is important to understand, because the differences in the value chains become visible only when the value chains are broken down to their individual tasks. Therefore, differentiation opportunities can be identified only when a firm completely understands its value chain activities. At higher levels of granularity, the value chains of individual firms within an industry segment look undistinguishable. At the highest level, for example, a value chain consisting of buy-distribute-sell activities represents all retailers. The differentiation opportunities are invisible at this level. But as these functions are disaggregated to the individual tasks, plenty of differences become visible because no two retailers have identical processes supporting the same business function. Such differences should be analyzed to establish if they can become opportunities for the firm to differentiate itself from its peers in the industry segment.

Figure 3.5 extends the example from the retail industry. The distribution activity is expanded into its constituent functions and the *store fulfillment planning* function is broken down into its constituent tasks. It is at this level that potential differentiating opportunities start to appear. For example, consider the inventory planning function in the stores. Most of the retailers follow different ways to execute inventory planning in stores. An inventory review can be conducted periodically or continuously, every other day or weekly; it can be segregated by product classes, ABC classification, or velocity-based classification; it can be conducted centrally or locally, with frequent physical verification or not, with real-time inventory data or with older data; or it can be based on automated inventory optimization algorithms or user inputs. The combinations of executing a simple inventory planning process in the stores are endless and if a firm can develop this function to achieve higher

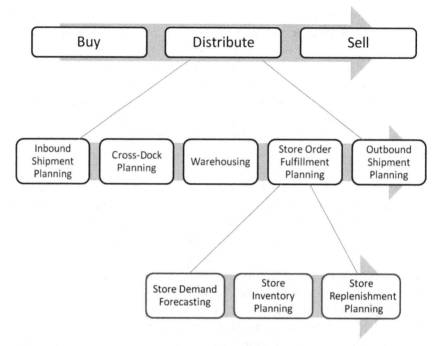

FIGURE 3.5 Deconstructing the Distribution Function

inventory turns and maintain more efficient in-stock levels than most of its competitors, then this activity can provide a distinct advantage for the firm. It can reduce the firm's cost of operations, reduce lost sales, and increase revenue and customer satisfaction.

Finally, we touch upon Porter's concept of linkages among these activities and their importance. These linkages have two overbearing characteristics:

1. They provide the ability to have integrated processes to achieve visibility across processes.
2. They provide the ability to react to changes with the objective of optimizing the results across the chain rather than focusing on improvements in a functional silo.

Such linkages can exist within the firm's value chain or may extend beyond its own value chain to the value chains of its partners. When viewed in the supply chain context, this basically means integrated processes that provide cross-chain process visibility, ability to detect real-time changes and assess their impact, and

WAL-MART's **INVENTORY PLANNING**

Wal-Mart has consistently achieved higher inventory turns than its competition by optimizing their inventories at their stores and warehouses. This provides Wal-Mart with the ability to continuously push the cost frontier by passing on savings to its customers that its competition is simply unable to match. What does it take for Wal-Mart to do so? Many things, such as the ability to have real-time inventory visibility across its network for on-hand as well as projected stocks, the ability to detect demand changes across stores and regions and react to such changes very quickly, and having a flexible distribution network with strategically placed warehouses and its own fleet of trucks for store deliveries. The important thing to understand is that any of the value chain activities can present an opportunity to differentiate; however, the firm must understand its own value chain and must have the ability to break it down to individual tasks to spot these opportunities. Of course, the willingness to invest in creating such differentiation is being assumed.

the ability to react to such changes in a globally optimal way. Notice that the process of detecting changes real-time, assessing their impact, and finding globally optimal resolutions can be automated using technology for commonly occurring business situations. This leaves the human managers to focus their attention on handling exceptional situations that the technology cannot handle.

For example, consider a situation where the corporate supply chain is integrated with its suppliers. As the purchase orders are sent to the suppliers, the supplier's supply chain sends back acknowledgments after planning these orders with the accurate projected date and quantity of supply. If this is different from the corporation's original needs, then the corporation can take several alternative actions: to buy the additional supplies from an alternate source, inform its own customers about the expected delay, or adjust its manufacturing plans to shift product mix. Some of these actions, such as ordering additional supplies from an alternate source or informing its own customers about the expected delay, can be automated, especially when the changes are within a predefined acceptable threshold. Others, such as changing the manufacturing plans, can be accomplished through user alerts and manual intervention. In all cases, the firm is reacting to a change in plan to optimize its global resources or customer service, both of which can be its differentiators created through the linkages between processes in its own value chain and those of its supplier's value chains.

This integration among the processes is, in fact, a very well-established practice these days. Enterprise resource planning (ERP) systems were created with this unique proposition in early 1980s and these remain one of the single differentiators among companies competing on process-based competency, increasingly supported through off-the-shelf technology solutions. We will revisit this aspect of technology-based solutions for automating business processes in our discussion on functional strategies.

DEVELOPING COMPETITIVE ADVANTAGES THROUGH CAPABILITIES

Now that we have reviewed the major concepts of the business strategy, it is time to dissect these concepts to establish the core precept of this book, that achieving strategic goals is really about building capabilities. Capabilities are simply functional competencies that a firm must develop and continuously improve to create and sustain the competitive advantages. *Functional competencies are a set of related business processes that are unique to the corporation in providing a specific capability and hence creating the competitive advantage.*

While several concepts of business strategy presented here may appear different, they all converge when seen from the point of view of strategic planning and execution. Regardless of the theory one subscribes to for the development of strategy, when it comes to realization of the business strategy, all firms must create specific business capabilities. Establishing this relationship between the different theories of strategies presented here and how all of them drive firms to create capabilities is the objective of this section.

To achieve this objective, we will present each of the major strategy concepts in this new context of how creating the right set of capabilities can help in achieving the goals set by the business strategy. We will review how each of the generic strategies drive a firm to develop specific business capabilities to achieve its goals. We will also review how the alternate views of business strategy, those based on resources and capabilities, converge with Porter's generic strategies when approached from the point of view of strategy driving the development of capabilities.

Porter's Generic Strategies

Porter defined three generic strategies: *cost* strategy is based on pursuing cost leadership, *differentiation* strategy is based on differentiation of the offerings (products/services/user experience), and *focus* strategy is based on creating a niche that can be further focused on price or product differentiators. We will explore how each of these strategies mandate the development of specific business capabilities that can help the firms achieve their business goals.

Cost Strategy: Creating Cost Advantages

Pursuing the cost strategy primarily drives the firm to reduce the cost of its products and services below the average cost afforded by its competition. As long as the firm has the capabilities to do so, it can continue to pursue the cost strategy. To determine what capabilities a firm must develop to reduce its cost, we need to understand the structure of cost in an organizational context.

Cost is one of the most important financial facts in an organization, so much so that it is the second line in a company's financial statements. That is quite sensible as well, because knowing the costs in comparison with the revenues of a corporation provides the quickest and most intuitive way of assessing a corporation's general health. Cost of goods sold (COGS) is generally made up of various cost components. Generally, the biggest component of COGS is the direct costs of raw materials for manufacturers and the cost of merchandise for the retailers. The second-largest component of cost in COGS is other direct costs, like the cost of manufacturing or the cost of distribution, including labor. Manufacturers add value by creating a finished product from its raw materials and this activity generally accounts for their second largest cost. Retailers add value through distribution of merchandise by getting the right product at the right place at the right time. Therefore, distribution costs generally account for the second largest cost for retailers. Some other industries may have their people as the biggest cost, for example, consulting, architecture, and design firms where value is added through the intellectual property created by their people.

In any case, controlling costs requires that the firm analyses its cost structure and establishes the main sources of cost in its COGS. Once that is done, the next step will be to analyze the activities related to those business functions that are the largest sources of cost and identifying the set of capabilities that affect these costs. These become the set of target capabilities that can be potentially created or improved. An organization may not be able to work on all the targeted capabilities simultaneously and may prioritize them over time. Organizational planning processes can be developed to prioritize targeted capabilities to drive capital investments and change management.

Expanding on the retail example, the cost strategy requires that one must focus on reducing the cost of merchandise and cost of distribution. This implicates the two business functions of the merchandise and supply chain. Merchandise must review its processes of sourcing, suppliers, contracts, product portfolio analysis, price optimization, and promotions to identify where these processes can be changed to reduce cost or be made more efficient to enhance resource utilization. Supply chain must review its processes on demand planning, inventory planning, replenishment planning, warehousing, and transportation to identify where the supply chain processes can be changed to reduce cost or be made more efficient to enhance resource utilization. The analysis of the merchandising and supply chain processes will allow the firm to shortlist the process capabilities it must focus on, to achieve the cost leadership. Once the target capabilities have been identified, the firm must have the *ability* and the *willingness* to create the capability to support their business strategy.

Cost leadership can be achieved through focusing on any part of the value chain since every activity can be reviewed for improvements. Of course, logic dictates that the biggest cost pie be addressed first since it will be the easiest to cut and make the biggest impact. Finding the biggest opportunities requires understanding and analysis of the firm's operations.

The process of analysis, prioritization, and creation of capabilities must be continuous, because all competitive advantages will erode with time as the competitors develop similar capabilities. Therefore, to sustain the cost advantage, the firm must find potential opportunities and continue to invest in the new capabilities and enhance existing ones to maintain their lead.

Differentiation Strategy: Creating Differentiation Advantages

Pursuing the differentiation strategy primarily drives the firm to distinguish itself either through its products and services, or through customer experiences that are valuable enough for the customers to pay a premium for the firm's products. Unlike the cost strategy that provides a clear definition of the target by identifying cost as the main success criteria, this strategy leaves that function to the firm, and for a good reason, as well: Cost is a common denominator across industries, but differentiation can be created along different dimensions and measured in several different ways. For example, differentiation can mean always-in-stock inventory for one retailer, or knowledgeable stores associates for another, or a next-day-delivery guarantee for yet another.

Like cost, there are many origins of differentiation in an organization. It can originate in firm's products and services or come from its many business functions.

Differentiation advantages can also originate from products.

FedEx: **ENHANCED CAPABILITY**

When FedEx launched their online parcel tracking service in mid-1990s, this differentiation advantage came from their capability to track the packages through transit and inform their customer electronically on the status of their deliveries. Having this advantage over their competitors allowed FedEx to grow and expand their market share quickly, but this also required that FedEx develop the capability of scanning all their packages at predefined events in their delivery life cycle, from receiving the package from the customer, to leaving their warehouse of origin, to reaching a transshipment point or destination warehouse, and finally to delivery. To produce this tracking information and relate it to a customer's specific package, FedEx had to integrate information from all their systems dealing with package acceptance, warehousing, shipment, and delivery. FedEx not only developed this capability when they introduced this service in 1990s, but continued to enhance this capability continuously when they introduced the hand-held devices carried by their drivers to capture real-time delivery information. The capability was enhanced again when these devices were able to electronically capture the signatures of the receiving party to provide proof of delivery. This differentiator allowed FedEx to charge a premium on their delivery services for a considerable length of time, until most competitors caught up with the technology and started providing similar services.

APPLE: **INNOVATIVE PRODUCT DESIGN**

Consider product innovations pioneered by Apple. Most of Apple's products are not based on any basic research breakthrough, but simply on creating a product design that is simple, elegant, and intuitive to use. When Apple introduced the iPod, all basic technologies going into the product such as the hard disk, battery, and the streaming audio had been available for quite some time. Even the product idea was not new, since the market already had a number of digital audio players. However, Apple found a way to combine these technologies together in an innovative product that was easy to use. Supported by a brilliant marketing strategy, iPod became an overnight success. Apple repeated this triumph with successive releases of iPods and iPhones. To do so, Apple must develop a capability to create innovative product designs, quickly bring them to market, and create marketing buzz, all before competitors can mimic their designs.

The process capability developed by Apple is very different from the process capability created by FedEx. While the functional capability created by FedEx is well defined and precise, the process capability at Apple is more likely a mix of culture, user experience design, and marketing. These basic differences between the two processes represent the differentiators in these two cases and also affect the sustainability of these differentiators. While FedEx's capability to track packages is now replicated by its competitors, to reproduce Apple's culture of innovation is more difficult, therefore providing Apple with a more sustainable competitive advantage through their capability of creating innovative product design.

Focus Strategy: Creating Niche Advantages

The focus strategy can be seen as a special case of the differentiation strategy in which the firm decides to target a specific group of customers. Depending on the profile of this targeted group of customers, the firm should create differentiators that will appeal to this group. These differentiators can again come from cost (as in cost strategy), or unique products and services (as in differentiation strategy). The key in this strategy is to be able to understand the targeted customer segment enough to know what differentiators will be valuable to them and therefore what differentiators a targeted group of customers will pay for. Understanding and establishing these facts is part of strategy formulation itself and therefore outside the scope of the current discussion.

However, once these differentiators have been identified, the same process as discussed earlier in the other two generic strategies must take over to identify the business capabilities required to enable the company to create and maintain the differentiators. Since we have covered ample examples in the previous two sections, we will skip replicating the discussion here and assume that the relationship between the goals of a strategy and their achievement by creating business capabilities has been clearly understood.

Resource-Based View: Creating Advantages through Resources

This view of strategy is based on the underlying assumption that a firm's competitive advantage originates from resources that are *unique* to it. The supporters of this concept identify resources in three categories: direct resources, indirect resources, and capabilities. The examples of direct resources are cash and assets and examples of indirect resources would be brand value and customer loyalty. Without any doubt, all of these, cash, assets, brand value, and customer loyalty can be used to create competitive advantages. However, having these resources at their disposal reflects an already successful firm, which raises the question of what made the firm successful in the first place, so that it would have resources such as cash, assets, brand value, and customer loyalty? The firm must have started its life as a small entity and made its way to its current eminent position. What did the firm do to get here? The answer to this question, in fact, points back to the unique capabilities that the firm must have created in its initial days that made it successful enough to have the resources at its disposal.

Therefore, while the RBV of strategy lists direct resources, indirect resources, and its capabilities as the sources of competitive advantages, I believe that the root of real competitive advantage is primarily *capabilities*. However, these capabilities can generate other resources, which in turn can drive more competitive advantages.

For example, extra cash can be a direct resource, but unless the firm is able to not only have extra cash today, but also have the *capability* to continue to have extra cash in the future, any competitive advantage gained through this resource is temporary and not sustainable. The same is true for indirect resources such as brand value. To build brand value, a firm must do things like build dependable products or provide superior customer service over a long period of time, both of which would be capabilities that the firm must build before brand value can be created. Once the brand value is created, a temporary advantage can be achieved, but the firm must work to maintain that brand value to create a sustainable advantage. Maintaining brand value means a continued focus on the product quality, customer service, or any other differentiator that was the key to creating the brand. This means that the firm must continue to maintain the basic capabilities that created the differentiators, which created the brand value. In most cases, the basic capabilities may actually require constant enhancements to sustain the brand value as other competitors enter the fray and try to replicate the success of the firm.

Therefore, possession of direct or indirect resources that can create competitive advantage is not an accident, but a deliberate and consistent effort that the firm has put together by investing in its capabilities allowing it to create these resources. While the resource strategy considers direct and indirect resources as enabling competitive advantages, and that is true, the fact is that these resources themselves are a result of functional capabilities that, over time, have delivered these resources in addition to their direct contribution to creating the competitive advantages.

While General Electric (GE) currently has a brand value, it created this value by building reliable products over a long period of time. However, to keep this advantage, GE must continue to build products that are reliable, durable, and simple to operate. This means that GE must continue to invest in its design and manufacturing capabilities to maintain its brand value. If GE stops investing in maintaining its lead in the design and manufacturing capabilities, then the brand advantage will certainly erode over time. Continuing to build better products requires GE to invest in maintaining and enhancing its design and manufacturing *capabilities*. While the *capability* to manufacture better products will eventually generate brand value, the reverse is not true—no amount of brand value will provide GE with the capability to manufacture better products.

Therefore, while a resource-based view puts a value on resources, the fact remains that sustainable competitive advantage can only be created through capabilities. When such capabilities are consistently able to sustain competitive advantage over a long term, they can also provide resources, direct or indirect, that will have a synergistic effect on the ability of the basic capability to create the advantage. This synergy can help either in sustaining the competitive advantage longer without enhancing the basic capability, or may create additional cost or differentiation advantages, allowing the firm to charge a premium for its products and services.

Capability-Based View: Creating Advantages through Capabilities

This view of strategy is based on the assumption that a firm's competitive advantage originates from its capabilities. Since this view is well-aligned with the core precept of this book and is adequately presented earlier in this chapter in the section on capability-based strategies, we will skip it here.

Summing up, the main objective of the corporate strategy is to create a competitive advantage for a firm. There are several different theories for understanding strategy and some of them have been presented here. The main concepts that have been discussed are the three generic strategies of Porter, the resource-based view, and the capabilities-based view of competitive advantages. While the resource-based view looks at direct and indirect resources as creators of competitive advantage, these resources themselves come from specific business capabilities. Therefore, while business strategies target creating competitive advantages, the advantages themselves are the result of a firm's capabilities (see Figure 3.6). These capabilities may exist, may be new, or may

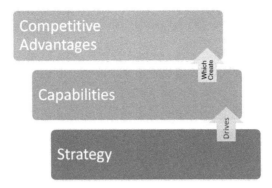

FIGURE 3.6 From Strategy to Competitive Advantages

be required to be enhanced to drive competitive advantages sought by the business strategy. Finally, the capabilities alone create the advantages to achieve the business goals of a firm.

UNDERSTANDING ADVANTAGE

Moving on with the understanding that capabilities are the origin of all competitive advantages, let us review what a capability must deliver to be able to have any value in the strategic discussion.

What constitutes advantage?

Earlier in the discussion, we used the word *superior* to identify a competitive advantage. A firm can have a competitive advantage, if its products are *superior* or if it provides *superior* customer service and so on. If the advantage comes from superiority, then what makes something *superior* to another? What creates superiority in a product or service?

Recall that we defined the capabilities as those that create or enhance business or functional competencies in a corporation. Business competencies are a set of related business processes and assets that are unique to the corporation in providing a specific capability and hence creating the competitive advantage. It therefore follows that it is the capabilities of a firm that enable it to produce superior products or services. Capabilities themselves consist of the business processes and assets required to execute those business processes (see Figure 3.7). Therefore, when firms have better business processes and assets, they have a superior capability. While a capability may consist of a process and related assets, the discussions here would refer to this simply as a process and

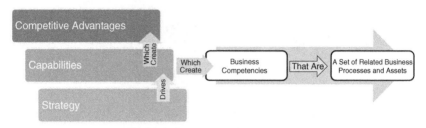

FIGURE 3.7 From Strategy to Competitive Advantages through Functional Competencies

assume that the related assets would always be included in the process as part of the capability creation.

Between two business processes supporting the same function, a business process is superior when it has at least one of the following advantages (see Figure 3.8) over the other.

Time Advantage

Time advantage is created when one of the business processes is faster than the other in achieving the same result. Time advantage is best exemplified with the time to market examples. Time advantage is typically created through careful analysis of all the activities supporting a process and elimination of those that don't add any value to the process, but only add lead time.

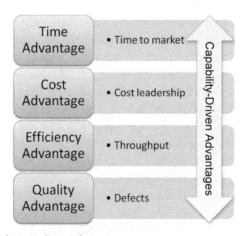

FIGURE 3.8 Understanding Advantage

TIME **ADVANTAGE: SATURN VERSUS HONDA**

Between 1991 and 1999, Saturn introduced only a single model of compact cars, the S-series, available in coupe, sedan, and wagon styles. During the same time, Honda introduced four completely new vehicles—del-Sol, CR-V, Passport, and Odyssey—and redesigned many vehicles, such as three generations of the Civic, three generations of the Accord, and two generations of the Prelude.

Time advantage can create product premiums, increased revenues, longer product life cycles, and intangible differentiator levers (such as brand value or an image of being innovative or agile). It becomes a competitive advantage when the firm develops processes that will enable it to quickly introduce new products in the market and portray the company as a pioneer and when the firm's business strategy leverages such differentiation through a premium brand image to grow market share and increase revenues.

Cost Advantage

Cost advantage is created when the superior business process is cheaper to operate than the inferior other. Cost advantage can be created through elimination of *waste* from the process, but also by optimizing the process within the process constraints. A lot of supply chain processes fall in this category and can provide finite cost advantages when implemented correctly. Inventory planning processes within the supply chain function is a good example in this category. A well-designed inventory planning process can leverage all these attributes of an item for determining optimal levels of inventory:

- Product segments based on the sales velocity
- Profitability profiles
- Product affinities
- Historical demand, supply, and lead-time patterns
- Projected demand, supply, and lead-time patterns
- Target service levels

However, depending on a firm's ability to collect and utilize this data, some firms may be able to create more favorable inventory cost structure than others, while maintaining comparable service levels. The firm with lower inventory and higher guaranteed service levels can then derive competitive advantages of cost as well as service (by guaranteeing product availability) from this *superior* capability. The firm can continue to enhance their capability to sustain these advantages by enhancing the algorithms for creating product segmentation, demand forecasts, using real-time data, increasing the frequency of planning, and so on.

Cost advantages in a manufacturing industry may arise from better manufacturing process, cheaper inputs, or higher levels of automation that increase efficiency. Reducing set-up change time, reducing the frequency of such changes, and increasing batch sizes are several commonly used methods to reduce per unit manufacturing costs. However, a superior manufacturing process will potentially have a comparable cost structure, but allow for short batch sizes to enable flexible factory schedules.

Every revised iteration of the original business process can potentially improve the existing cost structure and provide a continued superiority afforded by the process. These improvements are necessary to sustain the advantage over time. Cost advantage allows the company to become more profitable or expand its market share.

Efficiency Advantage

Efficiency advantage is created when the superior business processes provide higher throughput. Throughput measures the output of a process per unit time. For example, if a manufacturing station can produce 10 widgets in an hour, then its throughput will be higher compared to another station that produces only 8 widgets in an hour. Efficiency in this context also means asset utilization, such as the utilization of the assembly line in a manufacturing context, blast furnace utilization in steel production, or a jockey's utilization in the warehouse of a retailer. Assets in the context of efficiency can be people, machinery, or technology, anything that it costs to maintain and provides a useful function in the business process. The efficiency advantage can be created by automating, simplifying, or expediting a process. Efficiency advantage normally results in more favorable cost structure and supports a cost-based business strategy.

Think of the flexibility as part of the efficiency advantage. After all, there is no point in efficiently building widgets that no one wants. Therefore, flexibility of a process to change and adapt in response to the changes in the business environment is an advantage that should be built into the process. This flexibility in manufacturing environments typically shows up as set-up change time, while in nonmanufacturing industries, it may be the time required to respond to changing demand.

Quality Advantage

Quality advantage is created when the superior business process creates fewer defects than the inferior one. Quality advantage is generally a result of standardizing, automating, or simplifying a process. In the manufacturing context, a statistical process control (SPC) that allows companies to monitor the health of the process to reduce defects is a good example of this advantage. When compared to the conventional quality control processes that detect the defects after the product has been manufactured, the SPC-based approach prevents production of defective products by monitoring key process parameters. Quality advantage in the nonmanufacturing context relates to the ability of a process to consistently produce the same result (*dependability* and *repeatability*), and this definition can be applied to any business function, such as processing customer orders, fulfilling orders from a warehouse, creating replenishment demand, customer service, and so on. Quality advantage can reduce costs by preventing defects or introduce produce differentiators through better quality, such as increased customer satisfaction, customer retention, brand value, product durability, and so on. In all these cases, the quality advantage can support a business strategy by creating a differentiator with a potential value for which the buyer is ready to pay a premium.

For any process or capability to be able to create a real competitive advantage, the following two conditions must be fulfilled:

1. The value created through the superior process must be valuable enough to the buyer that she is ready to pay a premium for the differentiator created by this process or move her business to the firm to take advantage of this differentiator.
2. The cost of creating the process superiority must be less than the premium generated through the differentiator advantage created by the process.

Unless these two conditions are met, no advantage can be realized. If the cost of creating the differentiation is more than the premium it generates, then the system as a whole becomes less cost competitive, which is not desirable. If the differentiation, whether cost- or feature-based, is not valuable to buyers, then buyers will not pay any premium for the differentiator, which makes for a wasted investment. Therefore, when firms decide to invest in creating business capabilities, they must spend time to analyze the cost-benefit equation and clearly understand the differentiator created and the value generated through this differentiator from the point of view of the buyer. This is easier said than done. However, good analysis and logical inferences always help.

TOYOTA: **A BRIEF HISTORY**

Toyota Motor Corporation was founded in 1937. In fiscal year ending March 31, 2009, Toyota Motor Corporation and its subsidiaries sold over 7.5 million passenger cars, trucks, and buses worldwide under the Toyota, Scion, Lexus, Daihatsu, and Hino brands. The company manufactures vehicles and related parts in 26 countries and regions throughout the world and sells them in approximately 170 countries and locations.[10]

Toyota first started exporting cars to America in the late 1950s, but it was not until the oil crisis of 1973 that Japanese cars gained a noticeable presence on American roads. In the beginning, Toyota and other Japanese manufacturers continued to produce smaller, fuel-efficient cars for the American market. Toyota introduced their luxury brand, Lexus, in 1989, and started adding larger models, SUVs, pick-up trucks, and luxury models to its lineup in the 1990s. Today, Toyota makes 12 of its vehicles in North America. Since the company began manufacturing in North America in 1986, Toyota has built more than 20 million vehicles here and, today, Toyota builds more vehicles in North America than any other international automaker.

In 2005, Toyota ranked eighth in Forbes 2000 list with revenues of over $135 billion.[11] In January 2009, the *Washington Post*[12] reported that Toyota had become the world's largest auto manufacturer, surpassing General Motors: "Toyota outpaced its rival to sell 8.972 million cars and trucks around the world in 2008, about 616,000 vehicles more than GM's final tally of 8.356 million." On the way to becoming the world's largest automaker, Toyota managed to make its name through its famous Toyota Production System and its philosophy of consistent focus on quality, waste (*muda*) reduction, and continuous improvement (*kaizen*). It also pioneered in hybrid vehicle technology with the best-selling Prius hybrid and became well known for its luxury brand Lexus and its "pursuit of perfection" marketing pitch.

From late 2009 through the first quarter of 2010, Toyota recalled more than 8 million vehicles worldwide in several phases over claims of unintended acceleration in its vehicles. In April 2010, Toyota was asked to pay a fine of over $16 million by the United States government for its delay in notifying the National Highway Traffic Safety Administration regarding the defective accelerator pedals. In addressing the recall, Toyota took several actions including suspending its sales and production in spite of the large financial costs of doing so. While Toyota's initial response to the crisis seemed to be sluggish, the company quickly got its act together by organizing its dealers, resolving the underlying engineering issues, offering prompt repairs, providing huge financial incentives to lure new buyers back to the showrooms, and introducing the *star safety system* standard on all its vehicles to rebuild confidence in its vehicles. The result: their best-selling sedan, Camry, was still the number-one car sold in its category in YTD sales in May 2010, according to the *Wall Street Journal's*[13] data on auto sales. Toyota sold 125,804 Camry vehicles from January through May 2010, with the next domestic competitor being Chevrolet Malibu, at 87,597 cars in the same time period.

While the recalls have definitely affected Toyota's reputation for quality, the recent sales numbers show that the impact may be short-lived. Of course, Toyota's recent push to emphasize safety with its star safety system and its consistent message regarding reliability, along with the quality of its vehicles, should help as well.

BEYOND THE BUSINESS STRATEGY: FUNCTIONAL AND DEPLOYMENT STRATEGIES

A business strategy establishes the main direction for achieving the competitive advantages. It establishes the types of advantages that the firm decides to pursue to its benefit, in a given industry segment. The job of creating these advantages falls on specific business capabilities sought by the business strategy.

Identifying these capabilities needs a thorough understanding and analysis of the value chain of the firm. If the targeted capabilities do not exist, they must be created. If these capabilities exist, they must be assessed with respect to their superiority in comparison with similar capabilities of the firm's competitors. When there is more than one alternative to create potential strategic advantages for the firm, an objective cost-benefit analysis must be done to select the more desirable option. In addition to the cost-benefit analysis, the firm should also assess its skills and strengths in the functional areas to determine which capability would be easiest to create and maintain.

A functional strategy for the targeted business areas must be developed, similar to the formulation of the business strategy, to help prioritize potential initiatives to enhance the selected business capabilities. This is the subject of our discussion in Chapter 4, where we analyze the process for evaluating several business functions and create a prioritized sequence for the development of capabilities. Note that many functional strategies may exist to support the corporate strategy, each one mapping the evolution of a single business

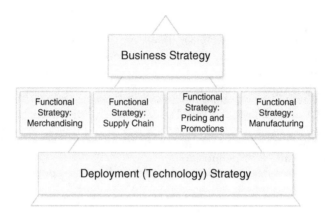

FIGURE 3.9 A Business Strategy May Drive Many Functional Strategies

function, and all of them together supporting the goals of the business strategy of the firm. The picture that emerges is shown in Figure 3.9: a business strategy driving many functional strategies that work together to support the goals established by the business strategy.

While we discuss the concepts of functional strategy, our main focus remains on the supply chain function in the firm. We review the existing thinking on different supply chain strategies and see how they are aligned to support generic business strategies to create competitive advantages. Where appropriate, we also discuss examples of functional strategies from other areas that may support specific supply chain strategy under discussion.

Beyond the functional strategies lies the realm of deployment strategies, which is the subject of our discussion later in the book. While there are more facets to deployment strategy, we primarily focus on the technology strategy that provides the enabling framework for the creation and maintenance of technology infrastructure required for successful deployment of functional strategies. We believe that technology is becoming a de facto enabler of business capabilities across the functional spectrum, and understanding how technology affects the quest of creating advantages is imperative for any company. Figure 3.9 shows the conceptual representation of the strategy model discussed here: business strategy is supported by many functional strategies that are enabled through a technology strategy.

The objective of the discussion remains to establish a working process to achieve an explicit alignment among the three strategies—business, functional, and technology—to create and sustain competitive advantages that support the business goals of a firm.

CHAPTER FOUR

Exploring Functional Strategy

I N THIS CHAPTER WE discuss what constitutes functional strategy and why is it important to have a functional strategy and ensure that it is fully aligned with the business strategy of the firm. As the business strategy of a firm can be established and understood only by understanding the business of the firm, the functional strategy can be understood only by understanding the functions of the firm that it must perform to operate. The discussion on the functional strategy of a firm is primarily a discussion of what Porter called its value chain or operations. Functional strategies cannot be formulated without a clear understanding of the firm's value chain, which describes its business processes and identifies those that are central to its business.

Once a firm establishes the business processes that are critical to its success, a well-thought-out functional strategy can be laid out to manage the evolution of the functional capabilities and to ensure that these capabilities will deliver toward achieving the promised competitive advantages. *Therefore, a functional strategy is the road map for development of functional capabilities that are within the scope of the identified business function.* Since most firms will have a few business processes that are central to their business, in this larger organizational context the multitude of functional strategies, each managing the evolution of a targeted business function, should leverage their relationships with each other so as to create a harmonious organization. *Functional strategy directs, controls, and measures the evolution of functional capabilities and its impact on the success of the stated business goals of the firm.*

Just as the firms within an industry segment may appear to be similar to each other when seen in aggregate, even though differences arise when their business models are dissected and magnified, the functions of their value chains also behave in a similar fashion. The value chain for a generic retailer, for example, has the three basic, generic business functions of buy, distribute, and sell. However, when expanding the underlying processes and reviewing specific operations, the differences among their individual processes become visible. As retailers, they look similar, but on a day-to-day operational basis they are most likely very different from each other. The process-logic that a Macy's warehouse supervisor follows when confronted with short supplies in the warehouse is different from the process-logic followed by a supervisor at a Ross warehouse under similar circumstances.

These functional differences become obvious when the functions are deconstructed into their constituent subfunctions, individual processes, tasks, transactions, and parameters. For example, the *buying* function at a retailer will consist of many processes to manage merchandising plans, assortments, sourcing, demand planning, supply planning, and purchasing. Each of these constituent processes can be further broken down into their components, even though some differences may start appearing even at this level. For example, a casual glance at the assortment at Macy's and Ross will be enough to know that while both firms must have merchandising capabilities to manage their business, they must have different processes for managing their merchandising and assortments. Ross follows a more opportunistic model for its assortment while Macy's main assortment is fixed, though seasonal, and easily lends itself to longer-term planning. Therefore, while both retailers will have to develop capabilities in the business functions of merchandising, assortment planning, sourcing, demand planning, supply planning, and purchasing, the similarities end with this enumeration. The actual processes at the two firms enabling these core functions are quite different. Similarly, their criteria for measuring the effectiveness of the business functions will also be different, their expectations from these functions will be different, and the relative rank of importance among these business functions will be different as well.

It is important to understand that the competitive differences arise through such differences in individual processes even though the business functions appear to be similar in the larger context. Therefore, to understand and assess the value created by a business function, it is imperative to drill down to locate these differences and analyze them for their relative impact on creation of competitive advantage for the firm. In doing such an analysis, firms will also realize that only some differences exist by *design*, while others simply exist— their origins unknown within the organic growth of processes that were invented based on the business needs of the firm at different times in its history. This is an important concept to grasp for developing functional strategies and will be revisited in the following pages.

By creating these differences by design, the firms enable superior processes aligned with their strategy focus that assist them to realize the goals of their business strategy, simply through execution of their day-to-day operations. These differences are the source of competitive advantages. Let us further review the concept of functional strategy.

WHAT IS FUNCTIONAL STRATEGY?

In Chapter 2, we define the business strategy as being a map of the business landscape. This map of the business landscape is created through careful analysis of the industry, products, customers, strengths, opportunities, and threats. This analysis helps the firm clearly identify its current position in the competitive landscape, as well as helps in defining its future destination. This helps the firm to outline a strategic path, identify the long-term direction for growth, and define how it wishes to reach its targets: whether through becoming a cost leader, an innovative pioneer, a unique niche provider, the largest merchandise selection provider, or best known for its customer service or most durable and utilitarian products, and so on. A business strategy identifies the differentiators that will position the firm competitively. A functional strategy identifies capabilities that will create the differentiators sought by the business strategy.

What a business strategy does for the business, a functional strategy does for the business function in question. We define the business function as a set of related activities from any part of the organization. For example, activities for demand and supply management can be thought of as a business function. A functional strategy consists of creating a road map for developing the capabilities for executing a business function so that it creates direct value for the firm. It starts with the assessment of the activities of a business function with respect to the firm's expectations for this function to provide specific competitive advantages. After the assessment, a gap analysis would identify the missing capabilities that must be created to enhance or sustain the competitive advantages. A prioritized list of all desired capabilities belonging to a business function forms the functional strategy for that function. Examples of such business functions are manufacturing, supply chain, merchandising, marketing, product development, and so on. The objective of the functional strategy is to compare the firm's capabilities with its competition and its strategic mandate, assess the gaps and opportunities, and establish clear priorities for development of these capabilities.

Therefore, a functional strategy provides a road map for the development of functional capabilities that are most relevant to support the business strategy. Since several business functions together enable the business of a firm, a good functional strategy must also consider how the capabilities in a specific business function affect others and ensure that any potential conflicts will be avoided. To accommodate such relationships, functional strategies should not be developed in isolation, but in combination with other related functions.

For example, to be effective, a cost reduction objective should consider not only the cost of buying raw materials, but also the cost of transporting them to the factory. This means that the sourcing and logistics functions should work together to develop capabilities because that alone will actually enable the firm to reduce costs. By considering all the activities required for enabling a specific capability, better strategies can be developed for evolving specific business functions. A holistic view of the business enables the firms to clearly understand the linkages in their value chain and identify the critical dependencies so that their efforts to develop individual process competencies have a greater likelihood of success.

The following attributes will help further define a functional strategy:

- A functional strategy starts with an overview of all the processes and their relationships within a business function. Through this overview, it identifies the specific processes that can be improved or enhanced to create advantages sought by the business strategy and the process relationships that are critical within the function as well as with other functions. For example, a functional strategy for a supply chain will not only identify the linkages between its own processes of demand forecasting and replenishment, but should also identify the relationship between the assortment plans (typically, a merchandising function) and demand forecasting processes.
- A functional strategy establishes the sequential dependence of processes within its purview. For example, a supply chain strategy should identify

the sequential nature of demand forecasting and replenishment processes because the output of demand forecasting drives the replenishment process calculations. Identifying this type of sequential dependence among processes helps in creating feasible deployment plans.

▪ A functional strategy establishes any prerequisites for the development of a business process. For example, historical demand data must exist for implementing a statistical demand forecasting process.

Together, these steps help create a functional strategy that provides a clear road map for the development of functional capabilities within the scope of a business function and its relationships with other business functions of the firm. If such analysis is available across all business functions of a firm, it provides an *integrated view of the company's value chain across its business functions*, of processes within each function, sequential and integration dependencies among processes, and the linkages among the business functions themselves. Thus, it represents the overall ecosystem of the firm's operations. Having this holistic view of the firm's value chain is imperative to the success of individual functional strategies, because only such a view can help create capabilities that promote global efficiencies.

Not all business functions are central to the stated business goals of a firm. Some of the business functions are simply required to run the day-to-day operations and having these capabilities simply brings the firm to par with others in the industry segment: These capabilities do not provide any competitive advantages, but are simply required for staying in the game. How can a firm determine the capabilities that are critical to its business strategy? How can it prioritize its investments when several different business capabilities may seem to be equally effective? The following three tests will help to identify and prioritize these business functions.

Test of Relevance: Is It Aligned with the Business Strategy?

Is the business function *relevant* to achieving the firm's stated strategic goals? The functional strategy must answer the question of the alignment of a business function to the business strategy in question. The capabilities of a business function may help the firm move toward its strategic goals, hinder it from doing so, or simply may be irrelevant.

Answering this question of relevance is the first test for investing corporate resources in any business capabilities initiative.

APPLE: **ALIGNMENT WITH BUSINESS STRATEGY**

Consider Apple and its primary strategy of product differentiation through innovation. A marketing capability that successfully highlights this innovative positioning is fully aligned with Apple's differentiation strategy. Therefore, this will be a business capability that Apple must develop, maintain, and enhance. Innovative product design, quick product development for faster time-to-market, manufacturing quality, and knowledgeable associates in the stores will all be capabilities that Apple must have in order to pursue its product differentiation strategy. In this example, the functional strategies for product development and product marketing must identify this fact and the critical relationship they have with each other and with the business strategy of Apple.

The question of *relevance* can be answered by focusing on the two keywords: *useable* and *capable*. Is the business function useable toward achieving the strategic goals of the firm? Is it capable of achieving the strategic goals of the firm? Sometimes, a business function may be useable toward achieving the corporate strategy goals, but not capable unless accompanied by other functions. The capability of a function may sometimes come through its interaction with another function. In the example of Apple, innovative product design is *useable* toward achieving the goal of having innovative products but, by itself, it may not be *capable* of creating differentiation, which is Apple's business strategy. To make it *capable*, Apple must simultaneously create product-marketing capabilities to highlight its product innovations and create a market for them. Together, the capabilities of innovative product design and product marketing allow Apple to pursue its business strategy.

Within the supply chain domain, another example exists to make the point: inventory optimization by itself is *useable* for cost reduction, but it becomes *capable* of achieving this objective only when integrated with replenishment process. This is an example of *synergistic dependence* for creating an effective capability. But the inventory optimization process requires availability of historical and forecast demand as one of its inputs, which requires a good demand-forecasting capability. The relationship between the inventory optimization and demand forecasting is an example of a *sequential*

CUSTOMER **SERVICE AT WAL-MART**

Should Wal-Mart invest in developing industry's best process for assisting customers at its stores? Given Wal-Mart's business strategy of being the price-leader, this is not directly relevant to their business goals. This capability is most likely not going to translate into any substantial competitive advantage, because continued branding and marketing focusing on Wal-Mart's low prices have already established customer expectations. Wal-Mart customers go to their stores for low prices rather than for the customer experience.

dependence that must be satisfied to make a function capable. These dependencies mandate that to create an effective cost-reduction capability using inventory optimization, the firm must consider creating capabilities for all the related functions, demand forecasting, inventory optimization, and an integrated replenishment.

Therefore, functional strategies can establish the most desirable business process competencies by identifying what functions are *useable* and what makes them *capable*. They should also identify any sequential or synergistic dependencies that may constrain the ability of these capabilities to create the desired competitive advantages.

Test of Opportunity: Assessment of the Competitive Placement

What is the size of competitive *opportunity* created by a specific functional capability? This question must be answered in the context of the industry segment that the firm competes in, because it directly depends on the average competency of the entire industry in conducting a specific business function.

As an industry matures, some of its functional capabilities become commonplace and lose their ability to provide any competitive advantage. These functional capabilities might have produced the competitive advantages for the first movers in the industry, but when almost everybody in the industry achieves parity on a functional capability, such a capability simply becomes a prerequisite to compete in that segment without any ability to create competitive advantages. Figure 4.1 clarifies this concept: Capability A has a big initial competitive advantage, but this advantage disappears with time as the capability becomes commonplace and everyone in the industry

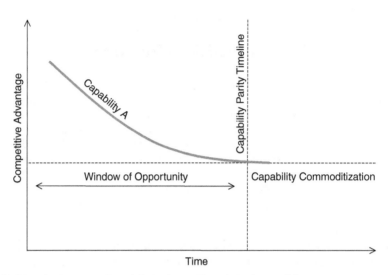

FIGURE 4.1 Business Capabilities Have Finite Windows of Opportunity to Create Competitive Advantages

achieves parity. Ability to accept and process payments electronically is an example of a business capability that has progressed from being a differentiator to becoming a prerequisite for all types and sizes of businesses. Self-checkout counters are fast gaining parity among large retailers and will soon lose their ability to provide any differentiation.

The size of the competitive opportunity created by a business capability directly depends on the difficulty of its replication by the firm's competitors. Incremental enhancements on existing processes are easy to replicate, but capabilities that are created through integration of several processes or that are a result of a process innovation that completely overhauls a specific process of doing business are harder to replicate. The functional strategy must assess the size of the competitive advantage potentially created through the development of a new capability. This requires a careful analysis of the capability in relation to its ability to create value for the firm's customers and the difficulty of a firm's competitors to replicate that value. The analysis indicates the size of opportunity in terms of the cost of creating this capability and the value for the firm created through this capability.

Once a business capability has become standard fare in an industry segment, all firms are expected to have that capability. Presence of the capability then does not produce any competitive advantage, though its absence will produce disadvantages due to the general consumer expectation. This

AMAZON's **EPOCHAL CHANGE IN APPROACH**

For example, when Amazon started their business model by selling books online in 1995, this was an epochal change in approach. While the capability of selling was not new, what Amazon had started through an online sales channel was truly historic in nature. The capability to sell online provided an opportunity for Amazon by creating a competitive advantage compared to its retail-store-based competition. It not only established Amazon as a retailer, but propelled it to be the largest among book retailers. At the end of 2009, Amazon reported sales of over $24 billion with a market cap of $60 billion, with Barnes & Noble at over $5 billion of sales and $1.3 billion of market cap.

is the process of *capability commoditization.* However, innovative enhancements to such capabilities will open up the opportunities for creating advantages and the cycle can continue. The impact of such enhancements will depend on whether they are just incremental or epochal. If the enhanced capability is incremental, then it may easily be replicated by the competitors and fail to create any sustained advantage for the firm. On the other hand, if the changes to an existing business capability are epochal, not very obvious, or complex to reproduce due to their linkages with other value chain activities, then they will create sustained competitive advantages for the firm and should be pursued.

However, even a change of that proportion has now been adopted by a large number of retailers and online retail is not quite seen as a differentiator any more. More recently, Amazon's introduction of Kindle is another major shift in terms of established models for selling and delivery of content. Competition from Google and Sony is already on its way, but Amazon has a definite first-mover advantage to be realized.

Sometimes, the opportunity may not be clear at the onset of a new competitive business capability. This is especially true when a newcomer in an industry breaks away from the conventional model of doing business and changes the paradigm. If the new business capability succeeds, it can provide the new firm with a huge competitive advantage. Such changes can be devastating for the incumbents, though evaluating all such shifts and addressing them proactively is also a risky venture.

WAL-MART: **INCREMENTAL ENHANCEMENTS**

In recent years, Wal-Mart's "ship-to-store" model for online sales is another example of enhancements to the online selling model that is incremental, but hard to replicate due to its inherent linkages with other value chain activities. To efficiently create a "ship-to-store" capability, Wal-Mart would require integration among its various business processes involved in customer order capture, order fulfillment, warehouse operations, transportation, store receiving, and finally customer service desk at the stores. Creating this kind of integration among operations is complex, but keeps Wal-Mart ahead of its competitors, who wish to replicate the capability.

The test of opportunity can also be seen in terms of *superiority* and *advantages*. A firm must determine if the capability being sought makes the firm's process superior to its competition and whether this superiority translates into the competitive advantages desired by its business strategy. The first part of establishing superiority identifies that the window of opportunity still exists for the business function and the second part of assessing advantages establishes the size of this opportunity.

NETFLIX: **CHANGING THE PARADIGM**

Blockbuster started the movie rental business in 1985. In 1997, Netflix emerged on the scene with its mail-based movie rental services and threatened Blockbuster's store-based model. Netflix provided value through direct home delivery, no late fees, and prepaid envelopes that its customers could use to send back the movies. Blockbuster eventually started its own mail-based services in 2004, but by then, it was too late. The window of opportunity for mail-based movie rentals was not an advantage anymore, but had already become an expected feature in the industry. In early 2010, Netflix had a market cap of almost $4 billion with a struggling Blockbuster with a market cap of only $52 million and an uncertain future.

Remember that superiority is not absolute and must be assessed in the right context. For example, let us try to answer which order fulfillment strategy will be superior when the demand-supply gap exists: the one that fulfills all orders short or the one that fulfills some orders fully, but shorts all others that can't be fulfilled? The answer depends on the industry and the customer context; and the right answer may involve an analysis of the type of customers (internal, external, business, consumer), service-level agreements, penalties for delay or nonfulfillment, probable loss of future business, probable value of future business, amount of demand-supply short-fall, seasonality of assortment, and so on. What is superior in one case may not be so in another situation. Therefore, answering the superiority question requires a clear understanding of the firm's business, the segment it is competing in, and the business strategy that frames the overall context for such an analysis.

The test of opportunity, therefore, identifies the business functions that have the largest opportunity to make an impact toward creating competitive advantages. It may also identify capabilities that do not create any advantages, but the lack of which may be creating disadvantages for the firm. The business functions in the first group should be pursued for creating advantages, but the firm may decide to pursue the business functions in the second group to eliminate any competitive disadvantages.

Test of Feasibility: Assessment for Likelihood of Success

This is essentially an assessment of a firm's strengths and resources to make sure that it can successfully develop a process capability. Does the firm have the skills? Does it have the resources? Does the pursued capability leverage the firm's strengths? Are the process and integration dependencies understood and resolved?

Developing new capabilities generally requires a host of organizational skills. Some are commonly understood, such as the ability to manage small and large programs, change management, and organizational impact of such capabilities as training and redeployment. Others may not be that obvious, such as the impact of the new capability on the existing ones: Which existing capabilities can be retired, which should be changed, or which should be integrated with the new one? What roles do these changes impact? How does the performance of people in these roles change? What is the impact of retiring the existing capabilities? Figure 4.2 shows these aspects of change management.

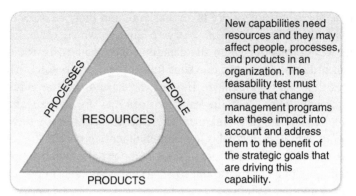

FIGURE 4.2 The Components of a Corporation and Change Management

These can be seen as organized around the same dimensions as in Figure 3.4, in the discussion on viewing the corporation as the sum of its components. Development of any capability requires resources and may affect people, processes, and products. Each of these should be analyzed for the expected impact of the new capability and change management programs organized to make sure that the deployment of the new capability is successful.

Many companies fail due to their inability to assess their ability to manage the change that comes with new capabilities and others fail due to their inability to provide adequate resources to develop new capabilities. In recent years, the failure of retailers Circuit City and Linen 'n Things and the struggles of Sears and Kmart are examples of firms that understood the capabilities they needed but just did not have the required skills or resources to create those capabilities. Dell is currently struggling with its new business model of selling through retail stores due to its lack of organizational skills to create the newly desired capabilities.

The test of feasibility ensures that the capabilities being pursued for strategic advantages can be successfully created and deployed with the organizational resources and that the investments in creating such capabilities will not be wasted.

WHY IS THE FUNCTIONAL STRATEGY IMPORTANT?

Functional strategy is the *missing link* in most corporations' strategic planning initiatives. While most of the firms may have a sense of direction for

ANNUAL **REPORTS: GLIMPSES OF FUNCTIONAL STRATEGIES**

It is not uncommon for corporations to think in terms of functional strategies. See the following examples with actual quotes from the annual reports of some of the largest corporations, which illustrate that thinking about functional strategies is very natural and an integral part of corporate strategy formulation. Almost all retailers in this example have explicitly mentioned their pricing, merchandising, and growth strategies. At the heart of these functional strategies lie some of the core capabilities that these firms have developed over time that enable them to pursue the functional strategies toward achieving the goals set by their overarching business strategy.

Lowes Annual Report 2008 (Fiscal year ending January 30, 2009)

- "A key tenet of our *Merchandising strategy* is keeping a sharp focus on the customer."
- "We remain committed to our *Everyday Low Price strategy*, which we will continue to emphasize."
- "Using our disciplined *expansion strategy*, in 2008 we opened 115 new stores in great markets across the United States and the Greater Toronto Area, down from 153 stores in 2007."

Target Annual Report 2008 (Fiscal year ending January 31, 2009)

- "Our newly launched *store and merchandise segmentation strategy* allowed us to customize our assortment . . . "
- "While our commitment to our *"Expect More. Pay Less."* strategy does not waver . . . "
- "Target's comprehensive *negotiations strategy* is key to our ability to deliver the latest trends at great prices."
- "An integral component of our *multichannel retail strategy*, Target.com provides us with deep insight into our guests' shopping preferences, allowing us to strategically interact with them through innovative direct marketing strategies and meaningful online experiences."

Wal-Mart Annual Report 2009 (Fiscal year ending January 31, 2009)

- "Our *strategy* is working, and we're building more and more momentum. We will maintain our focus on *price leadership* in every market . . . "
- "Samsclub.com is an integral part of our *growth strategy*."

their business strategy, they are not able to translate that to the required business capabilities. The strategic planning offices in modern corporations tend to directly leap from their business strategies into the individual capital projects, where various departments propose their projects for the capital investment budget of the corporation and provide justification on how their initiative is aligned with the corporate direction. As a result, many projects are approved and while all of them individually may add value, they don't necessarily align with a common evolution path for the core competencies of the firm. Such an approach creates what I call *organically grown* functional capabilities. Functional capabilities created with this approach may not be compatible with each other, are not likely to be well integrated, create inconsistent processes and underlying data models, and pose difficulty in creating meaningful firmwide operational metrics due to incompatible process design and data.

The underlying reason for this medley of business capabilities is the lack of functional road maps governing the evolution of business capabilities that are central to the strategy of the firm. Functional strategies are designed to create these road maps by explicitly designing business processes and building specific advantages within these processes. However, creating functional strategies requires good business and process skills, patience, and an executive commitment to create capability based competitive advantages in the long term. Our quarterly focus on Wall Street and a culture of immediate gratification are both detrimental to creating long-term strategies.

As a result, most corporations simply skip this step and move on to defining projects and individual initiatives that they believe will be most effective in achieving their strategic goals. This is what creates myriad problems that most corporations face by way of broken processes, insufficient returns on their most ambitious initiatives, and continued siloed behavior among various business functions.

Functional strategy serves the two very basic needs that firms have in the field of strategic planning:

1. The process of formulation of functional strategy forces the firms to understand their value chains, analyze the value chain in the context of their business strategy, understand the core business capabilities and their relationships among themselves, understand the sequential and synergistic dependence among these functions, and establish a coherent path of evolution for the whole business function. Contrast this with deciding the merits of one isolated project at a time which is the alternative.

2. It provides the firm with a clear direction to pursue strategic business capabilities, fully understanding the resources required, advantages expected, and any constraints when the dependence among business functions exists but not addressed.

A functional strategy or road map for evolving the functional capabilities provides an objective framework for prioritizing the capital investments in individual initiatives that are aligned with the firm's business strategy. It also supports the future growth of business by allowing the business strategy to leverage planned capabilities by analyzing competitive opportunities and threats and determining what is required to sustain the competitive lead.

As industries mature and firms within the industry achieve competitive parity, the process of *capability commoditization* erodes competitive advantages, till one of the firms breaks away from the pack and innovates a new business model. The new business model requires the development of new business capabilities and that, in turn, provides new opportunities for a new set of competitors subscribing to the new business model. Firms that continually evaluate their business capabilities through the practice of functional strategies are best positioned to know when industries reach functional parity and when they must reinvent their business model to continue their lead.

Trying to build competitive advantages without having a functional strategy in place is akin to starting construction on a building without having any structural designs for the building. This will become clearer as we go through the steps for creating a functional strategy and develop some of the tools for creating a functional strategy and review its deliverables.

STEPS IN CREATING THE FUNCTIONAL STRATEGY

Once a corporation has formulated their business strategy, they must identify the core business functions that are necessary to achieve their strategic goals. Each of these business functions consists of business capabilities that enable the firm to conduct its business. If these capabilities are superior to comparable capabilities of its competitors, then the firm has competitive advantages. Functional strategies establish the plan for development of such capabilities required by the business function. Therefore, creating a functional strategy is essentially an exercise in analyzing the value chain of the firm, understanding its core business functions, and creating a plan to design and develop competencies for a favorable positioning in its competitive segment. This exercise requires that the firm has resources that understand the firm's business and its operations clearly and have the required functional and operational experience to lead this exercise.

It starts by reviewing the firm's functional areas from the top and going down by deconstructing each of the functional areas into its subfunctions and eventually into processes and tasks comprising the subfunctions. The following steps provide a general outline of the process.

Develop the Functional Ecosystem Map

This is the first step in starting to understand the firm's value chain. The objective of this step is to create and catalog all core business functions required to support the firm's operations and identify the processes that together comprise these functions. The functional ecosystem is a high-level collection of all business functions that a firm must be able to execute in order to operate in an industry segment. At higher levels of abstraction, these ecosystem functional maps may not look very different from one corporation to another within the same industry segment. Figure 4.3 represents a logical representation of the corporate ecosystem. The boundaries represent the corporation's internal capabilities that must exist to be part of an industry segment and the arrows represent the interaction of the corporate ecosystem with the external world including the partners of the firm with whom collaboration is possible or desirable. This is the highest level of abstraction and does not specify any individual functional area.

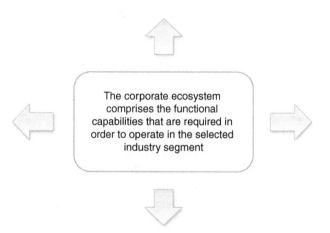

The corporate ecosystem comprises the functional capabilities that are required in order to operate in the selected industry segment

FIGURE 4.3 Corporate Ecosystem of Functional Capabilities

At the next level of granularity, the firm needs to identify the functional areas that are important to compete in their selected segment of the industry. These functions will vary from one industry vertical to another, but will be similar in a specific industry vertical. Variations of these functions may exist in different segments of an industry. For example, most retailers will have merchandising and supply chain functions, but depending on the retail segment they compete in, the individual functions within each of these may be different. Figure 4.4 shows an example of the next level of a functional ecosystem mapping.

This process of deconstructing the functional capabilities continues till every function is identified at a level that makes it specific to the operations of the firm and allows the firm to identify those functions that can truly add competitive value to their business. In the introduction to this chapter, we hypothesized that it is important to understand that the *competitive differences arise due to the differences in individual processes within the larger business functions.* The objective of deconstructing the business functions into individual process capabilities is to identify those capabilities where such differences can be designed to create competitive advantages for the firm. Not all process capabilities will create advantages, some are simply required to stay in the game, others are required to compete effectively because everyone within the industry segment may already have a similar capability, but beyond these will be the capabilities that can be developed for creating, enhancing, or sustaining competitive advantages. This hierarchy of capabilities is depicted in Figure 4.5.

For example, consider the capability to invoice the customers for a mobile phone company. This is a basic capability to conduct a business transaction, without which it will be hard to conduct this business. If a firm adds the capability of providing the details of individual calls to the customer invoice to enable customers to monitor their usage and verify the billing, this is likely to bring the firm up to par with its competitors. If this firm enables a proactive text-based alert as the customer is about to cross his or her plan minutes, that would likely be a competitive advantage for the firm, by creating a customer satisfaction differential. The three stages of the evolution of this business capability represent the three levels of business mandate, competitive parity, and the competitive advantage created by this capability.

Further extending this example, let us assume that the firm also provided Internet service to some of its customers in addition to the mobile-phone services. Can the firm create a customer service niche by creating an Internet service plan that is available across its cellular phone, land-based Web-access

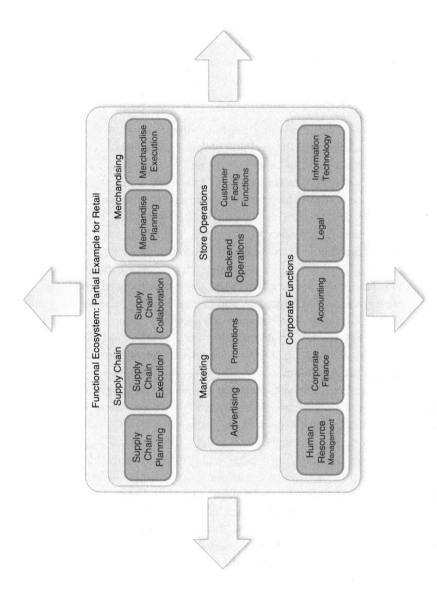

FIGURE 4.4 Functional Ecosystem Showing Partial List of Business Functions

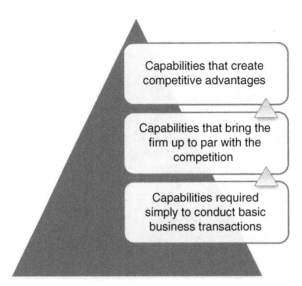

FIGURE 4.5   Hierarchy of Capabilities

lines, and wireless modems to provide the ultimate freedom to the user irrespective of the mode of access? If the market has this unfulfilled need and the firm's business strategy is driven by differentiation, then this will be a capability that will create competitive advantage for the firm. While the advantages in this example pass the test of relevance, that is, do they pass the test of opportunity? The latter depends on the difficulty of replicating the capability by the firm's competitors. If a capability is difficult to replicate or has intellectual property constraints, it will be much more valuable to create due to the longer window of time over which such an advantage can be sustained.

Creating a functional ecosystem helps firms to identify business functions that are critical to their existence. Deconstructing the functions into their constituent processes and tasks provides several more advantages in addition to assisting in creating functional strategies:

- It allows them to understand their business requirements and the functional capabilities they must have to exist, grow, and prosper.
- It allows them to critically examine their processes and functional capabilities to assess those that add value and identify others that do not add any value toward their business goals.
- It allows them to clearly establish their own hierarchy of capabilities into basic requirements that must exist simply to complete business transactions,

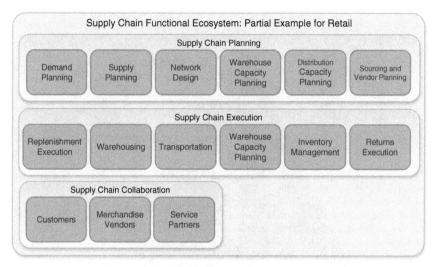

FIGURE 4.6 Deconstructing Supply Chain Functions

capabilities that bring them up to par with others in their industry segment, and capabilities that differentiate them and are capable of creating advantages that can be leveraged by their business strategies.

This understanding about the business requirements and desired capabilities is critical to create any functional strategy, including the strategy for the supply chains. For this exercise, we will take the supply chain functions as shown in Figure 4.6 and continue to expand them further in Figure 4.7.

Each function shown in Figure 4.6 can be expanded further. As an example, let us focus on the demand planning function. Demand planning function requires many processes, such as statistical forecasting, consensus forecast development, replenishment planning, pre-order allocation, and new product introductions. Some functional differences among companies in different industries will already become visible even at this level of abstraction. For example, the pre-order allocation process of managing demand is generally viable only for push-based store replenishments of seasonal or special merchandise. Another subfunction of consensus forecast development also shows considerable variation among companies: this is typically called sales and operations planning (S&OP) function in manufacturing industries and is used to keep the sales and manufacturing teams on the same page. Retailers may adopt the consensus forecast generation process differently to bring the two teams of merchants and inventory planners together. The conventional success

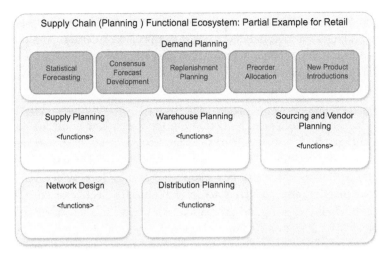

FIGURE 4.7 Deconstructing Demand Planning Functions

metrics for merchants (service levels) are generally at odds with those of inventory planners (inventory levels). Creating a consensus on demand provides an opportunity to reconcile the two teams to serve the common organizational goals rather than individual team goals. But again, consensus forecast function is not equally critical to all retailers. In fact, high-end retailers who compete on product differentiation and not cost may not have this functional ability because their objective is to create competitive advantages through product and service differentiation and not cost.

Similarly, while most firms may need to develop some basic capability in other subfunctions of forecasting, replenishment, and new products, the critical need for competency in each of them depends on their particular business model and strategic goals. For example, demand forecasting will be most critical for retailers and almost noncritical in an engineer-to-order business.

Establishing the importance of a business function to the firm's business strategy is exactly the objective of deconstructing the functions into their processes and tasks. The analysis helps firms to establish which baseline capabilities are required simply to exist, others that bring them up to par with the rest of the firms in the industry, and those that hold the potential for building competitive advantages. The explicit exercise of analyzing and evaluating each task individually also forces a firm to question practices that may exist historically, but which do not add any value to the process or cannot be justified with the changed focus on strategy.

Consider the ability to allocate pre-order demand. This capability enables retailers to allocate merchandise to its stores prior to ordering. As stores are serviced from their primary warehouses, allocating to stores allows identifying warehouse destinations for the orders. As advanced shipment notices are received, these warehouses can plan ahead and simply flow through the received merchandise to the stores using the planned allocations. The capability can be further enhanced by optimizing the allocations immediately prior to executing the flow-through to take advantage of latest-known demand at stores or by inviting store managers inputs on the demand or planned allocations. Having this capability allows the retailer to provide visibility of expected merchandise deliveries to local managers, who can then better manage their inventories and promotions. However, to successfully develop this capability, retailers would need demand forecasts at the store level, which requires demand history at the store level. This type of historical data can be consolidated from daily point-of-sale (POS) transactions by unique products, but requires additional processes to accomplish this. Furthermore, the analysis can help the retailer to understand their current processes, evaluate if they are adding value, and also understand related capabilities that must be developed for successful deployments.

Empowering the store managers by providing visibility to demand and allocations, and allowing them to manage it proactively, can create a better cost structure for the retailer. It also enables stores to better serve their customers. It allows the retailers to create better demand forecasts by combining a statistical demand forecast (leveraging science) with the intuitive knowledge of the store manager about the needs of their local customers.

A simple analysis of a capability allows the firms to evaluate its potential to create competitive advantages, evaluate organizational strengths and weaknesses, and an objective way to rank them in order of their ability to create value. A more formal method for creating rankings can make use of several criteria and is provided in the next step of the process.

The process of functional deconstruction should continue till every individual process has been identified. How deep should one go? In general, break a function down to its processes till the process description can establish a self-contained, cohesive set of tasks to execute that process and allows the subject-matter expert to create alternate sets of tasks to complete the same process. Generally, this is not the lowest level of tasks in a process, but an intermediate level where alternatives approaches become visible. Expanding the functions into such activities provides valuable insight into the value chain and may reveal areas of improvement and differentiation that may otherwise be invisible.

However, a reasonable assessment of such opportunities is quite possible at higher levels of process models, enough to differentiate one firm's operations from another, identify the core processes, and the potential areas for development of competitive advantages, which can then be detailed further. Therefore, while it depends on the individual firm's objective for this exercise, the deconstruction must be done to a level where a process can be clearly identified to be part of one of three levels of capabilities identified in Figure 4.5. Only then can the firm identify and prioritize the capabilities it must create to compete.

Continuing with the example of expanding the demand planning function, Table 4.1 shows another representation of the functional capability hierarchy. Presented as a table, this representation is more practical than the earlier graphical representations.

TABLE 4.1 An Example of Functional Deconstruction of Demand Planning Business Function

Supply Chain Function

  Supply Chain Planning

    Demand Planning

      Statistical Forecasting

        Ability to access assortment master data as a master input to the demand forecasting and synchronize the assortment masters with forecast

        Ability to collect historical sales data at store by day by product level and consolidate across time and locations as required

        Ability to model seasonality for seasonal merchandise

        Ability to model trending

        Ability to model causal factors affecting demand, planned and unplanned (internal and external)

        Ability to collect historical price data and associate to sales data to establish price elasticity and use this for future projections

        Ability to access projected pricing plans and use during the forecasting process

        Ability to create multiple forecasts with scenarios modeling several demand situations

        Ability to compare, contrast, and select the most likely scenario for demand forecasts

        And so on. . . .

      Consensus Forecast Development

(continued)

TABLE 4.1 *(Continued)*

Publish projected demand forecasts to stakeholder groups and alert them to availability of new forecasts

Ability to quickly present changes from last forecast (waterfall analysis)

Ability to allow stakeholder changes in draft in preparation for S&OP meeting

Ability to approve/disapprove/override stakeholder changes and create final forecasts for all downstream processes

And so on . . .

Replenishment Planning

—

—

—

The idea is to breakdown the functions into its constituents until the individual process of a function emerge at a level where one can intelligently analyze to determine their contribution to the business function and its ability to create strategic advantages.

These functional ecosystem maps for the corporate core functions help the firm understand their operations, the business functions required to support the operations, and the relative importance of these functions for the continuation and growth of the business. Understanding the functional capabilities and their role in achieving the goals of business strategy happens to be one of the least understood and least emphasized areas of strategy formulation. This inevitably results in investments in creating capabilities that do not directly contribute toward achieving the business goals of the firm. One of the reasons for this state of things is simply the lack of required skills to conduct such an extensive analysis of a firm's operations. As the analysis spans multiple business functions, individuals with relevant experience and competence across all the functions are required, but may not exist. To overcome such a gap in organizational skills, teams can be assembled with individuals representing only one or few functions rather than looking for individuals with expertise across all organizational functions. Together, such a team can assemble a functional capability picture of the firm that provides a systematic approach to understand, analyze, and prioritize the core functional capabilities of the firm's business.

Develop Assessment Scorecards

Once the functional capabilities have been cataloged as described in the previous step, the development of functional strategy needs a way to rank the functions in order of their importance toward the strategic goals of the firm. The objective of this step is to provide such ranking among the business functions using measures of their ability to create competitive advantages for the firm.

It is important to remember that the first step provides the processes that together constitute a business function. However, these processes are most often so mutually dependent that a pick-and-select on individual process basis may not be a practical idea from the point of view of enhancing the functional capabilities of the firm. Therefore, business functions need to be ranked in order to develop them as whole entities capable of providing integrated functions that are efficient, flexible, and address the requirements fully enough to contribute toward creating the competitive benefits. When corporations try to develop individual processes and ignore the whole picture provided by the ecosystem mapping process (or simply because they never had access to such information), the results often do not match their expectations, investments are wasted, and the competitive benefits don't arrive as predicted.

To create an ordered ranking of the core functions, the processes in a business function should be validated against the three tests—*relevance*, *opportunity*, and *feasibility*—mentioned earlier in this chapter. A composite score is then generated to rank the functions. The actual process of creating these composite scores is subjective, in part due to the relative weights assigned by different organizations to emphasize different aspects of importance to these three dimensions as well as the relative importance of the processes to the firm. However, validating these processes using common criteria provides the best method for making these decisions.

The *relevance* test primarily contemplates the following for a process and a numerical score assigned by a subject-matter expert (SME) provides the degree to which this expert agrees with the following statements:

- Is the process required (for basic business operations), desired (for competitive parity), or critical (for competitive advantage)?
- Is the process aligned with the corporate business strategy? Does it support or hinder the business goals or is it simply neutral to them?
- Does the process provide any capability that will create a competitive advantage desired by the corporate strategy?

The *opportunity* test and corresponding numerical score affords a chance to answer the following questions for the process involved:

▪ What is the current level of competence of the firm to conduct a specific process?
▪ What is the desired level of competence the firm must have in order to be competitive in the segment?
▪ What is the size of potential advantage (cost of creating the advantage versus the additional value produced) if the desired level of competency is achieved?

The *feasibility* test and the score necessarily answer the following:

▪ What are the gaps between the current and desired process capabilities?
▪ What process enhancements are required to get there?
▪ Does the organization have the skills and resources to create the desired enhancements?

This step helps in determining what business functions are most critical where changes must be made to survive, grow, and competitively position the firm now and in the future.

Develop Capability Maturity Maps

The previous two steps help catalog and prioritize the business functions and process capabilities of a firm. As individual processes seldom work alone to create a comprehensive business capability, their relationships and their dependence on other processes become critical to successfully creating competitive advantages. This step is designed to add the relationships among these capabilities to the output of the first two steps. Adding the dependence relationships enables the firms to establish coherent sets of capabilities that must be designed and developed together for best returns on the investment.

A capability maturity map (CMM) is simply a graphical representation of the business functions that simultaneously shows the relative competency of the firm in various business functions and the relationships among these functions by plotting their *sequential* and *synergistic* dependencies. The input from the assessment scorecards is used to determine the competency of the firm in a business function. The color coding shows a firm's desire to leverage the inputs toward building competitive advantage. The position of the function in relation to others shows the dependency relationships.

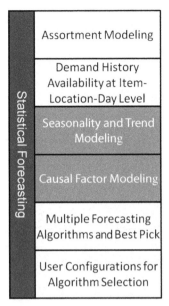

FIGURE 4.8 Part of a Capability Maturity Map Showing the Statistical Forecasting Subfunctions

The colors show the level of competency of the firm in each subfunction, and their relative positions from left to right shows their dependence. The subfunctions on the right either need or can be enriched from the subfunctions on their left side. The bottom box shows that all the subfunctions belong to the demand forecasting function.

Figure 4.8 shows part of a capability maturity map for statistical forecasting process that is one of the building blocks of a comprehensive demand planning capability. The figure graphically shows the individual processes identified as required for developing a statistical forecasting capability for a given firm. The shading of the blocks show how adequate the firm considers itself in these processes with respect to the desired competence. Any color coding can be adopted as long as everyone involved consistently understands and interprets it the same way. A typical representation can be used with green, yellow, and red colors to signify competence in a process:

▪ Red means the function is either not being performed, or is completely manual without any automation or optimization. These functional areas represent major opportunities for developing functional competence.

- Yellow represents inadequately supported processes; it shows that the process is semimanual, not integrated with other processes, or is not consistently used (variations exist for no apparent reason) across the enterprise. These functional areas represent abundant opportunities for improvement.
- Green shows that the process is adequately addressed and is automated to the desirable extent. It is an integrated process and is consistently used across the enterprise. These processes represent minimal opportunities for improvements.

The capability maturity map uses the *spatial position* to display the dependencies among the functions. The vertical axis is used to display sequential relationships and the horizontal axis for synergistic relationships. As a rule, functions that are at the bottom of another function are usually required to be developed before the functions on the top can be built. This dependence generally arises out of data or information that the functions share with each other. Functions to the right of another function enrich or extend the function on the left, and sometimes are also grouped together to signify the larger business process supported by them together. These relationships can be clearly seen in Figure 4.8: for example, demand history is required for using any forecasting algorithms, but the ability to model seasonality simply enriches any forecasting algorithm's ability to produce an effective forecast.

When all the subfunctions of supply chain are assembled on a capability maturity map, a visual picture of the corporate competence in that business function becomes immediately available. This is a powerful way of visualizing functional competencies, though it takes time and requires substantial knowledge of business operations and analysis skills to create. A sample maturity map for the supply chain functions for retail appears in Figure 4.9. While this provides a good starting point to provoke thought, the supply chain functions and their relative importance vary widely from one industry to another and within firms belonging to a single industry segment. The assessments of competency also vary widely. Therefore, firms are advised to create their own versions of the capability maturity maps after careful analysis and evaluation of their own operations, the industry segment, and their business strategy.

The colors of the functions show the level-of-competency of the firm in each subfunction and their relative positions show their dependence. CMMs can be built showing current as well as future capability assessments.

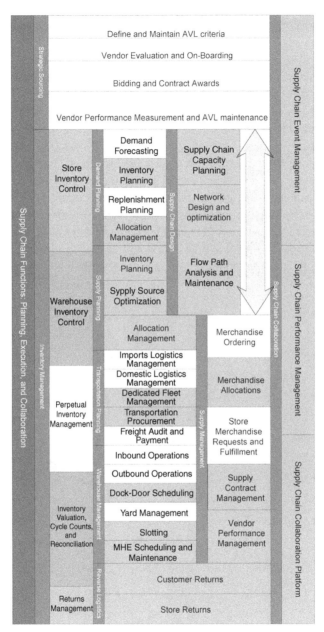

FIGURE 4.9 Example of a Capability Maturity Map for Supply Chain Functions in a Retail Context

Capability maturity maps can be created to not only assess the current level of process competence, but also for depicting how these functions evolve in the future to provide comprehensive support to the business operations. These time-lapsed maturity maps can then become one of the major inputs into the annual strategic planning exercises for corporations, targeted at identifying the priorities for capital investments. A sample of such time-evolving capability maturity maps for a hypothetical set of supply chain functions is shown in Appendix A.

The concepts of the functional strategy presented here are applicable across business functions: whether it is managing the supply chain, merchandising, or human resources, firms can use these concepts to analyze the relevance of the function to the business and their competency, and prioritize them to create a road map for building their capabilities. In Chapter 5 we follow-up with a discussion of these functional strategy concepts as they apply to the supply chain function and we also review the existing literature on supply chain strategies and their relevance to corporations.

CHAPTER FIVE

Current Thinking on Supply Chain Strategy

OW THAT WE HAVE a basic grasp of the concept of a functional strategy and how to develop one, we can proceed to discuss the supply chain function and strategies available to leverage supply chain competencies in a firm. Recall that the objective of a functional strategy is to *create a road map for the development of functional capabilities within the scope of a business function and identify its relationships with other business functions of the firm.* This definition motivates the practitioner to have a clear understanding of the business function before putting together a functional strategy.

In reviewing the concept of supply chain strategies, it is assumed that the reader is familiar with the individual supply chain processes, because this part of the book is devoted to understanding supply chains as a business function, their strengths, and how to leverage them to build competitive advantages. The details of supply chain functions are not covered here, but we will review the broad strategies that present opportunities for firms to leverage while designing their supply chains and aligning them to their business strategies. Readers who are not familiar with the supply chain functions or who need a refresher may refer to the author's book *Enterprise Supply Chain Management: Integrating Best-in-Class Processes.*

The scope of the supply chain is assumed to consist of all planning functions including demand planning, supply planning, inventory planning, logistics capacity planning, sourcing planning, and supply chain network planning; all execution functions of purchasing, warehousing, and transportation; and the collaborative functions with vendors, customers, and other partners. Appendix B presents a summary of supply chain functions relevant to these discussions.

Owing to their large scope, supply chains influence an extremely large part of a corporation's operations and directly affect their capital efficiencies by controlling costs and working capital. Almost all supply chain process improvements will directly affect the cost of goods sold (COGS) or impact working capital to enhance the return on assets (ROA). Appendix C presents a quick tutorial on the relationship between a firm's supply chain and financial metrics.

Before we present our way of thinking about the supply chain functional strategy, we will review some of the prevalent concepts that are often used in the context of supply chain strategy. While these concepts help in understanding the different aspects of supply chains, developing a functional *strategy* for supply chain extends beyond understanding these concepts. Most of these concepts focus heavily on a single aspect of supply chains and therefore fail to provide a balanced picture of required functional capabilities. We believe that a framework that views supply chains essentially as business functions that must support business strategy and create competitive advantages is currently missing. Defining such a framework is partly the objective of the following sections.

CURRENT THINKING ON SUPPLY CHAIN STRATEGIES

There is a bulk of literature available on supply chain strategies. We will review the major current concepts in the following sections. Most of the literature surveyed presents similar concepts by varying names in different contexts. They tend to typify the supply chains as being one of four types: lean, agile, speculation, or postponement-oriented. Hau Lee of Stanford identifies four types as Efficient, Risk Hedging, Responsive, and Agile, which are quite similar to the earlier characterizations but with subtle differences. Similar themes are repeated but all of them suffer from the same problem: They are all so generic that they frequently drive the business strategy rather than being driven by it. The level of abstraction precludes the possibility of going into specific details, which are useful in designing the business capabilities for a real-life supply chain. Being lean, for example, is viewed as simply a cost-reduction strategy and will be just as applicable to supply chains as it will be to human resource management or any other business function in a corporation. With that amount of directive, do these concepts really qualify as *supply chain* strategy?

Lean and Agile Strategies

One of the commonly known supply chain strategies directs firms to build lean or agile supply chains.

Lean primarily refers to elimination of waste and is the basic philosophy that originated as part of Toyota Production Systems, with its emphasis on the elimination of waste (*muda*). Therefore, this philosophy is based on reducing the cost by eliminating activities that do not directly add any value. Cost can be reduced in two ways: (1) by identifying and eliminating the wasteful activities that don't add any value and (2) by enhancing the efficiency of a required activity so that the throughput of the process can be increased. A lot of supply chain activities can directly leverage this thinking. Most execution activities in a supply chain can benefit from lean thinking, such as picking, packing, loading, and unloading in a warehouse; routing of shipments in transportation; labor activities on receiving docks at warehouses, stores, and manufacturing plants; and so on.

Agile, on the other hand, refers to the ability to react and adapt to the changes in demand and supply situations in a supply chain. To accommodate the inherent variations in demand and supply, supply chains need to react and adapt to such changes as they happen, to minimize the disruption and optimize the objectives, such as costs, fulfillment rates, inventory, and so on.

What does a lean design for a supply chain mean? A lean supply chain design requires that supply chains minimize the cost of operations at all levels. Lean requires that the supply chain uses the least amount of resources to efficiently complete its job. The primary resources in a supply chain are inventory, warehouses, trucks, people, and working capital. A lean supply chain will be designed to have minimal inventories in the system, minimal amount of warehousing space required to store these inventories, and well-optimized shipments to reduce the cost of shipments when inventory is required to be moved. A lean supply chain will also be designed to establish long-term, stable supply contracts with the lowest negotiated cost, but typically without any ability to change ordered quantities, delivery destinations, and required need dates after the order has been placed. Lean design will most likely not engage secondary suppliers, because a second tier of suppliers is expensive to maintain. All of these factors will reduce the costs of the supply chain operations, making it extremely cost-efficient, but will also constrain the supply chain's ability to adapt to any changes in demand, supply, or other resources, due to the built-in rigidity of the design. Low inventories make the supply chain vulnerable to not being able to fulfill orders if the demand suddenly spikes or if there are changes in demand that were not foreseen. Inability to change orders with the suppliers also constrains the supply chain's ability to react to any changes in demand and may saddle the supply chain with unwanted inventory. Having no secondary suppliers also limits the ability of the supply chain to reacting to spikes in demand and/or exposes it to supply failures from the primary suppliers. The focus on being lean prevents this supply chain from building redundancy by design.

An *agile* supply chain design, in contrast, will have redundancy built into its processes, allowing it to quickly respond to expected changes. This supply chain will be best to maximize the service levels for fulfilling demand, manufacturing personalized products, and providing excellent customer service. These objectives will drive the supply chain to keep higher levels of inventories to maintain order fulfillment targets, favor on-time deliveries over cheaper shipments, and favor quality inputs and personalized services over mass-produced, commoditized goods. These supply chains will have more flexible supplier contracts that enable them to change order quantities, destinations, need dates, and even cancel the orders altogether if the demand falls off a cliff. Suppliers will typically allow such flexibility for a cost. When demand suddenly rises and the primary suppliers cannot cope with the increased demand, an *agile* supply chain will go to a secondary set of suppliers that would have been established in advance for maintaining supplies for such an eventuality. As purchase volumes for the secondary suppliers will be low and demand uneven, the costs of such contracts is generally higher. However, having all these layers of extra inventories, warehousing, transportation, and suppliers will provide enough buffer to the supply chain to handle most variations in demand, supply, or lead time while maintaining its stated service levels.

Christopher, Peck, and Towill[1] propose a matrix of lead time and demand characteristics to select between the agile or lean strategies. For predictable demand, they propose a lean strategy. For unpredictable demand, an agile strategy is proposed when short lead times are the norm, and a *leagile* (lean and agile) strategy is favored when the lead times are longer. This makes common sense: when demand is stable and predictable, a supply chain can be designed with little or no redundancy. The deterministic characteristics of the demand create stable plans and low plan-volatility, therefore making it possible to operate with minimal shock absorbers, such as safety stocks, lead-time buffers, back-up suppliers, and other resources required to absorb sudden changes in demand-supply equation. This allows for a *lean* supply chain design that is cost-efficient, but may not elegantly support changes in demand when plans go awry. When the demand is unpredictable and lead-times are short, an *agile* design for a supply chain can work because the changes can be quickly responded to through shorter lead times. When the demand is unpredictable and lead times are longer, a combination of lean and agile designs is recommended.

While such distinctions in the supply chain design are fine in the context of a specific product group with similar demand and lead-time characteristics, such rigidity does not make sense for developing capabilities for the enterprise supply chain. One could not run a business with a *lean* supply chain with the lowest cost, but that cannot respond to any changes in demand or supply. Since all demand and supply has inherent variability, such a rigidly designed supply chain will quickly build up unwanted and obsolete inventories. To the same extent, one also cannot run a supply chain that is extremely responsive and manages the changes in demand and supplies precisely, because such a supply chain will have an unreasonably high cost to operate, quickly running out of working capital to support daily operations.

Therefore, we see both of these attributes as *core capabilities* of any supply chain design, being *complementary* rather than being *exclusive* to each other.

WAL-MART: **LEAN AND AGILE AT THE SAME TIME**

Wal-Mart is a prime example: Their explicitly stated business strategy of low prices has driven them to consistently reduce their cost of operations through supply chain innovations. Wal-Mart's supply chain is definitely among the most cost-efficient in the industry. However, it is also quite agile. Wal-Mart was the only major retailer to reorient their assortment with national colors and substantially increase their American flag-based merchandise after the 9/11 attacks in a very short time. Absence of any major clearance at their stores also points to an agile supply chain that can adapt itself quickly to changes, thereby avoiding overstocked stores and the need to discount merchandise to clear the shelves.

How can a supply chain be both lean and agile at the same time? A firm can regard both lean and agile strategies as *process drivers* for designing individual supply chain processes rather than as being all-encompassing strategies for developing a supply chain as a whole. In this context, they become the principles that practitioners can use to develop standard processes that leverage one of these attributes even as process exceptions leverages the other. For example, a firm may establish a store-based inventory policy using the *lean* principle to cover the supply lead time from the primary warehouse to the store. While the *lean* design drives their standard replenishment to the store, the process to handle exceptions to manage stock-outs may leverage *agile* principles, allowing priority replenishments to the store from a set of alternate sources in order to avoid losing substantial sales revenues. The example of Wal-Mart illustrates the complementary use of lean and agile design principles in designing a supply chain that is highly effective.

Therefore, the question of whether a supply chain should be lean or agile becomes a rhetorical question. Any large enterprise cannot have a rigidly designed supply chain that is either lean or agile. Both of these aspects of lean and agile are required in designing an effective supply chain to support the business.

Another way to look at these two design drivers is to think of supply chain functions in terms of planning and execution. Planning functions normally drive execution functions. For example, consider replenishment planning (part of supply chain *planning* functions) and warehousing (part of supply chain *execution* functions). Replenishment planning takes as input the demand requirements and creates the fulfillment orders against these requirements. These fulfillment orders are then executed in the warehouse. The replenishment function by itself does not result in any operations until fulfillment orders are acted upon by the warehouse. As demand changes, the replenishment process can frequently generate a new fulfillment plan without affecting any of the physical resources in the warehouse. Thus, an *agile* planning process combined with *lean* execution provides an effective way to design a supply chain that is both cost-effective as well as responsive.

Therefore, adopting an *agile* design philosophy for supply chain planning functions and a *lean* design philosophy for supply chain execution functions provides another viable alternative. These planning and execution functions are assumed to be tightly integrated so that as supply chain planning functions respond to the actual changes in the environment and adapt, they have the ability to drive the execution functions quickly to align with the new plans. This view of looking at supply chain in terms of planning and execution functions provides a practical approach that resolves the dilemma of lean versus agile. Remember that these characteristics describe the overarching process design philosophy for supply chain planning and execution functions, but do not exclude each other: That is, this design philosophy does not mean that supply chain planning functions don't need to be lean or that the execution functions don't need to be agile, rather that these functions have a *natural disposition* toward one of these two basic designs.

Let us extend the scope of this discussion to enterprise supply chains. While *lean* and *agile* can characterize the driving principle for the supply chain process design *within the context of similar products*, it loses its relevance in the context of an enterprise-wide supply chain design. Since most of the firms will have a mix of products with stable demand and with unpredictable demand, as well as a good lead-time spread with domestically sourced merchandise with shorter lead times and imported goods with longer lead times, therefore, an enterprise supply chain design must create supply chain capabilities that can cater to the diverse expectations of such business situations. Both these aspects are integral to the core supply chain capabilities and therefore not exclusive to each other in this context. *To that extent, an enterprise supply chain may be seen as a collection of smaller product specific supply chains, with each one of these individual chains being lean or agile, and the notion of the whole enterprise supply chain being either lean or agile becomes moot.*

Consider a typical retailer carrying a large assortment of seasonal products along with their nonseasonal merchandise. Some seasonal merchandise may depend on the weather, which is unpredictable, and as the onset of the season arrives early or gets delayed due to the weather patterns, the demand for such merchandise is directly affected. This unpredictability in the season-onset requires that the retailer must build up inventories in advance of the season so that they can be pushed to the stores at short notice to coincide with the season-onset. The length of the season, which is also an outcome of weather, affects the total demand over the entire season. This requires this retailer to have a good *open-to-buy* process so that merchandise orders can be changed to align with the actual demand in the stores. Regional weather adds another dimension of unpredictability to demand in specific regions that requires the retailer to be able to quickly shift their inventories across regions. This kind of demand unpredictability will drive the retailer to design an *agile* supply chain. However, a retailer's nonseasonal assortment has a predictable demand pattern and lends itself to a more *lean* supply chain design. To be effective, this retailer must design processes that are flexible enough to accommodate the wide range of product attributes and build several supply chains to address several product categories that form their assortment.

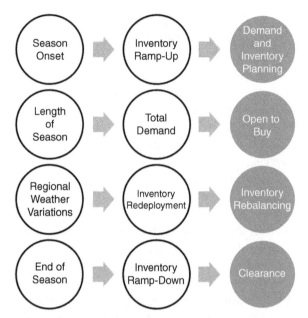

FIGURE 5.1   Effect of External Factors on Demand Management

Figure 5.1 shows how these external factors affect demand; for example, the length of season will affect the total demand, which is managed by having an effective open-to-buy process to control costs. Regional weather variations may require inventory redeployment requiring agility. Such factors, in turn, require specific supply chain capabilities for effectively managing the demand process, requiring the supply chain to be simultaneously lean and agile.

The need to build several supply chains for different product categories is not limited to the retail industry. It is true for a large number of manufacturers as well. Most businesses dealing with a combination of seasonal and non-seasonal products face similar requirements and should think about designing supply chains with different capabilities for different categories of products in their portfolio.

Product categories that generally have a stable demand (and therefore are potentially suitable for *lean* supply chain design) are functional products that address basic needs such as food, clothing, and gas. As the products in these categories are daily staples, their demand is almost inelastic and can be forecasted more accurately than others. Firms dealing in these products can definitely benefit from lean supply chains. However, these products also show seasonal characteristics that make a strong case for supply chain agility. In fact, there are few firms dealing exclusively in product categories with such stable demand characteristics to demand exclusively *lean* supply chains. Therefore, the opportunities for designing a supply chain with a highly pronounced *lean* or *agile* design are quite limited in practice.

So, is *lean* really a strategy for supply chains? The true answer is that *lean* is really a business model or a business strategy; in fact, this is just another name for Porter's cost strategy, because it is based on the identical principle of identifying unnecessary costs (cost elements that do not add any value in Porter's value chain) and cutting them. However, a business strategy based on building cost advantage can dictate that the supply chain design must be *lean*.

Is *agile* a supply chain strategy? It sounds good as a concept, but it is hardly new thinking on supply chains. Supply chains, after all, were invented so that firms can quickly react to changes along their value chains and be agile. If a supply chain is not agile, it is simply not doing its most basic function of reacting to demand and supply changes in the environment.

Summarizing the discussion so far, while understanding the concepts of lean and agile are helpful to establish individual supply chain processes using the demand and lead-time profiles of product groups, these concepts do not offer any actionable definition of a supply chain strategy that can be used to drive the capabilities of a firm.

Postponement and Speculation Strategies

These are two other strategies that have been mentioned in various supply chain strategy literature. The postponement strategy is based on the following two basic principles of demand forecasting.

1. The accuracy of the forecast demand decreases with an increase in the time horizon. The farther the time window for which the demand is being forecasted, the more inaccurate it will be. Figure 5.2 graphically represents this effect as a funnel: as time extends farther into the future, the forecast error grows, showing that the forecast demand will have larger and larger variations as time periods progress into the future.
2. Demand projections for a *product group* are generally more accurate than projections for individual products. For example, it is much easier to forecast the total demand for LCD TVs than it is for an individual TV of a specific brand, model, screen size, resolution, and color contrast ratio.

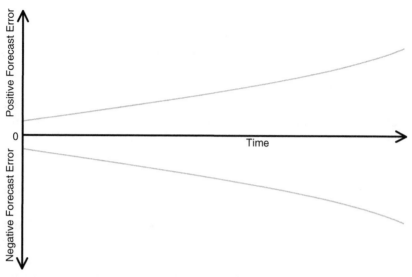

FIGURE 5.2   Effect of Horizon on the Accuracy of Demand Forecasting

EXAMPLES **OF DEMAND FORECASTING**

The first characteristic of demand forecasting is seen in action when retailers like Wal-Mart deploy cross-docking capabilities in their warehouses that allow them to push the decision of product allocation and shipments to stores to the very last minute. Generally, the supplier lead time for delivering the most merchandise from factory to warehouse is much longer than the transit lead time between the distribution center and stores, and since demand forecast is always more accurate for shorter time horizons, Wal-Mart can use this characteristic of demand forecasting to reallocate merchandise to stores according to their latest demand forecast, rather than shipping them based on the original forecast, which may have been created several weeks ahead for the purposes of generating replenishment purchase orders for its suppliers.

The second characteristic of demand forecasting is seen in action when Macy's uses the product groups for forecasting fashion apparel at the group level. Individual apparel SKUs have specific styles, colors, and sizes; for example, shirts will have unique style, color, and size designations even when they all belong to a single category, such as "men's shirts." However, forecasting demand for such items at the individual stock-keeping-unit (SKU) level is almost never done, due to the inherent forecast error in the process at that level of granularity. Instead, the forecast is created at the *product group* level that consolidates all colors and sizes and produces a forecast by style. This forecast is more accurate and is split into individual color and size combinations using predetermined ratios that are generally based on historical data.

Another example of this characteristic in action is seen in assemble-to-order businesses like Dell, which forecasts the needed inventory of computer subassemblies rather than the final products for computers. Computers typically have a finite number of variations in subassemblies, such as hard disk drives (HDD), memory modules (RAM), processor speed, and so on, which can then be assembled into a very large number of finished computers. Given this variety, Dell chooses to forecast the demand by subassemblies rather than the final product. This type of situation is graphically depicted in Figure 5.3.

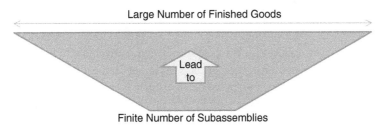

FIGURE 5.3 Higher Accuracy Results by Forecasting the Demand for Subassemblies

The postponement strategy leverages these characteristics of demand forecasting. It dictates that the firms should postpone the creation or delivery of the final product as long as possible. For retailers, this takes the shape of postponing the delivery of the final product to its destination, while for assemble-to-order manufacturers this means postponing the final assembly of the product. For manufacturing scenarios like build-to-stock, the postponement strategy may drive pushing the packaging or final assembly of the products, allowing the manufacturer to personalize, configure finished products to customer orders, and change the final product mix to suit any changes in demand. The postponement strategy effectively reduces inventory obsolescence and takes out the risk and uncertainty costs associated with having undesirable products, but it requires an integrated and agile supply chain to ensure that the latest demand forecasts can be frequently created and propagated through the supply chain to produce or allocate the right products for their customers.

The speculation strategy, on the other hand, is based on savings created through economies of scale, by creating and delivering the finished goods in bulk. The speculation strategy reduces the cost of logistics by maximizing the usage of resources like warehouses and trucks, and reduces the cost of manufacturing by running large production batches that improve throughput by reducing the cost of set-up changes and by reducing the raw material costs by buying in bulk. This strategy leverages the large lot-sizes to produce the economies of scale in manufacturing and distribution, but it is prone to having higher inventory costs due to higher inventory levels and obsolescence. As speculation strategy is based on creating economies of scale through mass production and distribution, the supply chain processes based on this strategy generally create stable plans without much volatility. The low volatility in plans does not require highly responsive supply chain design, especially when compared to the supply chains that cater to a postponement strategy.

While these two are also billed as supply chain strategies, a little thinking will dispel this notion. *Postponement or speculation is not a choice, it is an imperative forced by the type of industry, assortment, and demand patterns.* For example, a postponement strategy for delivering supplies to a trauma center or cereal to a grocery store are just not practical choices, even though it may allow for delivery of specific medical kits optimal for the type of trauma or the correct size of cereal packages in response to the actual demand. Therefore, medical supplies manufacturer cannot select postponement as their supply chain strategy any more than a grocer can postpone delivering their cereal. On the other hand, an assemble-to-order inventory such as custom-built gaming machines must adopt postponement, because the speculation strategy will simply produce too many unwanted machines, making the business model unfeasible. In real-life businesses, the business model, dependent on industry, products, and demand patterns, force either a speculation or postponement style of requirements on their supply chain.

The situations in which speculation or postponement is an explicit choice to be made for a supply chain are limited, but may become real options for specific categories of products or sales channels of a company. For example, consider Dell with their new business model to sell through the retail stores. In the changed scenario, Dell must master a speculation model of supply chain to fill the retail channels with prebuilt machines, but they can continue to use their postponement model of supply chain design to effectively build machines for their online sales of computers.

We summarize this section on speculation and postponement strategy with two statements:

1. In most situations, the choice of postponement or speculation strategies generally is a characteristic of the industry segment and not an explicit choice to be made by a corporation. Once a firm clearly identifies the products and services it wishes to provide and the industry segment it belongs to, their only viable option will be to pursue a speculation or postponement strategy to be financially successful, since the other choice will have clear disadvantages. However, pioneers will continue to define new *segments* and create new rules for themselves, as Dell did when it started its personalized computers business targeted at a new segment of individual consumers who were passionate about their computers, but could not afford to pay the high price of customization. Such pioneers with brand-new business models may have the option to follow a different supply chain model from those in the conventional industry segment.

2. Since the corporation must follow speculation or postponement as the primary business model driven by their industry segment, the supply chain strategy simply supports that business model option by providing required capabilities for the business model. This makes a clear distinction that the speculation or postponement strategy decisions are made at a higher level than the supply chain function and would require *all* business functions to align themselves with the demands of the selected business model, including the firm's supply chain. This will force a specific set of business capabilities for the firm's supply chain. This is simply the case of a business strategy driving a firm's supply chain capabilities, just as it should drive functional capabilities in other areas of business.

Understanding the postponement or speculation concepts and analyzing the type of product, demand, customers, industry, and operational costs are all good inputs to establish a direction for the supply chain design. However, developing the functional strategy for supply chains must go deeper and identify what process capabilities will allow the firm to pursue their selected (lean, agile, postponement, speculation, or a combination of selected flavors) strategy, identify how these capabilities depend on other functional capabilities and on each other, and finally establish a roadmap for the development of these supply chain competencies for the firm. In doing so, a supply chain may emerge that has characteristics of postponement for a set of products and processes and characteristics of speculation for another set of products and processes.

Summary of the Existing Thinking on Supply Chain Strategies

The discussions on the current strategic thinking on supply chains was centered on lean and agile, or postponement and speculation strategies. While they provide a relevant context for the supply chain design, they are not specific enough to be able to drive the design of individual supply chain capabilities. A supply chain strategy must provide a roadmap of evolution of supply chain capabilities, which requires a more in-depth analysis of the requirements and assessment of current and planned capabilities. The concepts of lean and agile lack that depth.

For example, why should *lean* be only a supply chain strategy? The origins of this concept lie in the manufacturing world, in which Toyota made a formal process for reducing waste in every activity on the manufacturing line. The concept is easily expanded to the rest of the enterprise activities, because the basic premise of the concept is to review every task and evaluate the value added by this task toward achieving the enterprise goals. In the case of manufacturing, this goal is relatively well defined in terms of the next subassembly or a finished product and therefore the analysis for establishing the value addition is relatively simple. In the case of a complex business process consisting of many steps and interrelated activities, such an analysis may not be quite as simple; however, the concept remains just as valid. Therefore, why should *lean* be thought of just as a supply chain strategy? *Lean* as a supply chain strategy does not provide any more input toward designing supply chain processes than a general reminder to evaluate each process for its value in the chain of activities that comprise the process. To that extent *lean* can be used as a strategy for all processes across the enterprise.

A similar argument can be made for *agile*. Responsiveness is not limited to supply chain alone, rather, it is a general measure of process agility. The efficacy of a lot of conventional processes is measured by their responsiveness: time taken to raise a customer invoice after a product is delivered, time to schedule service when a customer complaint is received, time to service customers on a register with varying load are all examples where process *agility* is highly desirable. Therefore, *agile* as a supply chain strategy also does not provide any more input toward designing supply chain processes than a generic desire to build processes that are responsive.

These two strategies, *lean* and *agile*, are too generic to be specifically useful in establishing a supply chain functional strategy, which must establish the roadmap for the evolution of supply chain competencies as competitive advantages.

Seen from another point of view, the *lean* strategy is equivalent to the generic *cost* strategy proposed by Porter. Both of these *lean* and *cost* strategies propose identical reviews and evaluations of all corporate activities. Porter called these activities the *value chain* and postulated that cost advantages can come from anywhere in this value chain and, therefore, the cost strategy drives the firm to review all value chain activities to find the opportunities for reducing costs to build competitive advantage. The *lean* strategy suggests the same argument when expanded beyond the production systems and into the whole enterprise. These two concepts are so similar to each other that calling *lean* a specific supply chain strategy is meaningless. *Lean* as a strategy is simply another way of following the generic *cost* strategy, even though this term has been generally used in the supply chain strategy context.

A similar case can be made for postponement and speculation strategies. These options define the underlying business model of a firm more than its supply chain strategy, which, in turn, must drive *all* organizational processes aligned with this business model, not only the supply chain processes. To that extent, these two options become a business decision that applies across all business functions. The decision of the business model itself is heavily constrained by the type of industry, type of product, demand characteristics, supply characteristics, lead time, and other similar factors. Plastic water bottles, for example, would almost never be a good choice for a postponement strategy, while custom-designed bicycles may profitably allow for a postponement strategy. (However, this would almost never be the case, if the corporation was trying to pursue a price leadership strategy from Porter's generic strategies.) Therefore, while the supply chain design for the firm must support the underlying business model of speculation or postponement, this is just one of several inputs for the design of a supply chain strategy.

Table 5.1 shows an equivalence of the Porter's generic strategies and the purported supply chain strategies.

Our main concern with these strategies is that while they are presented as supply chain strategies, they really are higher-level business strategies. Most of them depend on analyzing the factors that should be analyzed to establish a business strategy, not a support function like supply chain. They also tend to provide high-level direction similar to the business strategy and equally

TABLE 5.1 Comparison of Well-Known Supply Chain Strategies of Lean, Agile, Speculation, and Postponement to the Generic Business Strategies of Porter

Purported Supply Chain Strategy	Porter's Generic Strategy	Why They Are the Same	Why They Are Different	Generic Supply Chain Process Focus
Lean	Cost	Both are based on identifying and eliminating activities in the corporate value chain that do not add value.	There is really no difference at all except that *lean* has been referenced in supply chain context in literature and is therefore associated with supply chain strategy.	Process optimization to maximize resource efficiency and asset usage.
Agile	Differentiation and niche	Process agility is essential to create differentiation in product or processes.	Agility is more easily associated with supply chain processes that are based on flows, although it is not limited to supply chain processes alone. Process agility may be just one of the factors contributing toward creating differentiation/ niche.	Process optimization to detect and propagate changes throughout the supply chain.
Speculation	Cost	Speculation strategy is based on cutting costs by increasing the scale of operations.	Increasing the scale of operations is only one factor in developing cost cutting strategies.	Process optimization to maximize resource efficiency and asset usage.

(continued)

TABLE 5.1   *(Continued)*

Purported Supply Chain Strategy	Porter's Generic Strategy	Why They Are the Same	Why They Are Different	Generic Supply Chain Process Focus
Postponement	Differentiation and niche	Postponement leans toward addressing specific customer needs by customizing the product/service as close to the actual demand as possible. This is also the principle on which generic strategies of differentiation or niche are based.	Postponement is just one part of creating differentiation- or niche-based strategies.	A mix of process optimization to maximize resource efficiency and asset usage and to detect and propagate changes for producing finished products.

applicable to all the functional strategies. For example, a *cost*-focused approach to the business strategy will drive the firm toward building a *lean* supply chain, but it will also drive the firm's merchandising strategy toward cost-sensitive utilitarian product selection and cost-based sourcing. It is like a general guideline to create cost-effective processes rather than any specific inputs toward creating an effective supply chain.

On the other hand, the functional strategy assumes that the analysis of the industry segment, competition, customer demographics, product positioning, product, and demand attributes has been completed and a business strategy has been established. Unless the business strategy has been established, it is impossible to ascertain the desired business capabilities for building the competitive advantages, which alone are the inputs for creating a functional strategy; and they cannot be effectively determined in absence of a business strategy. This cannot be overstated—business strategy drives the required business capabilities, which drive the functional strategies. The industry is full of examples where firms have been trying to build their supply chains without having established what functional capabilities they desire to build or what business strategy they wish to follow.

A functional strategy does not replace the business strategy as the current supply chain strategies might lead one to believe. But a functional strategy needs the business strategy to outline the goals of the business in order to assess the functional capabilities that will help, hinder, or do nothing toward achieving these goals. Once these functional capabilities have been identified, the objective of the functional strategy is to build a road map for their realization. Therefore, *a functional strategy cannot and should not dictate business decisions such as postponement or speculation business models, but only constrain itself to build competencies to support the business model that has been established by the business strategy* as the model desirable for the firm. After all, business functions simply exist to support the firm's business and do not dictate the business model. Supply chain as one of the business functions exists simply to support the selected business model. This is a subtle but important distinction to make to understand the concept of functional strategies. This clarity is required for strategic planning, when considering functional constraints and confronting the scope of the strategy formulation.

So, what is supply chain strategy? How should it be understood and how should it be elaborated for a firm? What must a practitioner understand to successfully create a supply chain strategy to support their business and help create a road map to develop supply chain capabilities?

To answer these questions, we must first understand the supply chain *sphere of influence* (see Figure 5.4). Without understanding this sphere of influence clearly, we run the risk of creating supply chain strategies like lean and agile or speculation and postponement, which are higher-level business directives and are equally applicable to all business functions. While they set the tone for supply chain functional capabilities, they do so to no more extent than they set the tone for merchandising or financing or any other corporate functions. In this context, they serve no better purpose than reinforcing the business strategy's guidance for all business functions without offering any specific insights for creating supply chain capabilities.

The supply chain *sphere of influence* helps one to understand what supply chains can and cannot affect. Only then can one proceed to define how supply chain strategies can be formulated and how best to leverage them to create competitive advantages and support business goals.

FIGURE 5.4 Supply Chain Sphere of Influence

UNDERSTANDING THE SUPPLY CHAIN SPHERE OF INFLUENCE

Supply chains have a core sphere of influence in the firm's operations and a supply chain strategy must be formulated within those constraints. It is for this reason that we will ignore the strategies presented earlier since they are too broad and go way beyond the supply chain sphere of influence. Supply chains directly *manage* the following four basic components of a firm's value chain, which we call the supply chain sphere of influence:

1. **Management of demand.** While the end consumer demand is an independent variable, once the finished goods demand has been forecast, it is the supply chain processes that propagate the demand along the supply chain nodes. As the demand propagates through the network, supply chain processes may determine the optimal way to fulfill this demand, including where, when, and how this will happen. For the manufacturing supply chains, this propagation will take the demand to the warehouses, then to the assembly plants and factories, and finally to the raw material warehouses and vendors. Along the way, the finished goods demand will be broken down into its subassemblies, components, and raw materials using a bill of materials, as well as into its manufacturing operations and resources, using the bills of routing and resources. For retail supply chains, the propagation process will

take the demand to its warehouses and then to the suppliers. Thus, while the end demand may be independent, the supply chain processes have a huge impact in managing demand through propagation and determining the fulfillment methods throughout the supply network.

2. **Management of supply.** As the demand is propagated from the customer end to the supply end of the supply chain, the replenishment planning processes start creating the fulfillment plans, which results in an opposite propagation of supply to fulfill the demand at every node for every finished product, work-in-progress (WIP), or raw material. The replenishment plans finally drive the procurement process that replenishes the supply chain inventories from the firm's suppliers. Supplies from the vendors are managed through purchasing and logistics to replenish the supply chain nodes from where the supply propagation continues toward the demand end. These processes of demand and supply planning must work in concert for a smoothly run supply chain. Managing supply with demand is the most important function of a supply chain and since neither demand nor supply is static, the *agility* with which they are planned and re-planned *differentiates* one supply chain from another.

3. **Management of inventory.** This is the third part of the puzzle that supply chains directly control. Inventories make it possible for the supply chains to react to the changes in supply and demand while simultaneously maintaining acceptable fulfillment rates. However, inventories add cost that directly comes from the working capital of a company and therefore, needs to be reduced as far as possible while protecting the ability of the supply chain to service the demand. Supply chain processes of inventory classification and inventory planning help the corporations achieve that balance. The quality of the inventory planning processes depends on the underlying science, accuracy of historical and forecasted demand, supply and lead-time data, and cost models for inventory. The results of this process directly affect the *leanness* of a supply chain by affecting inventory costs and affect *agility* by maintaining demand fulfillment targets under varying conditions of demand and supply.

4. **Management of resources.** This is the last component of the corporate operations directly affected by supply chain processes. It is also the most complex and wide in scope since resources encompass so much in a corporation—they are the people, machinery, warehouses, trucks, fork-lifts, conveyors, and so on. A lot of these resources enable supply chain processes in the corporate offices, warehouses, factories, ports, in-transit, and stores. Supply chain processes create resource plans and affect the

efficiency and utilization of these resources. Throughput in a warehouse or factory is a direct result of efficient planning and scheduling capabilities. In a wider definition, one could consider inventory and cash as resources as well. We chose to consider inventory separately since there are very specific supply chain processes addressing inventory planning. Cash is a legitimate resource for a corporation and even though supply chains impact it through working capital (inventory and operations), receivables, and payables (cash-to-cash cycles), we do not consider this in the primary sphere of influence of the physical supply chain. The reason to do so is that while supply chain capabilities impact the financial results, they do not manipulate cash as they manage the other components of inventory, demand, supply, and resources.

The core objective of the supply chain is managing the flow of material from the supply end to the demand end through a network of inventory and resource hubs that are designed to stabilize this flow in spite of the natural fluctuations in the demand and supply signals at both ends of the supply chain (see Figure 5.5). The demand signals drive the supply chain plans for replenishment, resource, and inventory. As the demand signals are independent and change randomly, they affect all the supply chain plans. A similar pattern exists at the supply end of the chain though the variations may be less random, as supply changes are constrained by contracts, prices, lead time, and vendor relationships. A good supply chain uses its network of inventory and resources to absorb the variations in these signals to create a stable equilibrium for its operations. In this model, the inventory and resources act as buffers or shock absorbers to contain the natural volatility in demand and supply. In addition to inventory and resources, time can also be used as a buffer to maintain plan stability within manageable limits.

Depending on the firm's business model, supply chains can be designed to create differing levels of control (or constraints) on the four components

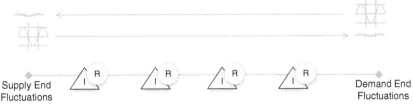

FIGURE 5.5 Supply Chain Core Objective

of supply, demand, inventory, and resources. These constraints reflect the objectives of the supply chain: a supply chain supporting a cost-based business strategy will place more constraints on the variables to control plan volatility and costs, while another supply chain supporting a business strategy of differentiation will focus on maintaining service levels or product quality but may allow higher plan volatility.

Understanding the driving factors and the overriding objectives in a supply chain is imperative to creating a supply chain strategy for a firm.

WHAT DRIVES YOUR SUPPLY CHAIN?

The objective of presenting the supply chain's sphere of influence was to establish the basic, though often missed, fact that supply chains can directly affect only these four components that they directly control. Therefore, any strategy we formulate for supply chain design must directly establish the behavior of one or more of these four components. One of these four components must also be identified as the primary *driver* to resolve plan conflicts and to establish the pecking order among the supply chain processes.

The next logical question to ask is: Which one of the four components should ideally drive the supply chain in a firm? Is it demand, supply, inventory, or resources? The answer depends on a number of factors, some of which we have seen in the review of the existing supply chain strategies. The industry segment, types of products, attributes of demand, attributes of supply, and finally, the selected business strategy are all factors that need to be analyzed to answer the question of what must drive a supply chain. A grocery firm with *cost* as the business strategy will have a dramatically different supply chain compared to that of a grocery store that selects *differentiation* as its business strategy. Both supply chains will have some common characteristics because they are both in the same industry segment (retail, grocery). For example, they will both require the ability to replenish their stores frequently for fresh produce and perishables, they will both have to develop temperature-controlled distribution capabilities, and so on. However, the grocer with *differentiation* as its business strategy may decide to differentiate itself by developing a supply chain for its produce that tracks its whole life cycle from the farm-to-the-shelf and provides this visibility to the customers to verify the claims of freshness, organic growth, sustainable farming, fair labor, or any similar differentiators that the customers may pay for. While development and maintenance of such capabilities will add supply chain costs for this grocer, it would also create a passionate and loyal customer base for them. In contrast, the supply chain capabilities for the grocer with the *cost*-based strategy may simply focus on more traditional ways of sourcing from the cheapest suppliers, optimizing inventories and shipping costs, and discounting products near their expiration dates.

The *differentiator* based business strategy, therefore, drives its own requirements for the supply chain capabilities that are different from those of the *cost*-based business strategy, while both the firms must also have a basic set of common capabilities. In this example, what is driving the two supply chains? While both of the grocery retailers need to be demand-driven, the one with *differentiation* as their business strategy must balance this against the supply-driven aspects, simply because they will have to manage many more constraints on the supply side, controlling quality through the assortment they carry, the sourcing that must support their policy of freshness, fair labor practices, organic fertilizers, and so on.

Unlike the current strategies that tend to conclude that the supply chain must be lean or agile, speculation- or postponement-oriented thinking through the core sphere of supply chain influence generally points to a *process group* belonging to one of the four components, which becomes the focus for creating competitive capabilities. This allows a specific guidance from the strategy to design, rather than providing a high-level general directive of being lean or agile. By *process group*, we mean the collective supply chain processes that are used to manage any one of the four components of the supply chain sphere of influence. In the example of the two grocers, the grocer with the *cost*-based business strategy will likely focus on inventory and resource process groups to leverage cost advantages, while the grocer with the *differentiation* business strategy will focus on supply process group. Remember though that these process groups only identify where the firm has the most potential to create advantages, even though they will have to develop capabilities in all process groups that bring them up to par with the competitors.

In this view of supply chain strategy, one of the four core *spheres of influence* is identified to be the primary sphere. This indicates where the firm can derive the advantages and where the impact of changes in the supply chain should be minimized. For example, the demand-driven supply chain will evaluate all alternatives in response to a change with the view of minimizing their impact on the demand plans, a supply-driven supply chain will do the same to minimize their impact on the supply plans, and so on. There are many reasons why a firm may design their supply chain to be driven by demand, supply, inventory, or resources, and they vary widely in scope, covering all relevant reasons like the industry, segment, products, demand patterns, supply conditions, and so on, in addition to the overriding business strategy that will affect such a selection. The following sections provide some guidelines.

Demand-Driven Supply Chains

In the demand-driven supply chains, the demand management processes take precedence over other processes that are designed to primarily support the demand processes. Consider an example: the supply chain creates the plans for the replenishment, purchase orders, and distribution using projected demand for a future time period. As that future time period comes closer and the demand forecast changes, then a demand-driven supply chain will react to such a change by re-planning all other dependent plans; that is, the plans for replenishment, purchase orders, and distribution will be re-created using the changed demand and maintaining the plan constraints. For example, some purchase orders may not be available for changes, if they have already been shipped, confirmed, or are contractually unavailable for changes.

A demand-driven supply chain for retail, for example, may use the latest store demand to create allocations when cross-docking in the warehouse. This means that even though the replenishment into the warehouse may have been planned using the store demand from two weeks ago (assuming two weeks supply lead time), the actual shipments to the stores will be made using the current store demand which may have changed from the demand projected two weeks ago.

A demand-driven supply chain is an industry standard in most retail segments that caters largely to undifferentiated assortments of utility items. An example where a demand-driven strategy may work well is manufacturing firms that are not constrained with large batch-sizes or high asset costs. The products will generally have characteristics such as low-brand value and a utilitarian nature, like disposable cups; an out-of-stock situation will certainly lead to a loss of sale. A demand-driven supply chain will have the characteristics listed in Table 5.2.

Choosing "demand-driven" as a strategy for a supply chain does not preclude the supply chain from being lean or agile; in fact, most retail supply chains will do well only when they are lean as well as agile. It also does not determine whether the business should select speculation or postponement models. These considerations, as we reviewed in the existing supply chain strategy discussions, are predetermined for a supply chain strategy to

TABLE 5.2 Characteristics of a Business Suitable for the Design of a Demand-Driven Supply Chain

Product	Demand
Utility or functional products, easily replaceable, little to no brand value, staple, certain loss of sale when out of stock	Largely stable and predictable demand even though it may be seasonal, little price elasticity due to staple nature of products with highly competitive pricing

Industry & Business Model	Business Strategy
Revenue-driven, fulfillment-driven Examples include retail and manufacturing industries with functional products	Cost leadership, speculation, lean, agile

support, since they are higher-level business directives. Thinking of the supply chain strategy in terms of being demand-driven actually establishes the process group that will react first to changes in the environment and then propagate these changes down the chain for all other processes to adapt. This establishes the process priority and a clear sequence to leverage in re-planning the supply chain activities in response to changes. Without such clarity, the supply chain as a holistic system may be paralyzed due to the conflicting responses to any such changes.

How does a *demand-driven supply chain* react to changes in supply, inventory, and resource availability? A demand-driven supply chain will always react to such changes by optimizing the *demand fulfillment* over any other objective. This affects what capabilities the firm should build and also provides guidelines to design such processes. For example, a change in supplies due to disruption of a vendor's operations may be addressed in several ways:

▪ The supply chain may simply decide to short the demand affected by such supply disruption, irrespective of the effect of such shortage on revenues. This option may affect revenues due to lost sales, but is the cheapest option because it does not add any plan volatility.

▪ The supply chain may react with a dynamic inventory rebalancing within the network to maximize demand fulfillment, even though such a dynamic movement of inventory may add additional operational costs. This option will save some lost sales and optimizes the fulfillment, but also adds to the cost of goods sold. In another variation, the inventory rebalancing process may optimize profitability rather than demand fulfillment.

▪ Alternately, the changes in supplies may trigger additional replenishment orders with second-tier suppliers or with expediting the existing orders.

In all these cases, the firm develops the required capability to respond to the supply disruption based on its own preferences. Some firms may develop all capabilities and select an option to react to the supply disruption depending on several other factors, such as supply lead time, inventory rebalancing process time, current projected demand, profitability, cost, and resource constraints. However, the key point of the example is that a demand-driven supply chain will consider all options to minimize the impact on demand fulfillment.

The firm's preferred response style directly affects the result of the same change in supply on its supply chain, and their level of sophistication in handling such changes directly depends on the superiority of their supply chain processes. Supply chains that can closely emulate and model real life and leverage mathematical models for optimization will be able to maximize demand fulfillment, while simultaneously keeping their costs of response to change to the minimum.

Figure 5.6 sums up the available response options in a demand-driven supply chain: While the impact of changes due to supply volatility is reduced during the propagation through the supply chain by using the inventory and resource buffers, the impact of changes due to demand volatility may be passed straight to the supply end or absorbed during the forward propagation based on other supply chain objectives. A demand-driven supply chain will try to accommodate changes in its demand plans by altering the supply, inventory, and resource plans.

AMR Research, now a part of Gartner Group, has made a religion out of demand-driven supply networks (DDSN). It is an easy-to-understand concept, since all supply chain planning starts from the demand end and reacts to changes in demand. This remains true for all supply chains, whether they are demand driven or not. The concept presented here differs from the DDSN

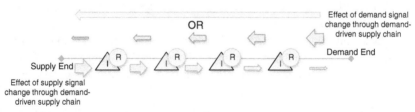

FIGURE 5.6 Demand-Driven Supply Chain

approach in that it recognizes all possible drivers of a supply chain and allows for a supply chain design that reacts to demand changes, even though such response may be dominated by supply, inventory, or resources considerations over the desire to align with the change in demand.

Supply-Driven Supply Chains

In supply-driven supply chains, supply management processes get the central focus and supply considerations override all other priorities. When a supply-driven supply chain detects a change on the supply side, this supply chain will react to reorganize the downstream plans for manufacturing, distribution, and sales to accommodate the changes on the supply side.

When would a supply-driven supply chain be strategic? It will be most desirable when the demand-supply balance in an industry heavily favors the suppliers, when supplies are restricted and monopolized, or where factors like contractual obligations, prices, lead time, cash flow, or credit severely constrain the buyer's ability to source from alternate sources.

Consider hospitals during the flu season: they must subordinate their vaccination plans and operations to the availability of the flu vaccine, the volume of the available vaccine, and the locations where it will be available. The vaccine supplies in this case are largely controlled through federal government departments and the hospitals have a limited role to play. An example we have all experienced is when a hot new item is introduced and the supplier chooses to decide where and how much of the product will be made available: think of introduction of new game systems like Xbox, Wii, and consumer electronics such as iPods and iPhones in recent years. In each of these cases, the supply chain for these products was driven primarily by the constraint on the supply side more than by any other supply chain consideration. Another example of supply chains that must be supply driven are engineer-to-order building industries, where every product is unique and custom-built. As the products are unique and volumes are relatively low, their production schedules depend heavily on the suppliers' ability to provide raw materials and subassemblies. Shipbuilders, industrial plants, and large commercial complexes are all examples of industries that have significant characteristics of supply-driven supply chains.

More examples exist where supply-side monopolies create situations for manufacturing industries for designing supply-driven supply chains. Rare earth metals, minerals, and other natural resources may fall in this category. Sometimes, the monopolistic situation is simply a result of geographic monopoly where the raw material resources may not be rare (as in a demand-supply gap that may not exist), but transporting them over long distances may be cost-prohibitive, creating a geographic monopoly. United States Geological Survey (USGS) identifies 16 rare earth elements (REEs). By several estimates, more than 90 percent of the world's deposits of REEs are in China. These elements are used in several applications from liquid-crystal displays for computer and television monitors to eyeglasses and permanent magnets. USGS notes that small, lightweight, high-strength REE magnets have allowed miniaturization of numerous electrical and electronic components used in appliances, audio and video equipment, computers, automobiles, communications systems, and military gear. A *New York Times* article in September 2009[2] reported that ". . . tighter limits on production and exports, part of a plan from the Ministry of Industry and Information Technology, would ensure China has the supply for its own technological and economic needs, and force more manufacturers to make their wares here in order to have access to the minerals," and that "Beijing officials are forcing global manufacturers to move factories to China by limiting the availability of rare earths outside China." Such supply constraints can push manufacturers to redesign their supply chain processes and networks.

In the well-connected global economy of today, the supply constraints have almost become nonexistent in most consumer-oriented industries and for most raw materials. However, there still are pockets where production, availability, distribution, marketing, or monopolistic considerations create supply constraints, and firms in those situations will do well with a supply-driven model. Lack of available materials or capacity is not the only reason for constrained supplies. Sometimes, suppliers may explicitly constrain supplies simply to retain product demand, generate curiosity-based demand, and retain price levels that may otherwise start tumbling down. Of course, these tactics would be possible only when the supplier has a monopoly or there is a small close-knit consortium of suppliers acting in unison to create artificial supply constraints.

Therefore, a supply-driven design works best when supplies are constrained, uncertain, or not directly controlled by the firm. This kind of supply chain will try to reallocate the available supplies against the outstanding demand to optimize schedules, fulfillment, resource utilization, and profitability. When cheaper supplies suddenly become available, a supply-driven supply chain may try to take advantage of that situation by hedging and benefiting from opportunistic pricing or supplies to protect against the future risks of shortage.

TABLE 5.3 Characteristics of a Business Suitable for the Design of a Supply-Driven Supply Chain

Product	Demand
Build or engineer-to-order manufacturing segments with heavy dependence on suppliers, luxury goods, highly-personalized items, regulated items, demand not easily shifted due to loyalty or monopolies	Firm demand generally available in advance

Industry & Business Model	Business Strategy
Supplies driven with focus on profitability, constrained supply, monopoly, artificially limiting supply to create specific brand image or retain pricing levels	Postponement, agile, customer segmentation by profitability

A supply-driven supply chain will have the attributes listed in Table 5.3.

Once again, a supply-driven supply chain does not exclude the lean or agile principles. In fact, a supply-driven supply chain will need to be agile to react to changes and influence all other plans to optimally leverage the changes in supply situations. Similarly, a supply-driven supply chain will also do well in a business model that lends itself to postponement so that the best price performance can be achieved with whatever supplies are available at the last possible minute when this decision must be made.

A supply-driven design will respond to supply disruptions by looking inward and re-planning their own operations, because the assumption is that the alternate supply sources are not available. The chain can react by reviewing and reallocating available inventory, postponing or canceling promised order fulfillment through selective customer portfolio optimization, or by re-planning manufacturing operations to optimize the available supplies and order fulfillment. If available supplies were to suddenly become abundant for a short period of time, this type of supply chain may react with hedging and hoarding supplies for the future, even though the future demand for these periods may not be firmly known.

Figure 5.7 sums up the probable responses in a supply-driven supply chain: While the impact of changes due to demand volatility is reduced during the propagation through the supply chain by using the inventory and resource buffers, the impact of changes due to supply volatility may be passed straight to the demand end or absorbed during the forward propagation based on other supply chain objectives.

FIGURE 5.7 Supply-Driven Supply Chain

Inventory-Driven Supply Chains

An inventory-driven supply chain has the greatest focus on controlling the inventory costs, even though this may affect the service levels, demand fulfillment rates, resource utilization, and supply plans. Any changes in this supply chain design will try to minimize changes to its inventory plans and hence protect the inventory costs and the working capital used in inventories.

This type of supply chain design is generally feasible when process variance is low, predictable, or well known. When the demand, supply, and lead-time variance is low, it means that low levels of well-planned inventories will be sufficient to support small changes in supplies and demand. A low variance in demand and supplies makes all the processes more stable and renders stocks of inventory less valuable due to low levels of plan volatility and a smaller magnitude of plan changes. Plan volatility refers to the frequency of changes to a plan and magnitude of plan change refers to the size of change to the original plan quantities, scheduler, or resource usage.

Such conditions for demand and supply can be found for staple, everyday essentials that form a substantial part of product assortment for many types of retailers and manufacturers. Supply chain processes for such product categories with a singular focus on inventory is quite a viable design. In fact, such a supply chain will provide the best working capital performance. This design can be combined with a discriminate focus on other objectives such as product profitability or demand fulfillment.

When inventory is not the central focus of the supply chain, as in supply and demand-driven supply chains, the inventory costs can be adopted as the second-most important objective for optimization. In a supply-driven chain, when inventory costs are high, profit margins are thin, and firms can afford to discriminate between fulfilling customer orders based on their profitability staying within their contractual obligations, an inventory-focused supply chain can be viable. In a demand-driven supply chain, the focus on inventory can drastically reduce the working capital investments in inventory holding costs by balancing the demand fulfillment rates against the inventory levels.

Another situation where inventory can play the central role for designing an effective supply chain is the maintenance of spare parts when the demand is sporadic and random. By positioning inventory in critical locations and optimal volumes, firms can address such a choppy demand situation more effectively than pursuing either of the other strategies.

This supply chain design will likely need to be supported with relatively sophisticated solutions to ensure that the opposing objectives of low inventory costs are balanced with the long-term interests of the firm through maintaining acceptable service levels for demand fulfillment. Most companies, when they follow an inventory-based supply chain strategy, fail to realize this and run into situations in which too little inventory affects their sales or too much inventory affects their costs. The reason for such an anomaly is that inventory alone is an internally focused process while the supply chains primarily exist for connecting the supply end to the demand end, both of which are directly affected by external factors independently. For this reason, an inventory approach is generally adopted as a secondary approach and subordinated to another primary driver of the chain, which may be demand, supply, or resources.

An inventory-driven supply chain will be characterized by the general attributes listed in Table 5.4.

In most supply chain scenarios, inventory *alone* may not suffice as a logical driver for the supply chain strategy, because the primary function of the inventory is to address the natural variance in other supply chain processes of demand, supply, and resource availability. Inventory alone ensures stable order fulfillment rates, but it also remains the largest cost driver in a supply chain. Therefore, any supply chain that is cost-sensitive must focus on inventory planning processes and create capabilities to optimize total system inventory without affecting

TABLE 5.4 Characteristics of a Business Suitable for Designing an Inventory-Driven Supply Chain

Product	Demand
Functional products, high cost of system inventory, maintenance parts	Stable demand with low variance, low supply variance (cost and lead time), or very low sporadic demand
Industry & Business Model	**Business Strategy**
Cost of operations driven with focus on profitability, competitive industry with low margins, efficient inventory transfers, or maintenance operations	Speculation, lean, agile, service levels by profitability

the desired demand fulfillment targets. To that extent, while inventory is clearly one of the core spheres of influence for supply chains, inventory plays that role more often in a secondary position to the primary driver of supply chain.

Resource-Driven Supply Chains

Some supply chains will be most effective when resource utilization can be maintained at a reasonable level and fluctuations in the resource requirements are minimized. A high cost of fixed assets, resources with rare skills, operations with steep learning curves, and high set-up time rendering key resources unproductive are all situations that characterize the suitability of such supply chains.

Resource-driven supply chains are primarily designed to react to changes such as to contain and minimize the impact on the resource plans. For example, when demand changes, a resource-driven supply chain may react by re-planning work so that the disruption to most critical resources is minimal. In a manufacturing scenario with high set-up change time, this behavior may lead the supply chain to react by changing the resource plans in a cascading priority:

▪ First, change resource plans at those work stations that are about to conclude their current production runs. This has the least impact on the resource utilization.

▪ Second, change resource plans at those stations that are in the middle of a set-up change. This impacts the resource efficiency by potentially adding to the set-up change time, but also ensures that the change will allow a longer production run and reduce incremental cost of production.

▪ Third, a firm may decide to continue executing the current plans for some products where these production runs have just been started. This protects batch sizes and reduces the incremental cost of production.

In addition to the high cost of set-up changes, two other characteristics of these supply chains are the requirements of maintaining high resource utilization rates and resource leveling to avoid wild fluctuations in the resource requirements. Both of these requirements may arise from the desire to ensure efficient use of expensive or rare resources. To achieve this objective, these supply chains may have to maintain inventories so that the changes in demand and supply do not disrupt the resource plans. The increased cost of inventory is balanced against the cost of set-up changes and cost of idling resources.

One example where this supply chain design will be most suitable is process industries where set-up changes are complex and time consuming, investments

TABLE 5.5 Characteristics of a Business Suitable for the Design of a Resource-Driven Supply Chain

Product	Demand
Batch production based process due to intensive asset investments and long set-up changes	Relatively stable

Industry & Business Model	Business Strategy
Driven by throughput rates, demand fulfillment constrained by resource plans	Speculation, lean, throughput driven

in fixed assets are high, and the profitability of the firm depends on its ability to maintain high levels of asset utilization to maintain throughput. Steel manufacturing is a typical industry example that fits the description.

A resource-driven supply chain will have the general attributes listed in Table 5.5.

Resource-driven supply chains, due to intensive investments in assets, higher set-up change costs, and requirement to maintain high resource utilization rates do not easily lend themselves to be very agile. This lack of agility means that these chains perform well under stable demand conditions and when long manufacturing lead times are provided to fulfill the orders. When demand volatility is present, the value of higher resource utilization must be balanced against the cost of set-up changes, cost of potentially unwanted inventory, and the cost of unfulfilled orders or lost sales.

For inventory or resource-driven supply chains, the impact of changes in supplies or demand signals may be propagated through to the other end without affecting any of the inventory and resource plans, or the supply chain may try to absorb the impact of these changes through the resource, inventory, or time buffers to achieve the targeted demand fulfillment. These options are shown in Figure 5.8.

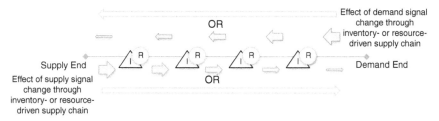

FIGURE 5.8 Inventory or Resource-Driven Supply Chains

In the following chapter, we continue to focus on the supply chain functional strategy, delving deeper into the process for creating an effective supply chain strategy that is actionable. In the proposed process for developing a supply chain strategy, unlike the conventional thinking on supply chain strategy, lean and agile are not exclusive to each other, but instead are viewed as integral requirements for any effective supply chain. Speculation or postponement strategies are not decisions affecting the supply chain, but rather are reflective of the industry and the product that the firm is offering—therefore, these attributes are merely inputs that are needed to design effective supply chain processes rather than supply chain strategies in their own right. The supply chain strategy begins with the business strategy, takes inputs from the industry and product characteristics, recognizes the peer-group capability parity, identifies the drivers of the supply chain processes, and finally, creates competitive advantages through an explicit focus on superior process design and deployment.

CHAPTER SIX

Creating a Functional Supply Chain Strategy

C REATING A FUNCTIONAL STRATEGY for supply chains depends on many factors. Some of these factors are established as part of a firm's decision to compete in a selected industry segment and others are established as part of a firm's business strategy to pursue competitive viability and growth. In the last category are the factors that are a matter of explicit choices from the many available design options. The factors in the first category are predetermined by the firm's decision to do business in a selected industry segment. The factors in the second category are determined by the firm's business strategy. Therefore, these factors must simply be taken as input for designing the supply chain strategy. The factors in the third category present a certain amount of choice in designing the supply chain. These were presented in Chapter 5 during the discussion on the core sphere of influence and include demand, supply, inventory, and resources. The categories affecting supply chain strategy are depicted in Figure 6.1.

A firm must consider all these factors to create a viable supply chain strategy that is aligned with its business objectives and complements the firm's industry positioning and their business strategy to create competitive advantages. The current discussion presents a summary of these factors and how they affect the formulation of supply chain strategy.

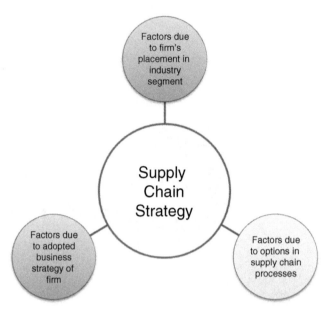

FIGURE 6.1 Factors Affecting Supply Chain Strategy

THE EFFECT OF AN INDUSTRY SEGMENT ON SUPPLY CHAIN DESIGN

The decision of a firm to compete in an industry segment affects their options in designing a supply chain. A firm in retail industry needs a very different type of supply chain compared to a manufacturer. Unlike retailers who must build efficient distribution systems, the manufacturing industries are typically more focused on maintaining the throughput of their manufacturing assets. Manufacturers also have several scenarios such as build-to-stock (BTS), build-to-order (BTO), assemble-to-order (ATO), and engineer-to-order (ETO). Each of these scenarios has characteristics that help in establishing common supply chain requirements for manufacturers. Manufacturing industry generally has its largest investments in factories and machinery and keeping their assets productive and maintaining the factory throughput is paramount for a manufacturer to remain competitive. These characteristics affect their choices in supply chain strategy. Within the manufacturing sector, discreet manufacturing has different expectations from their supply chains than a process-based manufacturer where the set-up changes may be extremely expensive to execute. Specific manufacturing models like BTS, BTO, ATO, and ETO also have different business models and should leverage their supply chains to help them achieve their business targets. For example, a BTS manufacturer must focus on throughput and efficiencies of scale, a BTO manufacturer would do best with a sharper focus on demand fulfillment and lead times, while an ETO situation requires focusing on achieving the promised delivery dates more than anything else. The varying degrees of focus on these objectives in different business situations drive the expectations and the design of a supply chain.

On the other hand, retail business is more focused on end-consumer demand, which is largely an independent variable. Retailers largely fall into two categories, store-based or non-store-based. The second category includes all online retailers, mail-order catalogs, and call-center catalogs. In general, the supply chains for retailers have few manufacturing assets, but they need complex distribution systems. With a large number of distribution points in their supply chains, retailers have a tendency to carry large amounts of inventory and must focus on optimizing their inventory and distribution costs to remain competitive.

Therefore, many factors limit the supply chain design options simply because a firm is competing in a given industry segment. These factors originate from the *existing capabilities* of other firms within the segment and *customer expectations* set due to these capabilities. For a firm to simply do business in a segment requires that they build *comparable business capabilities* to their competitors. This parity in capabilities is the baseline, unless the firm has a business model that is substantially different from other firms in the industry. In the latter case, when the business model is substantially different, *the business model differences may create competitive advantages* for the firm and may also drive a different set of required business capabilities, making parity with competitors moot. For example, Southwest Airlines in the 1990s did not issue seat numbers to their passengers even though this was an expected behavior for airlines at the time. They did not need to develop this capability because their business model was different from the existing carriers and focused on regional routes with limited flight choices and a keen focus on cost and service with customer interaction based on an informal and fun working environment.

Therefore, assuming similar business models, *it is only after achieving parity in business capabilities with its competition that the firm can start adding process differentiators that will make their capabilities superior and create competitive advantages.*

Belonging to an industry segment also places some of the common constraints that are common across all firms. For example, a firm belonging to a specific industry in a common geography will share many characteristics with its peers: the types of suppliers, the suppliers' control on the market (do they operate as a consortium or monopoly?), suppliers' locations, customer demographics, customer expectations, and so on. If the majority of the product or raw materials in this industry segment are imported, then all firms belonging to this segment must deal with a set of common problems like the following: effect of the increased lead time on the supply chain's ability to react and change plans in response to changes in demand, risks introduced due to the suppliers' overseas location, currency fluctuations, lead-time variance, and increased risk of damage during transit, and other disruptions due to the distances and lead time involved. All these characteristics will be common to all firms in this segment and will affect their supply chain requirements in a similar fashion. *This commonality drives some of the basic capabilities that each of these firms will have to develop, while each is also free to innovate and develop other capabilities driven by its business strategy. The first set of capabilities creates competitive parity and the second set creates competitive advantages.*

The existing thinking on supply chain strategy is relevant only in the context of common industry-level requirements and behaviors. It does not work on the second level where the competitive advantages are actually created by identifying and building process differentiators to create superior capabilities. That is why the general supply chain strategies—lean, agile, speculation, and postponement—are unable to create any differentiators for the firms. For example, functional products that have no or low brand value are typically suitable for speculative (BTS) manufacturing model, while products with a higher level of personalized attributes lean toward the postponement (BTO or ATO) manufacturing models. Products with seasonal and volatile demands tend to favor supply chains that can react quickly to changing demand, labeled as *agile* supply chains. *While these types of supply chain design establish the broad-based design paradigm for a supply chain, they do little in helping a firm to identify capabilities that will truly create competitive advantages for them.*

THE EFFECT OF A BUSINESS STRATEGY ON SUPPLY CHAIN DESIGN

The second category of factors that affects supply chain design is the firm's business strategy. We saw the equivalence of Porter's generic strategies and the conventional supply chain strategies in Table 5.1. The business strategy should directly guide the supply chain design. A cost-based business strategy should drive the supply chains to focus on reducing inventory and operational costs by balancing other functional objectives against these costs. For example, Wal-Mart reduces warehousing costs by continuously investing in automating its warehouse operations and cross-docking, reduces the transportation expenses by optimizing the loads and shipments, and reduces inventories through inventory planning and by reducing the fulfillment lead time to its stores. For a detailed discussion on supply chain processes that directly affect the costs, refer to Appendix C.

A differentiation-based business strategy will drive its supply chain to have a different primary objective other than the cost: it may drive a supply chain to consider demand fulfillment over and above other objectives or visibility of the customer order through the supply chain to create a sharp customer focus. It may have greater focus on services like white-glove delivery, installation, after-sales service and ease of returns if the customer does not like the product. It may have the customer involvement in design and expect its supply chain to provide real-time visibility into the inventories of underlying components and assemblies to project a realistic lead time for delivery. Mini Cooper with their focus on personalization, for example, will have a very different expectation from its supply chain than a GM or Ford that build standardized models for the mass market.

Later in this chapter, we revisit this subject and provide a more detailed view of what processes must be the focus of designing an effective supply chain for firms with different business strategies.

THE EFFECT OF THE PRIMARY DRIVER ON SUPPLY CHAIN DESIGN

Finally, the firm must decide what drives their supply chain. What is the overriding constraint and what is the overriding objective for the supply chain? Defining these objectives and constraints will depend on a clear understanding of the factors presented so far, as well as the firm's inclination to adopt a specific type of supply chain, for example, a demand-driven supply chain. In Chapter 5, in the discussion on *what drives your supply chain*, we covered the four possible drivers for a supply chain: demand, supply, inventory, and resources. Not all options may be available to all firms because some of them will be constrained simply by the type of industry or the business strategy being pursued or the current customer expectations. But, within the limitations of a defined specific driver, secondary goals for the supply chains must be established to drive the strategic thinking on the optimal supply chain design for the firm. For example, in a demand-driven supply chain that typically suits the retail industry, the supply chain design still has a lot of latitude in deciding how to react to changes in demand. Selecting a primary driver and prioritizing the other elements of the supply chain sphere of influence helps in designing processes that will be aligned with the organizational objectives and constraints. It also enforces a larger and integrated view of supply chain where individual processes must take the extended view to align themselves with the priorities of the *whole* supply chain.

Consider the following questions that can help drive a firm's supply chain design to create the desired advantages: When the demand goes up, what threshold of change should trigger new replenishment orders from the supply chain? How does the supply chain decide whether these new replenishment orders should be placed on the same suppliers as existing unfulfilled orders, or on different suppliers? What is the acceptable amount of risk that placing additional orders on the existing suppliers could delay the replenishment? When the new replenishment orders are created, does the chain evaluate constraints to ensure that enough warehousing, transportation, and operations capacity exists to process the receipts, stocking, and distribution? Establishing clear primary and secondary objectives for supply chain responses under different conditions provides the list of *functional capabilities* and guides the *process design* in order to achieve the strategic objectives of their supply chain functions. This list of functional capabilities helps establish the required supply chain processes, which, in turn, allows the firm to assess their current capabilities and develop a road map for supply chain competency development. We presented an overview of this process earlier in Chapter 4, through the three steps of developing a functional ecosystem, assessment scorecards, and capability maturity maps that can drive the supply chain road map in a firm. Combining the steps for the functional strategy with the other factors presented here, the following steps present a comprehensive guide for developing an effective supply chain strategy:

- Analyze the industry characteristics to understand the capability parity that must be built to compete with the other players in the segment.
- Establish a clear business strategy to survive and grow in the selected segment.
- Decide the primary and secondary drivers for your supply chain.
- Design specific supply chain processes to create targeted advantages.

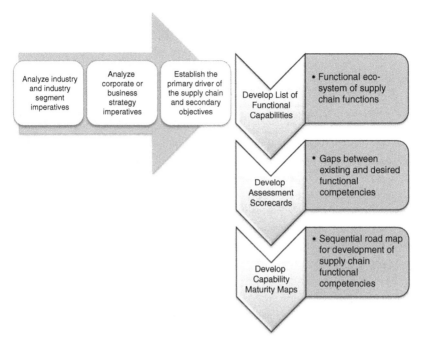

FIGURE 6.2 Process Flow for Developing a Supply Chain Strategy

Figure 6.2 shows an overview of the proposed process for supply chain strategy development. The steps on the left are analytic and subjective in nature and the steps on the right are more specific and tangible and can be standardized through templates such as the functional ecosystem and capability maturity maps, proposed earlier.

The assessment scorecards and the maturity maps are powerful tools to clearly identify the supply chain processes that the firm must develop to achieve the desirable functional capabilities that would result in a competitive advantage for the firm. Assessment scorecards force the corporation to drill down into all the processes and address the following:

- Identify their existing capabilities in a selected functional area.
- Assess the existing capabilities on specific functional criteria such as level of automation, level of configurability and extensibility. dependability, and ease of use and understanding, as well as technology criteria such as scalability, performance, compatibility with other systems, level of integration, master data, and so on.

- Compare the existing capabilities with the capabilities of their competitor and identify gaps in capabilities that must be filled simply in order to be competitive.
- Identify the new capabilities that the firm can develop to create competitive advantage for itself.

Once the assessment scorecards are available, the *capability maturity maps* (CMMs) can be created. The CMMs are the logical next step because they put together a feasible plan of building the desired capabilities. The CMMs offer a visual arrangement representing the evolution of the functional capabilities by taking into account the sequential and synergistic process dependencies and by incorporating any other desirable priority criteria. Together, the assessment scorecards and the maturity maps provide a long-term strategic road map for evolving the functional capabilities of the firm for maintaining and creating the competitive advantages necessary for growth. Capability maturity maps can be easily color-coded to create a visual image of the functional evolution of the firm for the selected function. These can then be used for prioritizing the capital investment plans of the firm. To ensure feasible evolution paths and to best leverage the investments, the following must be considered while building the maturity maps:

- CMMs must consider the sequential process dependencies. Some functional capabilities will depend on the existence of others and breaking the sequence will disrupt the evolution, making it infeasible or too expensive to implement. For example, consider the ability to automatically estimate and approve the freight invoices for shipments. This capability requires that the firm already has the ability to model the carrier contracts and electronically receive shipment data so that the carrier invoices can be independently estimated with the data on freight contracts and automatically approved when the two amounts fall within a user-defined range. Not having the ability to model carrier contracts or shipments will render any automation for freight invoices ineffective and useless. Having common master data is another example that makes the implementation of integrated solutions feasible and much more effective than working with many disparate sets of master data. Many firms fail to account for such dependencies or get discouraged with the effort involved in investing in such basic foundation blocks and end up wasting a lot of time and resources in finding solutions. Temporary solutions to support required process dependencies can be built as long as they are financially viable. Most such temporary solutions will need to be replaced and will require secondary investments for long-term competencies, and such replacement costs must be taken into account while justifying such short-cuts.

▪ CMMs must consider logical or synergistic dependencies among processes. In sequential dependencies, absence of a specific capability (such as the ability to receive shipments electronically and model carrier contracts) constrains the successful creation of another capability (the ability to automatically estimate and approve freight invoices). In contrast, synergistic dependencies don't constrain the creation of a specific capability by their absence; rather, if present, they may increase the value of the other process capability. For example, consider inventory planning and replenishment planning. While replenishment as a capability can be created in the absence of inventory planning, having the inventory planning capabilities will enhance the overall value of the replenishment solution by making it more accurate and useful. Related processes, when planned together for implementation of a solution, provide a better value because they allow the firm to select a common solution from a single vendor with a broader functionality and reduce the total cost of ownership (TCO), rather than the alternative situation when these are planned and implemented separately with disparate solutions from multiple vendors that may require additional resources, skills, technology stacks, and time to make them work in an integrated fashion.

▪ CMMs must reflect the organizational priority of the capital investments to support the core functional capabilities required to stay competitive. This reflects the organizational criteria for selecting initiatives from competing alternatives. Such criteria may involve typical cost-benefit analysis, return on investment (ROI) calculations, or any other process that the firm may use for prioritizing the capital investments. In addition to the financial aspects, most firms also have criteria such as regulatory compliance requirements, competitor parity, partner mandates, strategic alignment and value, that may affect the final priority of such investments. The strategic aspects of a potential investment can be brought into this consideration by plotting the investments on financial-strategic quadrants, as shown in Figure 6.3. Each quadrant represents the sustainability of the competitive advantage and a financial or organizational metric most critical to the firm. The investment proposals in quadrant 4 should be considered for implementation in the short term as these represent advantages with the longest sustainability and highest ROI

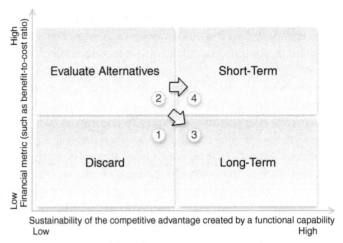

FIGURE 6.3 Sustainability Matrix for Competitive Advantages

(assuming ROI is the financial metric along the Y-axis). In general, capital proposals in the two right quadrants should generally be considered, those in quadrant 1 are highly questionable from the point of view of their ability to create any strategic advantage, and those in quadrant 2 should be evaluated to see how the competitive advantages created by them can be made more sustainable, or what costs reduced or benefits increased, with the intention of developing an alternative that would be moved to quadrants 3 or 4.

Once a supply chain functional strategy has been created with the deliverables described here, it can be used as a road map for evolving the functional capabilities, which, in turn, create and sustain the competitive advantages for the firm. This strategy must be reviewed frequently as the business environment changes in response to new opportunities, competition, the regulatory environment, and changes in the business strategy of the firm. The functional strategies can directly contribute toward the goals of the business only when they are continually aligned with the business strategy, and supply chain strategy is no exception.

SUPPLY CHAIN STRATEGY AND BUSINESS STRATEGY

How exactly are the supply chain and business strategies related? The mere fact that most of the existing literature on supply chain strategy focuses on strategies that are more applicable as business strategies, rather than with any specific relevance to the supply chain, points to a very intimate relationship between the two. There are good reasons for this; after all, supply chains have a very large footprint and cover so many corporate functions that they may simply appear to be the same as the business itself! However, that would be a mistake. Supply chains do have their fair share of control over opportunities for cost control and differentiation, and, therefore, the opportunities for creating competitive advantages, but supply chains are not the whole business. That was also our main argument against the existing literature on supply chain strategies, because these strategies reflect a higher-level business direction. While they drive the supply chain design, they are not specific enough to qualify as supply chain strategies.

On the other hand, thinking of a supply chain strategy in a vacuum of business strategy is meaningless. *While the business can be thought of as independent of the supply chain, the reverse is not true: supply chains do not exist without a business.* The sole reason for the existence of supply chain is to support the business. While it is true that supply chains come into existence to support a business, once born, the relationship must become symbiotic. This is to say that once the supply chain capabilities have been realized, they can and must be continuously reviewed to see what other business opportunities and competitive advantages they create.

Therefore, the *existential relationship* between the business and supply chains is one-way (supply chains come into existence only when a business needs such support), but their *sustenance relationship* is mutual and two-way (once existing, supply chain capabilities create new business opportunities, which, in turn, need more supply chain capabilities).

That brings us to the following attributes of the relationship between the business and supply chain strategies:

- Business strategy must exist and be clearly articulated before a supply chain strategy can be *effectively* formulated. All functional strategies including the supply chain strategy follow from a stated business strategy. While this may seem like a mundane statement to make, most firms grope in the dark trying to establish their supply chain priorities without having an articulated business strategy. This is equally likely to happen for large or small corporations with a Wall Street focus and little understanding of long-term strategic planning. Talking about a supply chain strategy in a business strategy vacuum is meaningless. Supply chain strategy is simply a road map of the functional capabilities required by the firm to operate their business and achieve the stated goals. These functional capabilities cannot be established with any clarity unless the business strategy has been established and competitive goals have been clearly identified.

▪ Just as Porter's generic strategies cannot be applied without understanding and analyzing a large number of external industry and internal organizational factors, the generic supply chain strategies cannot be applied without understanding the supply chain processes required to support the business strategy. The superiority of a capability is what creates advantage and that superiority must be explicitly designed into the functional process.

▪ There are some supply chain *patterns* that can be identified and that align well to support certain generic business strategies. For example, lean supply chain design is aligned to a cost-based business strategy. These patterns only help in identifying industry-wide best practices and may bring capability parity, but seldom create competitive advantages, unless some of these capabilities are enhanced through innovation. Sometimes, these innovations can be found in other industries. For example, consider Dell's use of vendor-owned inventory in their warehouses, which allowed them to substantially reduce their cash-to-cash cycle time. The same practice was later successfully adopted in retail when Home Depot created a similar arrangement for their lumber products with their vendors.

▪ To identify the generic supply chain direction, primary business requirements must be understood. The primary business requirements arise by virtue of the industry segment and the business model selected by the firm. These define the supply chain pattern that can be used for the supply chain design. For example, a retail supply chain will typically be designed as cost-focused, demand-driven supply chains. However, when new segments are created in old industries, such as when Dell pioneered the segment for custom-built machines (an assemble-to-order model) in a segment that was largely a build-to-stock segment at the time; the standard conventional supply chain pattern can be changed. Focusing on a new customer segment allowed Dell to create their supply chain niche capabilities (and their legendary cash conversion cycles) through vendor-managed warehouses, substitutable product assemblies, and just-in-time production. Such changes can warrant new functional requirements and new supply chain patterns are created.

▪ Having identified the primary business requirements, and therefore the dominant supply chain pattern, the secondary functional requirements are identified. These functional requirements are what would make the supply chain unique to the firm and are responsible for creating the competitive advantages. These requirements arise either because of competitive pressures forcing the firm to *react* or by a *deliberate design* to create competitive advantages. In the first case firms scramble to create functional capabilities to catch up with the competition and merely survive, while in the second case firms design their growth and lead the segment by creating competitive advantages where none existed before. Savvy businesses act in the proactive fashion, designing their competitive advantages rather than reacting to limit the damages when the external environmental changes force them to do so.

- Supply chain strategy must be considered in an end-to-end context and not in functional silos. This is an important concept for effectively developing a supply chain strategy. The supply chain functions are spread over many organizational groups and the strategy must be targeted to achieve a globally optimal solution rather than trying to maximize the objectives of the individual groups. Optimizing a single process in isolation rarely works. Decisions made in one step undoubtedly affect the other steps and the consequences of such decisions on all the steps must be understood. For example, if the purchasing department decides to buy cheaper raw materials to create cost savings, how does this decision affect production? Does it make the production more labor intensive or time intensive, thereby increasing the total cost of production of the finished goods? How does it affect the quality of finished goods? How will it affect the marketing strategy of the firm? Asking such questions to evaluate the impact of individual decisions across the *entirety* of the chain ensures that decisions are not implemented when they are good for only an individual processes, but at the same time are inefficient for the whole supply chain.

Not understanding the intricate and complementary relationship between business and supply chain strategies can lead to missed opportunities and conflicting investment priorities. There are many examples of such failures. While Kmart experienced disastrous consequences due to the misalignment between their business and supply chain strategies, Home Depot lost valuable time to build on its leadership position in the industry.

Unfortunately, there are no generic supply chain strategies that are equivalent to the generic business strategies proposed by Porter. As discussed earlier, supply chain patterns can be identified based on industry segments,

KMART: **MISALIGNMENT BETWEEN BUSINESS AND FUNCTIONAL STRATEGIES**

Kmart and Wal-Mart were both founded in 1962. Both focused on *cost* as a business strategy and adopted super-center retail formats. In 1987, Kmart had 2,223 stores and revenues of $25.63 billion to Wal-Mart's 1,198 stores and revenues of $15.96 billion. Kmart focused on marketing and merchandising to achieve the goals of their business strategy. Conceived as the bargain offshoot of the Kresge department stores, the chain blanketed the suburbs with stores carrying everything from Tide detergent to clothes, makeup, electronics, and housewares.[1] When customers started shunning its poorly made dishtowels, cheap makeup brands, and tacky clothes, instead of reducing costs by building supply chain capabilities (like Wal-Mart), Kmart went shopping, buying Sports Authority, OfficeMax, Builders Square, and Borders. The Big K and Super K store formats were introduced to lure customers back, but still no concerted effort was made to reduce the underlying cost structure. Most of Kmart's investments went into marketing and merchandising capabilities that do not directly help in reducing costs (both of these strategies are targeted toward increasing revenues rather than on reducing costs). The misalignment between the business and functional strategies cost Kmart heavily. In contrast, Wal-Mart chose to invest in the supply chain as a strategic advantage to support its business strategy of being a price leader. In 1991, Wal-Mart sales overtook the sales at Kmart. By the late 1990s Kmart was heading for bankruptcy and eventually merged with Sears. The functional strategies at Kmart were clearly not aligned with their business strategy. While the business strategy focused on cost, the functional strategies at Kmart were focused on creating a perceived differentiation through their marketing and assortment, while largely ignoring the cost. Kmart's inability to create capabilities for direct cost reduction and align their functional competencies to their business strategy eventually led to their bankruptcy.

product characteristics, and demand patterns, but actual supply chain processes must be designed with explicit differentiators built-in to create specific competitive advantages. However, some of the defining design characteristics for the supply chain can be established by correctly identifying appropriate priorities for the supply chain design.

Supply chain design directly controls the following five dimensions of a firm's competitive positioning: cost, quality, customer service, order-fulfillment,

HOME **DEPOT'S DIGRESSION**

Home Depot started with an explicit strategy to compete on cost and knowledgeable store associates since its inception and this showed in their warehouse-styled stores that focused on cost rather than the product presentation. The company grew with organically developed in-house systems to address their business needs as they arose. While this served them well in the initial years, the changing cost and competitive environment forced the company to renew their focus on technology. However, it quickly became obvious that the company had failed to align their business strategy to drive their functional strategies and their capital investments. During the years that Nardelli led the company from 2001 through 2007, Home Depot lost sight of its primary positioning as a retailer and tried to grow through acquisitions. Most of these acquisitions were to be spun off by Nardelli's successor in 2007. Nardelli also had an extreme Wall-Street-centric view on capital investments and projects were routinely reviewed before quarterly results and stopped or restarted arbitrarily to meet the numbers. In addition to losing sight of its primary business strategy of *cost*, the short-term focus on numbers further broke the link between the business strategy and the functional capabilities. The loss of focus cost the company precious time in building critical supply chain capabilities to strengthen its competitive positioning. With the ouster of Nardelli, the new CEO quickly reversed course, re-dedicating the company to its retail roots and investing to create business capabilities that would allow it to reduce costs and regain its competitive position. The company also started a big supply chain transformation initiative to reduce operational costs, though the sequence of initiatives under this transformation could be better.

While merchandising and supply chain form the two largest costs for a retailer, Home Depot's recent capital investments in technology in the United States were made in this sequence: self-checkout point-of-sale stations in the stores in early 2000s followed by freight payment automation in 2006, warehousing technology renewal that started in 2006 (and continues to be rolled out among their many warehouses), and, finally, shipment planning and inventory visibility in 2008. The self-checkout POS terminals may have saved a few cashier's salaries, but contributed in no way toward reducing the largest cost basis of a retailer—the cost of merchandise and distribution. The technology investments in optimizing transportation and warehousing address the operational costs, but do nothing toward reducing inventory or the cost

(continued)

(continued)

of merchandise through better planning upstream. In 2006 Home Depot also started building a cross-docking capability with the stated objective of increasing its inventory turnover. However, with no focus on creating better upstream capabilities of demand planning and optimizing inventory, the cross-docking effort is yet to achieve its stated goal. While Home Depot has been expecting potential improvements in their inventory turns, to be achieved through their cross-docking efforts, the numbers show they have been unsuccessful in achieving results so far. In four years since 2006, the inventory turns at Home Depot have actually declined from 4.76 in 2006 to 4.30 in 2009. See Figure 6.4 for the information on Home Depot's inventory turns.

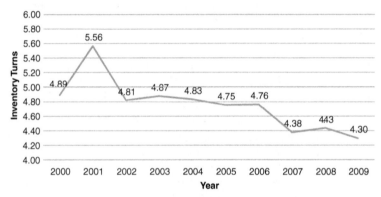

FIGURE 6.4 Inventory Turns at Home Depot

Source: Data derived from annual reports of Home Depot.

Home Depot's inventory turns have stayed flat, because the firm ignored the dependence among the supply chain planning and execution capabilities toward achieving their strategic goals. During the decade from 1999 to 2009, Wal-Mart's inventory turns changed from 6.43 in 1999 to 9.19 in 2009, which is an improvement of over 42 percent, while Home Depot's inventory turns have typically stayed flat between 4 and 5. Compared to most large retailers, Home Depot still has subpar functional capabilities in several supply chain areas, such as demand forecasting, replenishment, sourcing, and purchasing, which are core processes capable of significantly reducing the firm's inventory and merchandise costs. As the whole industry segment of hard-goods retailing is a laggard in leveraging supply chain as a strategic advantage, Home Depot is not in any immediate danger, though the firm has been under tremendous pressure for growth and profitability in recent years, which was further intensified by the collapse of the housing market.

The Home Depot has recently invested in enterprise resource planning (ERP) and supply chain management (SCM) systems for its Canadian operations. This is the first time that the Depot has chosen to deploy a largely integrated prepackaged solution for its enterprise functions, including demand forecasting, replenishment planning, and purchasing. While there are still some holes from the point of view of having an integrated supply chain, it is definitely a step in the right direction. The deployment was completed in 2008 and tangible results on its operations should be visible shortly, though it may be hard to tell because the firm's annual reports do not break the numbers down by the regions.

and efficiency/throughput. From the firm's point of view, notice that these five dimensions include cost and throughput, which are largely inward-facing, and quality, customer service, and order fulfillment, which are outward-facing dimensions. Unlike the existing supply chain strategy thinking that focuses on lean or agile kinds of supply chains, a real-life supply chain will always need to build capabilities to affect all of the following dimensions without exception. However, what differentiates one supply chain from another, and therefore allows targeted competitive positioning of a firm aligned with its business strategy, is the relative importance accorded to these dimensions during the supply chain design. For example, a cost-based business strategy will require a design that is cost-centric, but still creates supply chain capabilities to serve the other dimensions. A differentiation-based business strategy will most definitely be centered on quality, customer service, or order-fulfillment, depending on whether the differentiation is based on product or customer service. A focus-based (or niche) business strategy may select two dimensions that are central to the supply chain design to create a niche at the intersection of these two: for example, cost and order-fulfillment.

Figure 6.5 shows an example of the design priorities for a supply chain with a focus on cost. In this figure, the firm has explicitly decided to design a supply chain with the focus on cost and efficiency, where it would like to build the competitive advantages. It has decided to achieve parity with its peers on order fulfillment and quality dimensions, while maintaining subpar capabilities for the customer-service dimension. Understanding the objectives of the supply chain clearly help in designing processes to support these objectives.

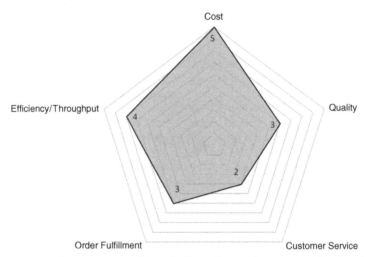

FIGURE 6.5   Relative Priority of Supply Chain Design Dimensions for Cost-based Strategy

Simply prioritizing and focusing on these five key dimensions for supply chain process design targets several supply chain metrics that are conventionally associated with supply chain. Fortunately, the large supply chain process footprint in the firm's value chain allows the managers to leverage several of these processes to support their business strategies. The following sections provide the supply chain characteristics for supporting the generic business strategies of cost and differentiation.

Supply Chain Characteristics to Support *Cost* as a Strategy

When cost is the main business strategy, several supply chain processes can help the firm reduce costs. These processes cover almost the whole spectrum of supply chain function and can be designed specifically with the intention of reducing the costs. Designing a supply chain with *cost* as the guiding philosophy does not exclude any of the other generic supply chain patterns. A *cost-optimized* supply chain can still be demand driven or resource driven, it can still be agile, and it can still support a speculative or postponement-oriented business model. The following characteristics can be built into a cost-optimized supply chain:

- **Better forecast accuracy.** Improving forecast accuracy *prevents* the creation of unwanted inventory. In turn, it saves the cost of all the operations that must be executed to create, buy, and distribute the unwanted inventory. Examples of such costs include the cost of obsolescence; the cost of manufacturing resources such as labor, material, and assets; delivery costs; stocking costs; and, eventually clearance costs to get rid of the unwanted material in the supply chain. Better forecasting accuracy is achieved with a better overall demand management process that is capable of leveraging historical demand data, but can also leverage other factors influencing demand, such as price, promotions, product-mix, season, weather, and so on.

- **Better inventory turns.** Improved inventory turns reduce costs by reducing the working capital needs of the firm and saving on the short-term borrowing costs. Reduced inventory in the system also reduces costs in less obvious ways, such as reduced warehousing space needs and reduced handling, allowing the supply chain resources to be more agile and productive. For a full discussion on the benefits of reduced inventory, refer to Appendix C. Inventory reductions are generally a result of better inventory planning processes that precisely identify inventory needs at specific locations to maintain the fulfillment rates throughout the supply chain.
- **Transportation optimization.** The movement of goods through the supply chain provides a big opportunity for better planning and reduced costs of transportation. A well-designed process can reduce miles driven, increase trailer-capacity utilization, reduce deadheading, leverage multi-modal routes, and increase asset utilization to cut unnecessary costs in the distribution network.
- **Warehouse management.** Well-designed warehouse management processes can optimize the space utilization and reduce unnecessary handling by better slotting and cross-docking. They can further reduce operational costs through better labor utilization and automation of handling activities where possible.
- **Manufacturing planning.** A constraint-based manufacturing planning process reduces waste by creating feasible plans within the constraints of the availability of materials, labor, and equipment. It can help increase the asset and labor utilization and reduce number of set-up changes (which is unproductive work) in the factories, making them more efficient to run.
- **Purchasing optimization.** Purchasing processes that take advantage of long-term supply contracts and larger consolidated volumes across business units of a firm typically lower the costs of materials. Developing capabilities like bid optimization and purchase planning can further reduce the procurement costs through better planning. Other processes like

reverse-auctions have also been used successfully by firms to reduce material costs, especially in the case of commodities.

Of course, a well-designed supply chain must be thought of as a whole entity. It must focus on building capabilities in several process-areas that are coherent with each other and integrated to deliver the expected results. Also remember that emphasizing the above characteristics does not exclude other supply chain imperatives such as the ability to quickly fulfill demand or provide visibility; it only means that the supply chain is being designed with cost-reduction as the main consideration that would take precedence over other normal deliverables expected from a supply chain. Table 6.1 summarizes the process focus for different supply chain functional domains for a cost- or differentiation-based business strategy.

TABLE 6.1 Supply Chain Design Focus for Cost and Differentiation Business Strategies

Supply Chain Function Domain	Process Focus for Cost-Based Business Strategy	Process Focus for Differentiation-Based Business Strategy
SC Network Design	Design the network with a focus on reducing the cost of distribution and stocking. Leverage multimodal opportunities, optimized loads, and optimized routes for transportation during the modeling and evaluation to understand the possible scenarios. Leverage automation and low-cost locations for warehouses.	Design the network with a focus on reducing fulfillment lead-time to customer-facing locations and warehouses that directly ship to the customers. Consider network characteristics that may allow better flexibility in dynamically redeploying inventory.
Demand Planning	Focus on increasing forecast accuracy to avoid costs associated with unwanted inventory. Enrich the process with modeling demand influencing factors such as price, seasonality, promotions, and weather. Create capabilities to manage the seasonal build-up	Focus on increased forecast accuracy to decrease out-of-stock incidences at warehouses, factories, and stores. Create better product assortment management capabilities to ensure better availability and wide selection. Create product *(continued)*

TABLE 6.1 *(Continued)*

Supply Chain Function Domain	Process Focus for Cost-Based Business Strategy	Process Focus for Differentiation-Based Business Strategy
	and ramp-down of seasonal products. Create capabilities to better manage product life cycle for introducing new products and retiring old ones. Invest in pricing and clearance planning processes and planning capabilities to increase the total lifetime returns on products.	and service personalization opportunities and develop capabilities for strong customer interaction to capture such inputs for design.
Replenishment Planning	Invest in inventory optimization processes to reduce inventory in all echelons of supply chain. Identify the best sources of fulfilling demand from within or outside the network. Deploy bid optimization and purchase planning processes to find cost-reduction opportunities. Create capabilities in hedging (currencies and commodities based on scope of operations). Optimize product mix in manufacturing for best profitability scenarios when capacity constraints exist.	Focus on maintaining high service levels through better inventory planning. Develop capabilities for flexible inventory deployment across the network. Optimize product mix in manufacturing for fulfilling high-priority customer orders when capacity constraints exist.
Supply Management and Manufacturing	Identify critical suppliers and develop collaborative relationships with them. Reduce errors, increase process efficiency, and create real-time visibility by developing capabilities for automated real-time data exchange with partners. Develop capabilities for reverse-auctions to find cost-reduction opportunities. For manufacturers, focus on optimizing production runs and reduce set-ups to increase throughput. Develop capability to	Develop unique sources of products to create differentiation, develop partnering programs and leverage partners for creating differentiated products and services, create collaborative long-term relationships to share plans and create a highly *responsive* extended supply chain. Create partner incentives and scorecards to strengthen collaborative behavior and extend collaboration across

(continued)

TABLE 6.1 *(Continued)*

Supply Chain Function Domain	Process Focus for Cost-Based Business Strategy	Process Focus for Differentiation-Based Business Strategy
	level resource plans for fulfilling given demand to manage plan changes and schedule volatility. Automate and de-skill operations where possible to increase resource efficiency and reduce waste due to quality issues.	processes for product design and post-sales where applicable. Develop visibility and control across the extended supply chain. In manufacturing scenarios, develop capabilities to support product personalization and design inputs from the suppliers.
Transportation Management	Focus on reducing costs through optimization to reduce miles driven and increase load utilization. Leverage multimodal routes to reduce freight costs. Automate the processes for shipment tracking, freight invoice validation, freight payment, and settling carrier disputes.	Develop tracking capabilities for material-in-transit to create real-time visibility of shipments and inventory status. Develop partnerships with critical carriers and create collaborative processes with automation to create flexibility in operations.
Warehouse Management	Reduce costs through warehouse automation and optimized labor scheduling. Enhance warehouse space utilization and lower overheads through optimized slotting. Develop cross-docking processes, planned and opportunistic, to reduce stocking time and touch points for inbound inventory. Automate process for capturing in-transit damages on inbound orders and develop certified receiving processes to cut down on receiving quality checks and quantity validations. Consider vendor-managed inventory where possible to reduce cost of carrying inventory. Adopt advanced shipment notices for inbound and outbound	Develop capabilities for value-added services in the warehouse to cater to personalized products and services. Invest in automating yard-management and dock-scheduling processes to create complete visibility of inventory at the warehouse. Provide customer pick-up opportunities or other personalized delivery options to customers to reduce fulfillment lead time. Enrich delivery with value-added services such as removal, disposal, or recycling of old product or installation of new items. Develop capabilities to preconsolidate orders for a single complete delivery against customer orders.

(continued)

TABLE 6.1 *(Continued)*

Supply Chain Function Domain	Process Focus for Cost-Based Business Strategy	Process Focus for Differentiation-Based Business Strategy
	shipments to plan shipments, receipts, labor, and equipment at the warehouses, stores, and factories.	
Collaboration	Focus on automated interactions for reducing manual touch points and related costs where possible.	Focus on automated interactions to reduce errors and increase real-time visibility of orders, inventory, and resources throughout the extended supply chain.

Supply Chain Characteristics to Support *Differentiation* as a Strategy

When the firm's business strategy rests on differentiated products and services, an emphasis on a different set of processes can provide the opportunities to build a supply chain aligned with the goals of the business strategy. Differentiation can be created through better products, quality, and service capabilities and better designed supply chain processes can help create such capabilities. Once again, designing a supply chain with *differentiation* as the guiding philosophy does not exclude any of the other generic supply chain patterns. A *differentiation-driven* supply chain can still be demand driven or resource driven, it can still be agile, and it can still support a speculative or postponement-oriented business model. The following characteristics can be built into a differentiation-driven supply chain:

- ▧ **Order accuracy and fulfillment.** In a supply chain supporting a differentiation strategy, the customer-orientated processes take precedence in building capabilities. The ordering process is one of the main focus areas for this supply chain. The customer order life cycle consists of order capture, fulfillment planning (activities such as manufacturing, purchasing, shipping from warehouse), fulfillment execution (activities such as picking, packing, value-added services, shipping), tracking, and post-sales services. Supply chain processes actively support the fulfillment planning, fulfillment execution, tracking, and some post-sales services of the equation. Maintaining order accuracy and fulfillment rates is one of the primary service differentiators that can be built into the supply chain by designing better processes.

- **Visibility.** Providing visibility across the supply chain creates many differentiators, some of which provide customer-facing capabilities and others provide internal control. The customer-facing capabilities allow the customers to be in full control of tracking their orders as the orders move from one phase of their life cycle to another. The internal capabilities allow the managers to control the flow of orders, ensure timely delivery, and take proactive measures to address any issues that may arise during the order life cycle.
- **Personalized products.** Allowing the customers to customize their products is another way to create differentiation. The extent of this personalization may vary depending on the firm's business. It may be limited to monogramming the shirts with their initials and selecting paint colors and interiors on a car. It may be more involved, as in selecting specific design and memory features in a laptop. Or, it may be extensive, such as would be the case in designing a luxury yacht or customizing homes. In all cases, supply chain processes must be designed to take the personalization inputs and ensure that the manufacturing, assembly, stocking, distribution, and shipping processes are suitably modified to accommodate such personalization.
- **Personalized delivery.** Some industries may allow for building personalized delivery options for customers to create differentiation and supply chain processes must be designed to support that. Deliveries can vary from several options for shipping service levels to white-glove delivery at home that includes installation services, if required. A personalized delivery may require all products to be delivered together or in a specific sequence and specific time as may be the case for project-based building environments. All of these capabilities can be built by carefully designing the underlying supply chain processes to create differentiation.
- **Sourcing.** Superior sourcing processes can help create differentiation in many ways. There are many characteristics that make a product unique for the customers who may pay a premium for such differentiation. The uniqueness may come from many sources, such as the product quality, geographic source, tradition (such as handmade products), superior design, engineering, better raw materials, better manufacturing practices, fair-trade practices, green manufacturing and packaging, recycling

opportunities, and so on. Sourcing processes that help in locating such suppliers and creating partnerships may help a company's supply chain to directly help create differentiation.

Supply chain characteristics to support a focus strategy will have a mix of the characteristics discussed earlier for the cost and differentiation scenarios. In each case, what is important is that the supply chain capabilities are designed to drive specific advantages that the firm seeks to create to sustain its business models. Only such explicitly designed supply chains can pass as supply chain strategies that are fully aligned with the business strategy and capable of creating the competitive advantages. Of course, the design of supply chains evolves over time as the business focus and its needs change, but the important goal is to have a supply chain strategy that guides this evolution through design rather than one that grows organically as a reaction to the business needs and, therefore, simply supports the mundane operations rather acts as a competitive weapon.

7

Technology Strategy

Y OU WALK DOWN THE grocery aisles, fill your cart with breakfast cereal, bread, and wine, then go to a self-check-out counter, scan the items, swipe your credit card, and you are done. At home, log-on to your bank account, pay a few bills, check your statement, stop payment on a check—all within a few minutes and without having to call anyone and be put on hold and forced to hear "easy listening" music. Or better yet, log-on to your favorite retailer on the Web, browse their latest fall assortment, order the silk slacks you have been wanting for some time, and ask for next-day delivery. All these interactions enable firms to do business with their customers and all of this is enabled through technology.

Technology has become an integral part of the businesses. Technology allows the businesses to be effective and efficient. It allows them to be more productive, provide better customer service, and create innovative new ways to interact with their customers, vendors, and partners to collaborate and conduct business. While the examples here related to the day-to-day situations for customer interaction, businesses routinely use technology to manage their back-end processes as well. Supply chains, merchandising, production scheduling, sales plans, and any number of business functions are enabled by technology. Technology creates the functional capabilities and allows the businesses to execute their operations effectively. As the business needs change, technology also enhances these capabilities and sustains them over time. When firms design superior functional capabilities to create competitive advantages, technology provides them with the infrastructure to realize those capabilities.

In Chapter 2, in the section on *Understanding Advantage*, we presented the four dimensions of advantage, which are time (to market), efficiency, cost, and quality. We said that a process was superior to another, if it delivered better results along any one or more of these four dimensions. Technology support for a process can create such advantage along all the four dimensions: it can reduce the time to create a process capability (*time* to market), it can increase the *efficiency* (typically through automation), it can reduce the *cost* through increased efficiency, and it can increase the *quality* of a process by preventing errors or enforcing process constraints through data quality, validation, and real-time verification.

But, *technology is no panacea.*

While technology has the ability to add all of these benefits to the functional capabilities of a firm, it also adds a level of complexity and cost to the operations that must be managed successfully to leverage the advantages of technology. But, this is a competency that all businesses need to acquire— *technology is no longer merely an option.*

Technology is so ingrained in the basic requirements of any business operation today that businesses must develop the skills to manage technology to their advantage or perish. In fact, it has become so ubiquitous that not only do we take it for granted, but we don't even notice it unless it fails. Therein lies the importance of technology—it is fast becoming the underlying *basic infrastructure* for business, just like the power and communication systems that are taken for granted in a modern office building and noticed only when missing. Just as one cannot think of designing a modern building without plumbing, electricity, or climate control, one should not think of creating a business without thinking of the underlying foundation of technology infrastructure. The extent of technology competency that a business needs depends on the size and operations of the business. A small individually owned retail store may do well simply with the technology to accept credit cards and electronic checks, though a little technology for organizing their payroll, inventory, orders, and invoices would do wonders to the amount of time spent on these processes. But, when you increase the size of this business a few million times to reflect the size of today's larger corporations, the complexity of their operations increases as well. To manage that complexity of operations efficiently and profitably, firms depend on technology for almost everything they do.

Even though technology plays such a central role in a firm's ability to run its business profitably and sustain its competitive advantages, for most firms it remains an afterthought rather than being a proactive part of their overall strategy. That remains true for supply chain technology as well. Technology is indispensable: not for its own sake, but rather as an active tool toward building functional capabilities that create and sustain competitive advantages. In fact, thinking of functional capabilities without the underlying technology, or vice versa, is just not optimal any more. This is especially true at the strategy planning level where these two components actively interact with each other, where they affect and enhance, or limit and constrain each other.

Technology enables almost all business functions. Enterprise resource planning (ERP) systems, for example, can enable enterprise functions for finance, human resources, sales, production, order fulfillment, purchasing, maintenance operations, distribution, and so on. The benefits of the enabling technology range from simple automation, to an integrated ability to instantaneously affect all related processes, to providing real-time visibility to changes in business, to processing large amounts of data to provide consolidated corporate metrics from trillions of transactions and solving complex mathematical models simulating millions of business variables to optimize business efficiencies.

As supply chain functions are among the more complex of the business processes, they offer unique opportunities for optimization and differentiation. On the flip side, of course, the complexity also means that these solutions are generally harder to understand, difficult to implement and maintain, and may sometimes require an advanced level of user education to be successful. Supply chain solutions routinely employ statistical forecasting and time-series analysis, mathematical programming, data-mining, probabilities, queue theory, and so on. While the advanced modeling techniques provide the ability to squeeze ever more savings from the business ecosystems, they may also require better skills and education levels of the users of such technology. The right technology can help by hiding some of the complexities of the solutions through simpler user interaction, automated decision-making, and integrated processes; however, selecting and maintaining the right technology requires that the functional strategy for building the process capabilities is planned together with the technology strategy so that the two complement and leverage each other rather than constrain and limit one another. That is where the technology strategy becomes important to understand and critical to plan.

WHAT IS TECHNOLOGY STRATEGY?

To describe *technology strategy* we will leverage the generally understood scope of the enterprise architecture that includes the data (alternately called information), applications, and technology. Data is key to any process executed through computer-based solutions and data technology relates to things like databases, data-integration technologies, data-warehousing, reporting and analysis, master data management, data access control, data history management, and so on. The second aspect of a technology strategy is applications—these include business applications such as enterprise resource planning (ERP), back-office applications, specialized custom-built applications to support specific organizational processes, business applications supporting functions such as warehousing or forecasting or inventory optimization, and even systems applications monitoring other applications and servers to help maintain the availability of critical systems across the enterprise. Applications use data and automate the processes, making them more efficient and less expensive to run. Integrated applications can provide extended benefits in terms of automation across functions that affect each other or may depend on one another for information sharing. The last aspect of the technology strategy relates to hardware and software technology components and includes things such as servers, networks, and infrastructural software such as operating systems, databases, programming languages, compliers, and so on.

The objective of a technology strategy is to provide an evolution road map for all the technology components for an enterprise, typically including technology standards, adoption plans for newer technologies, and retirement plans for the older ones, as well as the policies and guidelines for data modeling, application building, quality assurance, solution development, and so on. Finally, all these policies, guidelines, standards, and road maps (collectively known as the *technology strategy*) must support the functional and business strategies of the enterprise to create a technology environment that has the following attributes:

- **Flexibility.** Technology must be able to support changing functional needs to support the changing business environments and objectives.
- **Efficiency.** Technology must enable such change in a timely and cost-effective manner.
- **Sustainability.** Technology must be sustainable and cost-effective over the long run.

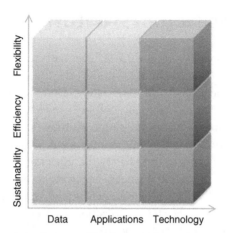

FIGURE 7.1 Technology Strategy Matrix

The technology strategy can be viewed along the two dimensions of its scope and objectives as in Figure 7.1. The scope consists of data, applications, and technology, as shown along the horizontal axis, and its objectives of sustainability, efficiency, and flexibility are shown along the vertical axis. Because businesses do not use technology for its own sake, these two dimensions are repeated for every critical business function that the technology supports in an enterprise. That adds the third dimension to the visualization of technology strategy in a firm. The picture then changes to the one shown in Figure 7.2. This visualization of the technology strategy with the third functional dimension is closer to reality because the primary purpose of technology in a business remains to support the business functions of the firm.

A good technology strategy must provide a *common* viable structure for the three technology components so that they can be leveraged across *all* business solutions, rather than defining each of them for every process in the enterprise. This is better represented in Figure 7.3, where the individual business functions have been merged and appear as a continuous dimension along the Z-axis. This is the visual representation of what a successful technology strategy must achieve for the firm: it must be able to define a common sustainable technology road map that can support all of the firm's business processes in an integrated manner and allow them to evolve as the business environment and the process expectations change.

This is the technology strategy view that we will expand upon in the rest of the discussion on the subject. This is similar to the conventional view of enterprise architecture in the corporations and borrows heavily from the discipline. It adds to

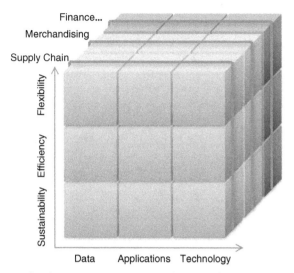

FIGURE 7.2 Technology Strategy Matrix with Business Functions

the enterprise architecture view of technology strategy in that it is inherently developed from and simultaneously supports the functional strategies of the firm. It is therefore in complete harmony and alignment with them.

So finally, what is technology strategy? *Technology strategy is the road map to identify, evolve, and sustain the technology required to support the business functions of the enterprise.* Since this is a book about the alignment of the three strategies, we will view the technology strategies only in the context of the business and functional strategies as follows.

A business strategy identifies the differentiators that will position the firm competitively. A functional strategy identifies capabilities that will create the differentiators sought by the business strategy. *Then, a technology strategy must identify the technology that will support the functional capabilities required to create the competitive differentiators targeted by the business strategy.* Because technology exists only to support the business processes, the technology strategy can be justified only in this context with the business and functional strategies. However, as argued earlier, technology is so prevalent in the operations of the firms, that it must be seen as the underlying infrastructure without which the firm will collapse. On the other hand, when properly planned, technology can support, expedite, and sustain the creation of competitive advantages by enabling, enhancing, and maintaining the desired business capabilities.

Most firms miss the role of technology during the strategic planning exercises due to their lack of understanding of how technology can enhance

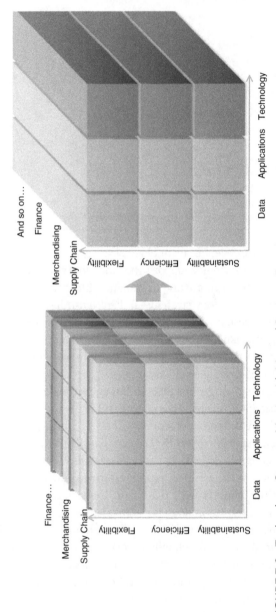

FIGURE 7.3 Technology Strategy Matrix with Merged Business Function

or constrain their ability to build functional capabilities. Technology is typically an afterthought to strategic planning as simply the collection of hardware and software that is expected to deliver the results demanded from it. This narrow-minded view often results in missed opportunities, short-sighted and un-sustainable technology investments, mismatched expectations, and deep dis-satisfaction with the enterprise technology. It is not uncommon to find firms that continuously struggle with technology, don't seem to be able to leverage it, consider it as a necessary evil, and invest to build technology that only constrains their growth and flexibility, and kills business innovation. We believe that there are two basic reasons for such situations.

1. Technology is an afterthought when it comes to strategic planning. Most firms conduct their strategic planning exercises to evaluate the projects and prioritize their capital investments, but this is done in absence of any understanding of the technology requirements of such initiatives and the impact on the existing technology landscape of the enterprise. That exercise of evaluating the technology impact is typically left for later, for the information technology (IT) teams to explore. In most cases, it is too late by then, as the project dollars may have been committed to specific solutions with no or little flexibility left for the IT team to leverage.
2. The scope of technology strategy within the enterprise strategic planning process is either very limited or not clearly defined in most firms. In both cases, technology often gets short shrift due to the lack of clearly defined scope, responsibilities, and controls. While they may look innocuous in the short term, such attitudes lead to process capabilities that are too expensive or too rigid to create any competitive advantages in the long run.

Both these reasons require creating a corporate strategy planning process that includes all the three components of business, functional, and technology strategies when evaluating the projects and prioritizing corporate investments in long-term business initiatives with the intention of creating competitive advantages for survival and growth.

COMPONENTS OF A TECHNOLOGY STRATEGY

Most technology-based business solutions have three common aspects. They need data to model the business objects and scenarios, they need application logic that simulates the business process and enables specific functions, and they need technology infrastructure like the servers and networking equipment to run the applications and provide users with a way to interact with the systems. When these three components work well together, they create solutions that successfully support business functions. As the functional requirements change and evolve, flexibly designed and deployed solutions can adapt such changes and provide enhanced returns on the original capital investments.

These three components also constitute the technology strategy with the objective of selecting and maintaining a landscape that is extensible to support new solutions and business functions as they become necessary for the business to maintain its competitiveness. An enterprise-wide view of technology helps the firms break open the project-specific silos of technology that invariably result in an assortment of unsustainable and expensive technology growth in pursuit of business solutions.

Data, applications, and technology infrastructure are three basic components of the technology strategy. The objective of this section is to discuss the importance of each one of these components in building the technology strategy as well as their impact on the ability to create and maintain functional capabilities.

Data or Information

Data provides the basic foundation for all computer-based application systems that dominate the enterprise and virtually support all their functions from human resource management and payroll to customer order fulfillment and logistics. As computer applications cannot deal with fuzzy data or instructions, the quality of data directly affects the ability of the applications to model the enterprise and provide decision support or automation of the enterprise processes. While this seems to be a pretty obvious fact, most of the firms struggle with creating, harvesting, maintaining, harmonizing, and sharing consistent data among its applications. In fact, few firms have explicitly defined and implemented processes for data governance. This affects their ability to effectively leverage technology solutions or to adopt their existing solutions quickly in response to evolving business processes or changes in business environment. The lack of common data models and data-governance practices also makes it unnecessarily expensive to integrate different applications to create seamless process flows or to get a single reliable view of their operations due to the inability to consolidate incompatible data.

For example, consider a large enterprise with several business units that share raw materials to produce products. Without a common item master for their raw materials, this firm cannot easily develop an enterprise-wide view of their total spend on these raw materials from their key vendors, even when the business units may have the same vendor in different parts of the world. This will certainly constrain their ability to negotiate prices, credit, and supply terms that could have resulted in substantial savings. In another situation, consider a retailer with independent customer masters for their mail-catalog business, Web channel, and stores. As customers divide their business among these sales channels, the retailer loses all visibility into customer behavior despite having the data from individual channels due to their inability to identify specific customers consistently across these channels.

LACK **OF CONSISTENT CUSTOMER DATA**

These are not far-fetched scenarios; rather, these are situations that most of the larger companies struggle with on a day-to-day basis and issues that continuously cut into their returns on technology investments. Consider AT&T and their inability to leverage customer master data. While AT&T has quite a few Web-based account management tools, they are unable to provide their customers with a single application to access all their accounts. This affects AT&T negatively in many ways: it negates their product bundling strategy by creating a gap between what the customer expects based on bundling of services and what they get when they try to manage their "bundled" account. It also negates the marketing hype built to promote the bundling strategy. The inability to see a single consolidated view of their customers also frequently results in misdirected marketing efforts, in which AT&T tries to sell services that the customer has already purchased from another AT&T division. This is not only ineffective, but also very expensive. A consolidated customer master data, in this case, would allow AT&T to focus their marketing dollars effectively, while simultaneously creating an environment of trust with their customers. The trouble with the visibility of customer data is almost ubiquitous across industries and pervades almost all firms that have more than one large division under the same brand. There are many more examples of companies that have failed to manage their customer data consistently across their business lines, such as the Internet service provider Comcast and the Servicemaster group of companies that owns Terminix, TrueGreen, American Home Shield, Merry Maids, and more. Most of the conventional retailers who have started their Web retail channels in the past few years provide more examples of broken data with their inability to merge the customer data from their retail stores and online channels.

As a business changes and emerges, mergers and acquisitions happen, and the business expands into new geographies; data needs to be managed to continuously support the new needs of the firm. There are many dimensions of managing data in the technology strategy. While data strategy is not quite synonymous with master data management, the technology solutions marketed under the master data management umbrella provide a well-structured opportunity to the firms to streamline their data management processes, create common data models, and manage the data life cycle consistently.

To start with, firms must understand their basic master data elements. This is the data that is used across many applications and keeping it consistent enables effective process integration, automation, and analytics. Products, locations, customers, and vendors are common examples that are typically used by many disparate applications across the enterprise and should be managed as enterprise master data to leverage the information produced by these applications. Firms need to analyze their own operations and processes to establish the basic common data that they would want to model as enterprise level master data. Once established, they need to create data governance processes for creating or harvesting such data, cleansing and harmonizing, maintaining, and sharing this data with all the enterprise applications that may need it.

Firms must also identify the use of data in the enterprise. Some common uses are the business applications, data warehouses for reporting and analytics, and process integration that requires moving data between applications, processes, and partners. The firms must also analyze how the data is used in each of these applications; for example, some applications will create it, others will only use it, while yet others may also modify and enrich it. Understanding *how* the data is used allows the enterprise to establish data governance and maintenance processes that are not in conflict with the data usage patterns. Firms must also create a data archival and purging policy to address regulatory and process requirements. For example, financial settlement data with vendors may be required by law to be maintained for a minimum number of years. While there are no regulatory requirements for maintaining historical demand data, the firm may decide to maintain this history to use it for demand forecasting and product planning purposes. Inability to archive data and retrieve it when required may jeopardize the legal rights of the firm and business process efficiency or both.

Finally, firms must also develop a clear organizational view of the data. Who owns master data? Who owns transactions? Who uses it, who needs it, and who can access it? The organizational view of data for master data and transactions is extremely important. The access to financial data, for example, may be restricted based on the role of a person in the organization. Similarly, the merchandising department may decide when a product record should be published in their products catalog so that it can be sold only after all relevant data on the product has been captured including its price, promotions, discounts, assortment locations, supplier, replenishment cycle, and so on. Having a clear picture of data ownership and data needs allows the firms to accommodate these requirements while developing the technology strategy.

We conclude this section by summarizing the main reasons for an enterprise to manage data as part of their technology strategy:

- Data provides the common language to the enterprise applications.
- Common master data allows the applications to work seamlessly and support the business processes in a naturally integrated fashion. This allows process visibility across the enterprise, enabling everyone to respond to unplanned events and minimize disruptions to the business.
- Common master data also allows for consolidation of information from disparate applications into consistent metrics that can be used for supporting and measuring business process effectiveness. It allows management to get a single overview of the enterprise and supports objective decision making.
- Common data allows for a streamlined approach to archiving, retrieval, and purging of old data across the enterprise.
- Common data management streamlines enhancement to the data models to support new processes, upgrades of technologies and solutions, and changes to integration requirements, reducing the total cost of ownership of the affected business solutions.

Applications

In recent years, packaged business applications have become standard for managing most of the enterprise processes. Enterprise resource planning (ERP) systems have continuously expanded their functional footprint in response to the increasing complexity of businesses and their desire to enhance organization efficiency. For a large number of industries, these packaged solutions offer truly valuable alternatives to custom development. The evolution in application design and Web-based technologies enables these solutions to provide flexibility in deployment, performance, maintenance, and operations across a globally distributed user base. On the flip side, the amount of underlying technology infrastructure that is required to build, test, and run these complex applications has grown exponentially as well. While the applications of yore might have only required a dumb terminal and a mainframe, most enterprise applications now require an underlying technology infrastructure consisting of a large number of components such as database servers, application servers, Web servers, client terminals, integration servers, messaging servers, directory servers, and so on. Each layer adds to the overall complexity of the technology landscape and creates a formidable challenge for most companies.

This complexity of technology affects the solution vendors as much as it affects their customers. Since the solution providers must also contend with the same constellation of available technologies to build and run their solutions, they must pick up specific technology stacks to do so. When these solutions are tested and certified for specific technology stacks, they may not run on others. This poses a great challenge to their customers, since the technology stacks selected by the solution provider may not be the same as those selected by the client firm. To reduce situations of incompatibility, the solution providers test and certify their wares on multiple popular technology stacks. Most of the larger firms also end up having many possible combinations of such technology stacks even though this multiplicity increases the complexity of their technology landscape and pushes the cost of building and maintaining it.

Therefore, when an enterprise decides to invest in a specific application from a selected solution provider, they must also invest in all the underlying technology that this solution will need, for hardware, software, networking, integration, monitoring, and security. This means that the firm must have the required skills for all these supporting components of the solution or develop them to successfully deploy the selected solutions. Once deployed, the firm must maintain these skills over the life of the solution. All these costs add up toward what is generally known as the *total cost of ownership* (TCO) for the solution.

For all the previous reasons, applications become a critical component of the technology strategy. Business applications directly affect the functional abilities of the firm as well as the technology landscape. Technology strategy must be balanced between the value created by these applications and the cost of deploying them.

Often, the decision of selecting one application over another is strongly governed by the desirable functionality and its usability by the business and the technology implications are generally not a priority. While this process may seem logical, an integrated approach is more productive in most cases. Firms must learn to assess the impact of business solutions on their technology landscapes to establish the TCO. They must rationalize and standardize their investments in the underlying technology layers to constrain the technology proliferation, which otherwise is guaranteed to push the costs of initial capital investments as well as the costs of maintaining these solutions in the long term.

Once a business application has been deployed, it will most likely require upgrading as the solution providers come out with newer application releases that may be functionally better, faster, more stable, or address specific business issues raised by clients. In most cases, the solution providers also stop supporting the older versions of their applications based on a published schedule. In response, the firms must plan to upgrade the business applications in a fashion that is compliant with the vendor's support plans. Since such upgrades introduce a level of risk due to the changes in the business applications, they may cause business disruptions. On the other hand, not upgrading leaves the firms with the risk of applications that are no longer supported by their vendors. Therefore, firms must plan for such upgrades complying with the vendor's support plans, but also minimizing the business risk. It requires an assessment of change and its impact on the business and technology due to such upgrades. One of the objectives of the technology strategy is to enable such risk assessment and allow for managing it adequately.

The following points summarize the discussion on application component of technology strategy:

- Firms need to limit the technology proliferation to be effective. Standardizing technology stacks is a way to achieve this objective.
- Firms must develop an application policy that allows them to leverage their technology standards to leverage in-house skills for operating and maintenance and lowering the total cost of ownership of the business solutions.
- Firms must also develop guidelines for selecting solution vendors so that applications for different business functions are tested and integrated on common stacks or are compatible with each other to allow for building naturally flowing processes that don't need expensive manual touchpoints.
- Firms must often assess their business applications and the processes they support to evaluate the gaps and establish the best way to create extended functionality.
- Firms must develop road maps to upgrade the business applications to enhance and maintain their functional-capability parity with the competition and to continue to leverage the competitive advantages created through these applications.

■ Firms must develop and implement processes to assess and control the business continuity risks during accidental failure, transition, and planned upgrades of their applications supporting critical business functions. Examples of such processes are archival and back-up processes, disaster recovery processes, and high-availability deployments with built-in redundancy to support partial outages in system resources.

Technology Infrastructure

The technology component represents the technology infrastructure that is required to host all the technology solutions required by the firm to operate. These include hardware and system software required to host the business applications that enable the firm's operations. This includes the required hardware such as the servers, routers, network switches, optical fiber, desktops, disks, memory cards, and so on, and system software such as databases, operating systems, application containers, Web browsers, integration engines, messaging software, directory servers, software compliers, editors, monitoring applications, high availability software, and so on.

As noted in the applications section, the technology stacks required to host the business applications can multiply rather quickly unless they are standardized as part of the larger strategy that includes considering the hardware as part of the criteria during the selection of business solutions. Standardized technology stacks constrain the allowed combinations of servers and system software. Therefore, most large corporations define such standards to keep the proliferation of hardware and software within manageable limits.

Technology is another fast-changing component of the technology strategy. Moore's law predicts the development of faster machines that in turn drive newer operating systems, databases, and other infrastructural software to take advantage of the faster processing power of the computers. The fast-changing technology means that a firm will have technology proliferation over time as their processes evolve and technology expands to enable them. In addition to the natural evolution of technology, the required business capabilities may themselves proliferate as companies grow, change, and innovate their products and processes, which may result into ever more undesirable technology diversity and complexity. A long-term strategy can ease the situation by establishing a road map for evolution of the technology layer as the business requirements and technology emerge. Having a clear plan for such upgrades also enables the firms to assess and control the risk caused by technology obsolescence, which typically leads to inflexibility of the business to innovate, change, and effectively respond to the changes in its competitive environment.

The following points summarize the technology component of the strategy:

- Firms must develop technology standards to control the technology proliferation to control undesirable escalations in cost and complexity of their technology landscapes. Such standards must include all hardware and software infrastructure needed by the firm.
- Firms must develop clear upgrade paths to maintain their technology parity with the competition as well as the solution providers to continue to leverage the competitive advantages created through their business applications.
- Firms must have processes to assess and control the business continuity risks during failure, transition, and planned upgrades of their technology supporting critical business applications.

There are several enterprise architecture (EA) approaches that have been established in the last few years that may be used by the firms on developing their own enterprise architecture disciplines, of which the technology strategies form a large part. An overview of a process that is based on a collective review of such frameworks is presented later in this chapter. However, it is presented only with the intention of making the user familiar with the general progression of steps in the process. It does not conform to any specific framework nor does it present a detailed process to guide the development of an EA practice. If the development of technology strategy is the prime objective of the reader, then the reader is advised to find other sources of help. There exists a wealth of material on the subject and even a casual search will uncover many available methodologies and processes.

Before diving into the process overview for developing a technology strategy, we will present the case for why a technology strategy is important part of the quest for creating competitive advantage.

WHY DEVELOP A TECHNOLOGY STRATEGY?

Why is technology strategy necessary? We have established so far the need for the business strategy as well as a functional strategy for a firm and we have also established that technology is an essential component to create and maintain competitive advantages through functional capabilities. But we have not yet answered this question Why should firms develop a technology strategy?

In Chapter 2, we discuss the subject of *understanding advantage* and define four dimensions that create advantage: time, cost, efficiency, and quality. These are the criteria used to differentiate processes that create competitive advantage from those that don't. To answer the question on technology strategy, we will use the same four dimensions to make the case for why firms must create a technology strategy to support their quest for creating competitive advantages through functional capability.

The realization of business goals depends on developing the functional capabilities, and these functional capabilities themselves are often supported by the business solutions that need technology to be deployed, operated, and maintained. In short, technology enables the capabilities that, in turn, create competitive advantages. The advantage itself originates through one or more of the enhanced process characteristics of cost, time, efficiency, or quality, and a well-thought-out technology strategy can help create these process characteristics along all the four dimensions of time, cost, efficiency, and quality. It can reduce the time to deploy a solution and enable a functional capability, reduce the cost of deployment, make the deployment more efficient, and enhance the quality by making a process more reliable or less error-prone by creating a consistent and repeatable process. Conversely, lack of a technology strategy may impact these dimensions negatively and reduce or eliminate the positive impact of the competitive advantage. Let us see how this happens.

Most firms don't have an organizational view of technology, but rather look at technology in terms of requirements for deploying individual solutions. While this project-based view may work in the short term, in the long term it creates a very complex and unsustainable technology landscape in which legacy systems exist side by side with the latest technology, creating inflexible and hard-to-integrate systems. Such landscapes are replete with multiple technologies for supporting the same or similar business processes and may have incompatible technologies that are hard to integrate and expensive to maintain. The landscape grows organically into a disparate collection of technologies that is expensive to operate, renew, and replace. The cost of operation goes up due to the diversity of maintenance skills required to support the diverse technology. The cost of renewal is linked directly to the number of licenses that must be renewed for every piece of deployed technology and the cost of replacement goes up as such replacement typically requires large-scale changes to the affected systems and processes due to obsolescence and their impact on business.

The situation described here is not limited to specific companies, but rather quite rampant in most industries. Such short-sighted practices cause the technology to proliferate rather quickly because a company has no clear policy on the selection and deployment of the technology required to host their myriad business applications. This multiplicity and the attendant complexity is, in fact, reason enough for a firm to develop a technology strategy so that their technology landscape evolves in a planned fashion that fully supports their business needs, but is also sustainable in the long run. This multiplicity or proliferation affects all four dimensions of advantage creation negatively. Out-of-control technology proliferation soaks up organizational resources without enhancing any of the dimensions creating the advantages. As the primary purpose of technology remains hosting the business applications required to enable functional needs, the following four dimensions are interpreted in the same context.

1. **Time of solution deployment.** Technology proliferation increases the time of solution deployment. There are many reasons for this; some are direct, such as the inability to quickly recruit the new skills required or retrain existing staff in different technologies, and others are indirect, such as the extra time required to model integrated processes using applications hosted on different stacks of technology. For example, if a company has standardized on using Webmethods as their enterprise Web server but then decides to buy business applications that would run only on Websphere, then they must now not only learn the new skills for the second Web server technology, but it has also become more complex to integrate these two systems, if the business process mandated such an integration. Of course, installing, configuring, and maintaining a brand-new technology takes extra time as well, without any corresponding reduction of the time required to maintain the older parts of the existing landscape. All these factors will increase the time to deploy the new functional capability that reduces the total value created through the competitive advantage by reducing the window of opportunity, as shown in Figure 4.1.

2. **Cost of solution deployment.** Technology multiplicity increases the cost of owning technology. This cost covers the direct cost components such as the cost of obtaining the initial license and the cost of renewal, as well as the indirect costs of subscription and support. The proliferation also deprives the firms of their ability to negotiate with technology vendors by

consolidating their technology spend with lesser number of vendors. It also requires more people to maintain disparate technology due to the specialized skills required to install, configure, and maintain them. The people costs are further increased due to retraining costs and longer ramp-up times due to turnover. If the new technology happens to be software that needs a specific platform, then there may be additional costs due to new hardware, operating systems, monitoring tools, and so on. When the cost of solution deployment goes up, it reduces the potential value created through the functional capability by undermining the return on the investments made to create the competitive advantage.

3. **Efficiency of deployment solution.** There are two aspects of efficiency. The first one deals with the efficiency of the solution usage in a day-to-day environment and the second deals with the efficiency of returns on the investment made in the solution deployment:

    1. This point deals with the solution efficiency as it relates to the performance, scalability, and responsiveness of a solution. Technology proliferation increases the touch points as well as the need to process data and transactions multiple times simply to integrate solutions on multiple technology stacks. Such conversion wastes computing cycles, makes the process slower, and affects the overall usability of the applications by their inability to perform, scale, and respond.

    2. This point deals with the efficiency of the financial investment. When the cost and time of deploying a solution goes up, the efficiency of deployment goes down. It becomes less cost-effective and directly affects the return on investments. The increased costs and time required for the solution deployment reduces the ability to create sustainable competitive advantage and, sometimes, may eliminate the advantage completely. Recall that if the cost of creating the competitive advantage is more than the value of the advantage or if it unsustainable over the long term, then these factors make the advantage undesirable and the strategy flawed. Technology proliferation, through its impact on cost and time of solution deployments, can actually void any competitive benefits in some cases.

4. **Quality of the deployed solution.** Finally, technology multiplicity can affect the quality of the deployed solution and therefore lead a firm to question the value of the competitive advantage being pursued. The deterioration of quality generally results from a lack of standards among the competing technologies that may manifest itself through their inability to integrate smoothly. This lack of integration may show in many

ways, for example, inability of the applications to interact in a real-time fashion injecting process delays, inconsistent data, and transactions that cannot be used without transformations, extra computing costs, and delays, and the inability to detect events and raise alerts, which require real-time user intervention. All of these issues may, in turn, add costs and delays, further reducing the projected benefits and inflating the cost of achieving them.

It is for all these reasons that corporations need to evaluate their existing technology and establish a technology strategy that not only supports their business strategy, but actually enhances it by reducing the time and cost to create the functional capabilities supporting it. This brings this discussion to the next subject of how business solutions (which create the functional capabilities) are evaluated and selected by most corporations.

Most of the business solutions in large corporations are enabled through business applications built for them. These applications may be custom-built internally by their information technology teams or purchased from a solution provider. They may be hosted in-house or may be subscribed to in a SaaS (software as a service) environment. While the impact of technology on business solutions varies in the different scenarios mentioned here, it nevertheless substantially affects business capability. On the positive side, technology solutions provide standardization for the business processes, bring consistent decision-making discipline, and can reduce dependence on an individual's skills to execute a specific process. On the other hand, technology solutions can constrain the business process by reducing its flexibility and by forcing users to go down rigidly defined paths, which may cause frustration and poor service.

However, in all scenarios, technology has an integral role in determining the final outcome of the deployment of a business solution, its overall success, usability, and its ability to support business requirements and enable functional capabilities. This integral view, in which the business solution and technology together create a functional capability, is what is often missing when corporations evaluate their needs.

Very often, when firms make decisions on business solutions, the functionality and usability (ease of use) of the solution is their only focus and they don't necessarily consider the technology aspect of the solution. This leads to an unbalanced view in which the corporation is unaware of the possible changes to their existing technology landscape due to the introduction of this new business solution. This further leads to their inability to understand the impact of the potential technology changes or their ability to effectively manage such changes. The absence of the process of impact and change assessment on the existing applications and technologies when a new solution is planned leads these firms to make decisions without fully understanding the impact of such actions. Such short-sightedness frequently causes cost and time overruns on technology-based solution deployments, which have become quite rampant.

The impact of such short-sighted decision making typically becomes obvious when the technology solutions fail to deliver the expected benefits through their failure to enable promised business capabilities, through the high costs to maintain the solution, limited options for enhancing the business capability as the environment changes, and so on. The impact of such unplanned changes in technology and their resultant costs are generally evident shortly after the deployment is started, but the financial and organizational costs of making any changes to the decision at that stage normally eliminate any real options for the firm.

In contrast, a well-established technology strategy provides an enterprise view of the technology as a business enabler rather than as a tool to deploy a specific solution at a certain time. It supports a structured organizational decision-making process to consider the impact of changes due to technology integrated with the business requirements driving the deployment of the solution. This integrated evaluation of the technology solutions prevents some of the problems presented here by considering the existing technology landscape and assessing the costs of change mandated by the potential introduction of the new solutions. Therefore, an effective technology strategy must allow a firm to clearly assess and understand the impact of change: How will the introduction of a new business solution affect their current technology landscape and affect the planned evolution; how will it impact their ability to sustain the deployed business capabilities in the long run? The technology strategy also helps by clearly defining the path forward for the evolution of technology based on consolidated organizational requirements, rather than the model where technology simply grows organically in reaction to the isolated understanding of business requirements, one project at a time.

For a successful alignment of technology strategy with the functional and business strategies, another important aspect to consider is the organizational structure and the interplay of the three groups in the firm. While a well-articulated technology strategy is definitely helpful in identifying the impact of changes to the technology landscape, the firm's ability to utilize this assessment is limited by its organizational constraints. It is not unusual for companies to have enterprise architecture teams who have the ability to establish and provide such direction, but who do not participate in the decision-making process or have any avenue by which to make any meaningful contributions toward ensuring that the technology strategy stays aligned with the functional and business strategies.

TECHNOLOGY STRATEGY AND ORGANIZATION

Based on the arguments presented so far, it would follow that for optimal organizational performance, the technology strategy must evolve from the business capabilities required by the firm and, correspondingly, the business solution decisions must be made taking the existing technology strategy into account. However logical this may seem, this does not happen very frequently in real-life corporations. For most companies, it is a struggle to keep the two aligned, much less in a position to leverage each other. The two decisions are made almost in complete isolation from each other and the culprit almost always is a broken organizational structure.

Typically, the business and technology groups are separate organizations with different objectives and leadership. The business organizations generally have a small group of specialists focused on assessing the business requirements and the gaps in the current functional capabilities to decide what capabilities should the firm build. Based on these gaps, business teams move into the next phase of evaluating the solutions and vendors who would be the potential suppliers of technology to build these enhanced capabilities. Technology teams generally have no active part to play in this process, until after most of the decisions have been made, the solution has been selected, and the fate of the technology required to support that solution has been sealed. While the technology teams may have a strategic road map for the evolution of technology to support a business, these road maps have almost no significant impact on the business team's decisions, due to the broken organizational process that prevents the teams from working together as partners.

Of course, this misalignment is exacerbated by the fact that the two groups specialize in their own areas and do not have many obvious common skills that can be leveraged across the two teams. The business teams typically don't understand the technical concerns and the technology teams are equally ignorant about what the business team is trying to do and why. In most cases, the two groups have no common forum in which to share information, educate each other, and collaborate in the decision-making process, to make choices that will mutually affect them for a long time to come. All these factors contribute to the two groups working in isolation, while they should actually be very actively collaborating in prioritizing capital investments that will sustain the firm in the marketplace.

Next, consider the current funding model for technology solutions. In the last few decades, almost all larger firms have moved to a model where business groups exclusively fund the technology solutions to be built. On the face of it, this model makes good sense because technology, after all, is there simply to support the business and does not merely exist for its own sake. But things are never that simple. Even though the dependence of business on the ability of technology to enable business processes has grown exponentially, the current financing model does not provide any incentive to the business teams to involve technology teams early on in the process, to allow them to have a meaningful impact on the decision-making process. The breadth of technologies involved and the specialized skills required to contribute effectively, prevents any reasonable expectation of technology competence to be built within the business teams. This leaves the active collaboration between the two teams as the only viable option to make optimal decisions. However, mistrust, lack of mutual appreciation, and missing organizational structure, all contribute to the unwillingness of the business to include technology as part of their decision-making process. In the end, having such a broken decision-making process for the most critical decisions directly affecting a firm's capabilities impacts the firm's ability to create competitive advantages in a cost-effective manner.

The bottom line: Business and technology solution groups don't have any common success metrics and, therefore, no stake in each other's success or failure. Even though it would make the most sense, organizationally, to optimize the process of planning and creating business capabilities, by working together and by sharing the objectives and constraints of the two groups, most organizations today fail to provide a forum where the two groups can share common objectives. Unfortunately, this causes obstacles to optimal decisions when it comes to building competitive advantages that address the business needs in the most cost-effective and flexible manner.

To address these organizational issues, firms must reconsider their organizational structures and the prevalent funding models. But, most of all, firms must invest in cross-functional resources that are competent enough in both the constituencies of functional knowledge about the business solutions as well as the technologies required to support them. This is quite possibly the biggest underlying reason for the mismatched organizational behaviors of firms when it comes to strategy. Unless the executive leadership is trained in cross-functional areas, understands the constraints, and appreciates the contributions made by the two groups toward building and sustaining competitive advantage, the situation is likely to continue without significant improvements.

Enterprise architecture (EA) has evolved as a separate discipline in many corporations in recent years. The concept behind EA was to build precisely the kind of competency that we have mentioned so far: a cross-functional team that understands the business of the firm, the functional capabilities required by the firm, and the role of technology to create and maintain such capabilities. Such a team, in theory, would have been able to assess the capability requirements of the firm and balance them against the desirable technology strategy that would allow the firm to seek, build, and maintain competitive advantage in a cost-effective manner that is sustainable over the long term.

Until now, the EA has obviously failed to deliver. Several reasons can be attributed to this failure, but the biggest reason remains organizational structure and the lack of cross-functional resources. So far, EA has been a technology initiative, it has always been part of the technology group, initiated by the CIO, and therefore disowned by the business leadership. Some other reasons for the failure that deserve to be mentioned here are lack of cross-functional skills and a lack of executive leadership's interest in focusing on strategic planning. The latter itself is likely a reflection of Wall Street's laser-sharp focus on the next quarter, which discourages firms from pursuing any long-term strategic planning process and executives from instituting a consistent business strategy.

Even so, the conceptual framework for enterprise architecture remains relevant. However, organizations must recognize this relevance and correct the organizational structure to leverage the basic concepts of EA to effectively execute their strategic planning processes. The current placement of the enterprise architecture groups within the technology teams, their narrow focus on technology, and their low business savvy continues to frustrate effective planning efforts and produces questionable results. There are three distinct reasons for corporations to change the organization placement of the EA to a more central and elevated structure, such as directly under the office of the CEO:

1. **The cross-functional nature of the EA concepts.** The natural scope of work for the enterprise architecture organizations cuts across the traditional functional and organizational silos. The EA teams not only cut

across technology and business competencies, they also need to have considerable cross-functional knowledge across business areas (such as finance, supply chain, and merchandising) to effectively plan strategic growth paths for a simultaneous functional and technology evolution across the entire business. The need for effectively managing the organizational landscape across several groups makes it desirable that EA teams are organized directly under the strategic initiatives group and above all individual groups.

2. **Long-term focus of their deliverables.** EA teams typically are forward-looking and focus on long-term initiatives that will be implemented over the next two to five years' time. This long-term focus requires them to clearly understand the corporate strategy for growth and business initiatives that will support such growth. The need for access to such information also requires that EA teams are organized so that they can get direct inputs from the corporate leaders and contribute to such decisions when their input is desirable.

3. **Capital-intensive nature of their projects.** Since EA teams are generally involved in strategic planning, they are routinely engaged in evaluating projects with large multiyear capital outlays targeted at creating distinct competitive or regulatory advantages for the business. The nature of their projects makes it desirable for them to have a good understanding of the corporate financial projections and objectives. Once again, that creates the need for the EA teams to be organized in a manner that allows them to have access to this information when relevant to long-term planning of the capital investments.

PROCESS OVERVIEW AND DELIVERABLES FOR CREATING TECHNOLOGY STRATEGY

While a detailed discussion on the process for creating technology strategy is out of scope of this book, an overview of the basic process outline would not only help in understanding the need for a technology strategy, but also provide a tangible list of deliverables expected from such an effort.

The basic process for creating a technology strategy starts with creating an "as-is" picture of the technology landscape, comparing this with the requirements derived from the functional and business strategies, conducting a gap-analysis between what exists and what is required to support the business, and finally developing a "to-be" picture of the landscape. Once the two pictures of current and future landscapes are available, the strategy can be put together by creating a road map of finite work-packages that will get the firm from its current position to the desired future position. The strategy primarily establishes the sequence of steps, time lines, and constraints within which the evolution takes place.

Before proceeding further, we would like to emphasize that any technology strategy created in isolation will be worthless and lose credibility, because technology primarily exists to support the business processes. This is also the main premise of the existing EA frameworks like The Open Group Architecture Framework (TOGAF). This notion is discussed in Chapter 8, on supply chain strategy, where we make the final arguments on keeping the business, functional, and technology strategies aligned, and show how this alignment can be achieved and leveraged beyond the current EA and strategy frameworks prevalent in the enterprises.

There are several enterprise architecture frameworks available to create a technology strategy; however, the basic steps remain the same. The actual deliverables from such an effort are generally developed by individual corporations as the need for information on specific entities and level of detail required for describing each of these entities remains specific to the individual corporate needs.

Therefore, in the following pages, we will describe the basic steps and provide examples of the types of deliverables that are generally suitable for each of these steps. EA is based on collecting data about the technology and information assets of an organization and leveraging this data to develop a sustainable technology road map. Examples of this data are catalogs, the attributes of assets such as business applications, servers, network equipment, operating systems, databases, Web servers, application servers, service registries, testing and quality assurance applications, security applications, and so on.

While these steps are basic in nature and can be completed without any special tools, there are software solutions available that will help create and maintain the EA artifacts quickly and ensure their integrity over time. These tools are especially useful for larger enterprises with more complex landscapes. Since there are no standard data and information models that would serve everyone, EA teams generally develop their own information models to collect and analyze the technology assets of a corporation. The packaged EA solutions allow the users to easily develop such models and configure them to optimize a firm's objectives for developing this information. The tools allow the selection of the entities to be modeled, the design attributes for these entities that are

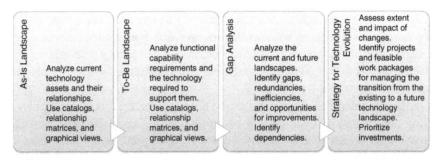

FIGURE 7.4   Overview of the Process for Creating a Technology Strategy

most useful to the organizational artifacts, and create entity relationships that help in change assessments. The tools allow the users to create multiple data-views for creating various EA artifacts including the catalogs, relationship matrices, and process flow charts that address questions from several different points of views.

The first step (see Figure 7.4) toward creating a technology strategy is to understand the current technology landscape in the enterprise, the "as-is" picture. This step requires that firms define the most critical entities of their technology and information assets that should be modeled for this exercise. While the technology components—such as the infrastructure elements of severs, networking equipment, and other hardware—are obvious choices, there are other entities—such as business units, data centers, users, business applications, master data entities, system applications, and business functions—that can be modeled to create a comprehensive picture. Some firms may also like to extend the model further and include the ongoing projects that will impact the landscape in the immediate future.

The deliverables from this step are generally captured in the catalogs, relationship matrices, and several other artifacts as follows.

- **Catalogs.** Catalogs are simply a listing of the functional and technology assets of the firm. Catalogs typically help in taking stock of what exists. This helps in creating the "as-is" picture and in creating the relationship matrices that are key to understanding and assessing the impact of changes due to extensions and evolution of the current landscape. Catalogs are typically compiled for business applications, servers (and other hardware assets), and business functions. For each of these entities, the attributes captured depend on the scope of questions that the EA may need to answer. Some examples of attributes captured for applications are vendor, dates (installation, last upgrade, contract validity, subscription, support), cost of license, cost of support subscription, type of support, location, data center, server, business functions supported, and so on. For servers, attributes collected may be their specifications, vendor attributes, cost attributes, build attributes, applications hosted, location/data center, and so on. For business functions, one may record business units, enabling application, user roles, and so on. These attributes help in quickly understanding their costs and the impact on users and the business, if this entity was to be removed or changed.

▪ **Relationship matrices.** The relationship matrices show how an entity is connected to others in the enterprise. The objective of creating relationship matrices is to establish the relationships among the information assets of a corporation as well as among their users and business units. The information enables a quick understanding of how the changes in one entity may affect other. For example, a relationship matrix between the business applications and business functions can quickly identify business functions that will be impacted if one of the business applications were to be brought down for maintenance or upgrade. The matrix can also be used to understand the gaps in technology by identifying business functions that are not automated through any application. Relationship matrices can be multidimensional. For example, the matrix showing the business applications and functions can have additional dimensions of user roles and business units added to it to identify the impact on users and business units if any of the business functions were to be redesigned. In another example, if a server hosts the business applications for demand forecasting and finance, then these relationships will be captured in the matrix and a change assessment report will alert the technology strategists of the impact on the business through these two applications, if the specific server were to be upgraded.

▪ **Views.** Views enable the information compiled in the catalogs and relationship matrices to be presented in several different ways to address specific questions. For example, the change impact reports can be produced to understand the effect of changing a business application or a hardware server on its stakeholders. These stakeholders may include business functions, users, and business units; similar reports may identify the impact of a planned upgrade of a technology asset, business application, system software upgrade, and so on. In a different view, similar change assessments can be presented to identify systems and servers that could be affected due to changes being planned to a business capability.

The number and types of views developed depend on the nature of questions to be answered and can be customized by the firms. Of course, the richness of data captured for the assets in the catalogs constrains the views that can be created and their use.

- **Landscapes.** The landscapes are generally an alternative presentation of the catalogs and relationship matrices. They are visual and easier to understand by large audiences who may not be as familiar with the underlying data in the catalogs and relationship matrices. They are typically created to visually show entities of the same type: for example, business functions and their relationships. The landscapes enable users to quickly understand the as-is and desired future pictures and spot major gaps in capabilities and support infrastructure that need to be filled. The landscapes can be created for the current state of technology assets as well as the future target state. After the current landscape information is available and well understood, it becomes easier to share this information with executives and business stakeholders, and the enterprise can begin to appreciate the complex nature of technology and its impact on the firm's business. With richly defined attributes in the catalogs and relationship matrices, the firms can also start to understand the costs, dependencies, redundancies, gaps, and the opportunities for changes.

- **Assessment scorecards.** The assessment scorecards are used in combination with the catalogs to compile additional information on business functions and applications with the objective of measuring their adequacy or desirability. This helps the firm understand its competency in the selected business capability and allows it to focus on those that are most critical to it for achieving its business goals and profitable growth.

- **Road maps.** Road maps are created to understand the evolution of business capabilities or technology in the firm. Putting together a road map helps the firm understand its capital investment requirements for building and/or maintaining its competitive position. Visual road maps developed using Gantt chart presentations provide a quick view of planned changes and allow the users to analyze and assess the impact of such changes in capabilities or technology.

All the preceding artifacts help a firm in understanding their existing technology assets, gaps, and requirements. All this information can be used to create the "to-be" or the target landscape for the enterprise. This is the target technology landscape that the firm believes it needs to build based on its current known business requirements. This is a more complex initiative and requires cross-functional skills and direct inputs from business teams. The basic input for this step starts with the assessment of future functional capabilities required by the business, which is derived from the functional and business strategies. Other inputs for the future landscape come from the enterprise's desire to standardize its technology and from external influences such as product life cycles published by solution and hardware providers, the desire to update obsolete technology, changes in policy, changes in partnerships, mergers and acquisitions, and so on. The "to-be" picture is then an ideal technology landscape that will create, support, and sustain all the functional capabilities identified by the business teams. This "to-be" landscape will change as the business requirements change and emerge. Often, the business requirements build upon their current strengths and therefore are incremental in nature. This helps in creating a smoother evolution of the "as-is" landscape to the future technology landscape in the enterprise. Of course, there will also be opportunities for planned significant changes that may not be incremental in nature: for example, consider a large enterprise that has traditionally grown using their own custom-built applications and then decides to implement an enterprise resource planning (ERP) solution that may replace the majority of their custom-built applications within a two- to three-year time frame.

During the analysis to create a "to-be" picture, most firms also create technology standards and the architecture principles to *govern* the changes that will inevitably result from such an evolution. If such standards and principles already exist, the analysis phase to create the desirable future state provides the best opportunity to review the existing technology standards and the architecture principles so that they can be fully leveraged and actively contribute in the firm's evolution rather than becoming bureaucratic constraints.

Comparison of the current and future landscapes provides the "gap analysis" to the firms and an opportunity to create a strategic road map to go from the current to the projected landscape in the future. The gap analysis will not only take inputs directly from the two landscapes, but also from the investment priorities, logical dependence among business processes, sequencing, changes in regulatory environments, changing investment priorities, changes in competitive landscapes, and the business environment. The purpose of the gap analysis is to assess and understand the impact of change and manage the risks to the business associated with the change. The technology road map is not static in nature and should be evaluated at least once a year to adopt changes in the operating and external environment of the firm.

Finally, the next step for any road map consists of creating feasible work-packages that are manageable and sequence them over time creating a path for the evolution of the technology landscape from its current state to the future state. Such a road map will have identifiable, well-defined projects in the short term and larger change packages for the longer term that can be reviewed and broken down into individual projects as time rolls by. Technology projects can also be part of the larger business initiatives targeted at creating business capabilities or independent projects. The choice really arises from whether a technology project is specific to enabling a business capability or forms part of the technology foundation common for all business applications. In both the cases, the sequencing and dependency constraints would govern its actual realization. The technology road map also defines the planned schedules for retirement and upgrades of existing technologies and introduction of new technology components. It identifies the impact of changes due to each of these events and the impact to the business teams. It provides a plan for the future capital investments required to maintain and enhance firm's competitive position. It allows the firms to create a well-planned path of transition to the technology future in a proactive and engaged manner rather than merely reacting to changes in a haphazard fashion.

Governance

As described in the process for developing an effective technology strategy, the deliverables and their contents are typically unique to an organization, even though there are some common information themes in the artifacts developed. The main objective of the artifacts is to enable the understanding of the current technology, information, and business capability assets of the firm, create a future target picture for these assets, and then define a road map to go from the current state to the desired future state.

This is facilitated through a well-thought-out governance process, which is the other large part of an effective technology strategy. A good governance process ensures that all the individual projects making up the building blocks of the enterprise's technology capabilities comply with the stated direction of evolution. The governance process typically takes the shape of toll-gate reviews of capital projects at key stages of their life cycles. These reviews can be organized at the following stages: project proposal, business requirements, solution selection or design, testing and quality assurance, and finally at the time of final deployment. Reviewing the projects through their whole life cycle provides an opportunity to validate that their design, technology, service providers, and the targeted business capabilities are all aligned with the objectives of the guiding technology and functional strategies in place.

To achieve this objective of compliance and to communicate the firm's targeted state, technology strategies develop sets of principles and standards. These principles and standards are published and guide the project teams during the deployment initiatives. The following are some of the tools that technology strategies use to ensure such compliance.

Architecture Principles

Architecture principles are statements of policy, guidelines, standards, and intentions for managing the technology and information solutions that drive the technology architecture and hence the strategic direction of technology in a firm. Therefore, while they are not quite as tangible as the data, application, and technology infrastructure, we will cover them as a distinct component of the technology strategy because they are an integral part of setting the corporate direction toward following a disciplined strategy.

The architecture principles can be created to guide various areas of technology and business solution architectures. For example, a firm can have architecture principles for its data, applications, and technology components. Firms may choose to develop these principles for other areas such as information security and application testing. It really depends on what technology assets are most critical to the success of the firm and, therefore, important for a planned evolution over time.

The objective of establishing such principles is to provide guidelines to all the teams involved in making decisions for managing technology. To create effective principles that will help decision making, these principles must be direct and relevant to the task at hand. Mark Schultz[1] of IBM sets the following criteria for defining good architecture principles.

- **Simplicity.** Key points must be clear and understandable by different groups throughout the organization. Take care not to have too many principles, or it leads to confusion.
- **Consistency of interpretation.** A robust principle includes policies and standards that allow support of governance in a consistent manner. To support this concept, words that define a principle must be carefully chosen so there will not be multiple interpretations of a principle.
- **Relevancy.** Principles must cover all relevant and important constructs of an organization. The value of a principle is that it fits in the realm of what is needed to support the architecture applicable to the IT needs of an organization.

- **Granularity.** Principles are large grained. Care must be taken not to define principles that are too fine grained and too narrowly focused.
- **Flexibility.** Principles must be expressed in a way that they can adapt to other principles with only some degree of conflict. No principles should be in conflict where one invalidates the intent of the other.
- **Stability.** Principles should be enduring, yet able to accommodate changes. Principles have a life cycle; a process must be developed that ratifies changes to a principle that will allow for adding, deleting, and updating of the principles.

Once the architecture principles are established, articulated, and adopted by the firm, they should be used for driving creation, changes, and retirements of any technology asset. They can also be used for making decisions when multiple options are available. The architecture principles are often used for governance and compliance validation for technology initiatives to ensure consistent evolution of the technology landscape aligned with business strategy and requirements.

The Open Group Architecture Framework (TOGAF) is an industry standard framework that may be used freely by any organization wishing to develop an information systems architecture for use within that organization. This framework specifies four components[2] of an architecture principle for defining effective principles.

1. **Name.** Should both represent the essence of the rule as well as be easy to remember. Specific technology platforms should not be mentioned in the name or statement of a principle. Avoid ambiguous words in the Name and in the Statement such as: "support," "open," "consider," and for lack of good measure the word "avoid." itself, be careful with "manage(ment)," and look for unnecessary adjectives and adverbs (fluff).
2. **Statement.** Should succinctly and unambiguously communicate the fundamental rule. For the most part, the principles statements for managing information are similar from one organization to the next. It is vital that the principles statement be unambiguous.
3. **Rationale.** Should highlight the business benefits of adhering to the principle, using business terminology. Point to the similarity of information and technology principles to the principles governing business operations. Also describe the relationship to other principles, and the intentions regarding a balanced interpretation. Describe situations where one principle would be given precedence or carry more weight than another for making a decision.

4. **Implications.** Should highlight the requirements, both for the business and IT, for carrying out the principle—in terms of resources, costs, and activities/tasks. It will often be apparent that current systems, standards, or practices would be incongruent with the principle upon adoption. The impact to the business and consequences of adopting a principle should be clearly stated. The reader should readily discern the answer to: "How does this affect me?" It is important not to oversimplify, trivialize, or judge the merit of the impact. Some of the implications will be identified as potential impacts only, and may be speculative rather than fully analyzed.

As examples, TOGAF provides several principles, one of which is reproduced in the following list. This should typically be a valid principle for all firms.

1. Name: *Compliance with Law*
2. Statement: *Enterprise information management processes comply with all relevant laws, policies, and regulations.*
3. Rationale: *Enterprise policy is to abide by laws, policies, and regulations. This will not preclude business process improvements that lead to changes in policies and regulations.*
4. Implications:
   a. *The enterprise must be mindful to comply with laws, regulations, and external policies regarding the collection, retention, and management of data.*
   b. *Education and access to the rules. Efficiency, need, and common sense are not the only drivers. Changes in the law and changes in regulations may drive changes in our processes or applications.*

A direct implication of this principle, for example, will be that all business applications handling personal identifying information about the firm's customers may have to implement secure data creation and access processes. They will also have to comply with the data retention issues when the customer relationship terminates. An indirect implication of this principle will be for applications handling the credit card data. The firm may decide that all such applications must be enhanced to comply with the payment card industry (PCI) standards. While PCI standards are not a law unto themselves, they provide the best guidelines for securing the customer credit card information, because the laws around such information vary by states and are still evolving. This principle may drive significant changes in the way the firm creates, retains, and uses personal and credit card data from its customers.

Technology Standards

Technology standards consist of lists of approved technology that can be purchased and used in the organization. The concept is similar to having an approved vendor list for purchases. If a specific technology is not approved for use, then the organizational processes will prevent purchase, renewal, subscription, and sourcing of such technology for use within the enterprise.

If an enterprise decides to maintain technology standards, they must develop processes to evaluate, on-board, maintain, and retire technology. This is typically achieved through frequent technology review meetings, where all new technology is presented along with the business requirements driving such needs. The meetings are generally hosted by the technology and solution architects. This forum presents a great platform for any cost-benefit analysis, as well as a platform to evaluate alternatives for technology and their providers. Once a technology is approved by the group, it is added to the approved technology list that is widely published. The purchase process is tied into the approval process so that unauthorized technology purchases are prevented.

Once a technology has been approved and becomes part of the enterprise standards, the team of architects generally follows the provider's recommendations on renewal and support. It is a good idea to review each technology standard at least once a year to evaluate the continued business need, comparison with the latest alternatives, and to ensure continued vendor support. With time, technologies will become obsolete, and a disciplined standards process enables a firm to establish guidelines for technology renewal and allows it to budget for such renewals.

Evolution Road Maps

Technology evolution road maps are the other common deliverable of technology strategies. These road maps are what define the technology strategy as they bring all the other deliverables together to create a single driving document for the technology evolution and management in a firm.

Each of the other deliverables—such as the catalogs of technology assets, relationship matrices, technology standards, and the architectural principles—brings its inputs to create the technology road map. Technology road maps are driven by evolving business needs for new solutions, planned solution upgrades, vendor's product support schedules, and other internal considerations such as changes in standards, mergers, and acquisitions. Technology road maps ensure that all stakeholders are aware of the planned changes in the technology landscape and have enough time to plan so that these changes can be managed safely and without creating any unexpected business disruption. They also ensure that everyone is informed of the technical capabilities of the firm that are available for them to leverage as they see fit.

However, the technology strategy is not static. The strategy itself evolves, adapts, and changes in response to the requirements of the business, environment, and innovations in technology. Conventionally, the strategies typically allude to a long-term plan or vision of the firm and are not evaluated very frequently. However, technical advances in recent years have shrunk the cycle of changes affecting business innovation and hence the competitive pressures. This has, in turn, driven more frequent evaluation of the strategies themselves to keep them current and relevant. Technology strategy is no different, and as the changes in the technology landscape occur even faster than the changes in the business landscape, it is imperative that firms keep up with changes and update their technology strategies more frequently. Technology strategy has two powerful drivers: business requirements and changes in technology. Obsolete technology loses its ability to adapt to changing business requirements, constrains business innovation, and eventually becomes a liability. It is typically easier to plan and update technology assets on a regular basis rather than to revamp the whole technology foundation because of its obsolescence and effective worthlessness to the business. Such extensive change is not only expensive, but also presents significant disruptions to the business that may prove fatal.

Figure 7.5 shows an overview of the technology strategy process that uses the governance processes and the architectural deliverables to achieve its

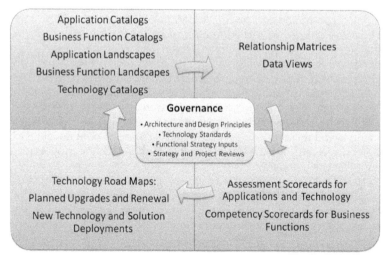

FIGURE 7.5 Technology Strategy Process Life Cycle

objective of creating technology infrastructure that is fully capable of enabling the business needs of the firm and also continues to renew itself to keep up with the changes in technology, potentially opening new ways to do business for the firm and thereafter maintaining the competitive advantages thus created.

WAL-MART **AND KMART: ROLE OF TECHNOLOGY**

While both Kmart and Wal-Mart had similar goals when they began in the early 1960s, the course of their businesses took radically different routes. In 1991, Wal-Mart sales overtook the sales at Kmart. While there were many factors at play, as is always the case for any corporation of this magnitude, Kmart's inability or lack of inclination to adopt technology was one of the big reasons that the company declared bankruptcy in 2002.

Wal-Mart started investing in technology in 1966, an innovation that was championed by none other than Sam Walton himself. During the next two decades Wal-Mart invested in several store-based technologies such as computers, electronic cash registers, and UPC scanners for nongrocery items. Wal-Mart continued its investments in technology by building a satellite-based communication system in the mid-1980s and investing in technology that would allow them to get real-time sales and inventory data from their stores. In addition, Wal-Mart spent heavily on technology that enabled their legendary supply chain capabilities, automated distribution centers, optimized transportation, supported vendor collaboration, and so on. Wal-Mart leveraged technology in all its business operations and adopted it to enable their functional capabilities while directly supporting their "every day low prices" business strategy.

In contrast, Kmart never quite believed in technology. *Kmart's Ten Deadly Sins* states that "Kmart needed an IT champion at the top and it never had one. Even during CIO Dave Carlson's tenure, from 1985 to 1995, he worked with a CEO who 'prided himself on never having used an automated teller machine and used an assistant to print email.' Such admissions clearly demonstrated that information technology was not a priority for the company."[3]

Most likely, it was because Kmart never really understood the role of technology in building their business capabilities, even though they had been investing in it, probably because of competitive pressure. During the 1970s, Kmart was opposed to any major investments in technology.

Kmart did not take up any substantial technology investments until 1978, when it started installing computers in its stores—a full 15 years after Wal-Mart started investing in technology. In the late 1980s, Kmart invested $3 billion in technology that provided them with scanners in 500 of their stores, a satellite-based credit-card processing system, and the ability to monitor sales and inventory. However, this covered only a fourth of their stores, unlike Wal-Mart who had the ability to track sales and inventory in all their stores.

In the 1980s, Wal-Mart invested in electronic data interchange (EDI) for operational collaboration and then created a collaborative network called RetaiLink enabling it to share its current and projected demand data with its suppliers. Kmart adopted EDI only in the early 1990s, pushed into it through their suppliers' initiatives. Wal-Mart also kept its supply chain strategy keenly aligned with its business strategy to cut operational costs by building a lean distribution network. Company practices such as owning their own fleet and cross-docking drive Wal-Mart's technology investments in supply chain. In contrast, Kmart had a mixed distribution network and never quite invested in their own fleet for distribution, losing the opportunity to design their own processes or improve operational efficiency beyond what their service providers supplied.

In addition to not being able to leverage technology, Kmart also simply did not seem to have a coherent business or functional strategy to drive the technology strategy. While Wal-Mart identified operational efficiencies early on as their key to reducing costs, there is no singular theme in Kmart's history that can be seen as an equivalent strategy. In 1990, Wal-Mart sales overtook Kmart for the first time; by then, it was amply clear what Wal-Mart had been doing right—Wal-Mart had invested heavily in the automation of distribution centers, communication between stores and headquarters, real-time sales and inventory visibility, collaboration with vendors, and planned investments in technologies like EDI. Kmart's response: to expand through unrelated acquisitions such as Borders, Office Max, and Sports Authority—only to have to shed these assets in the mid-1990s. Kmart had tough competition on pricing through Wal-Mart's laser sharp focus on operations and cost reduction, and on assortment from Target's high-end image. Whereas technology enabled Wal-Mart to create highly effective logistics and supply chain capabilities, Kmart simply stagnated due to a lack of strategy and antipathy toward technology. While Wal-Mart continues to squeeze value from its operations and its investments in the technology systems, Kmart simply gave up.

Former CIO Dave Carlson depicts Kmart's information systems in 1985 as one that was "cobbled together over time."[4] This is an example

(continued)

(*continued*)

of the organically grown supply chains that we have mentioned throughout the book as something to avoid, in favor of explicitly designing supply chain processes that in turn drive the technology that enables them.

When Chuck Conaway took over as chief executive of Kmart in 2000, he identified the company's supply chain as the main target for improvement. In 2001, he announced that Kmart was writing off $195 million of assets that no longer had value. This included $130 million worth of supply-chain hardware and software that was being retired and $65 million for the replacement of two outdated distribution centers. He also had to write off 15,000 trailers full of inventory, sitting behind the stores. The inventory existed because the management did not believe its own information systems.[5] Although Conaway got rid of the unwanted inventory, the inherent systems problems continued, consistently showing up as out-of-stocks and pushing customers away from Kmart stores.

In 2002, Kmart announced it would invest $1.4 billion rebuilding and refurbishing its operational infrastructure and implementing IT changes. At the time, its spokesperson characterized the investment as being "more money than Kmart spent in the last decade on IT."[6] While the statement was supposed to underline the big investment, it also says a lot in terms of previously anemic investments in technology for a company the size of Kmart—which had reported revenues of over $37 billion in 2001.

In the meantime, time had run out for Kmart. Their revenues continued to falter and the declining sales resulted in a liquidity crisis and halts in shipments from major vendors, leading the company to file for Chapter 11 bankruptcy protection on January 22, 2002, becoming the largest retailer ever to do so. In March 2005, Kmart was merged with Sears to form Sears Holdings Corporation.

CHAPTER EIGHT

Supply Chain Nirvana

Bringing It All Together

S O FAR, WE HAVE reviewed the basic concepts of corporate, functional, and technology strategies. Quick refreshers were provided on each of these strategies, including overviews of the current thinking on each of these strategies. While the work available on corporate and technology strategies sufficiently addresses the subject expectations, there is very little said about the functional strategies that connect the corporate strategy to the technology and are actually responsible for the creation of the functional capabilities of firms that provide them with competitive advantages.

I believe this directly reflects a lack of time or willingness to understand the close relationship between the functional and business strategies on the part of the practicing managers, who should be in a position to fill the gap caused by the absence of functional strategies. Functional strategies establish the business capabilities that must be built by the firm in order to achieve the goals of the corporate strategy by creating the desired competitive advantages. While a conceptual framework can be built to define the scope of functional strategies and the process to develop one, the actual strategy for specific business functions, including the supply chain, requires a deep knowledge of both the business function and the business objectives of the firm. The lack of resources with such deep process knowledge in various enterprise functions is another major reason for such thin coverage of the subject. It is also necessary to keep a clear perspective of which decisions belong to the business strategy and which belong to the functional strategies. The decisions at the business strategy level must drive the evolution of all functional capabilities, while those of functional strategies simply drive the evolution of such capabilities. This distinction between the business strategy and functional strategy is specifically lost for the supply chain business function. This is obvious in the discussion on the supply chain strategy in Chapter 3, where the existing literature on the supply chain strategy falls short because it is unable to grasp these boundaries and portrays as supply chain strategies what must be seen on a higher level as the business strategy.

To refresh the discussion on strategy so far, let us review the definition once again. A business strategy identifies the differentiators that will position the firm competitively. A functional strategy identifies capabilities that will create the differentiators sought by the business strategy. A technology strategy identifies the technology that will support the functional capabilities required to create the competitive differentiators targeted by the business strategy.

This summary describes the direct links that the three strategies have with each other. It also clearly establishes the *driver* and the *driven* relationships. Business strategy establishes the corporate goals that drive the functional capabilities required by the firm, which typically drive the technology required. Figure 8.1 shows this *top-down view*.

In a *bottom-up view*, the technology at the bottom provides the foundation upon which the functional capabilities are built, which creates the competitive

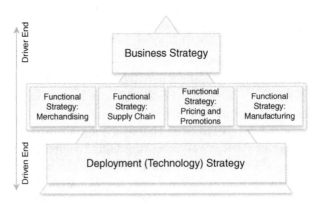

FIGURE 8.1 Top-Down View of Business, Functional, and Deployment Strategies

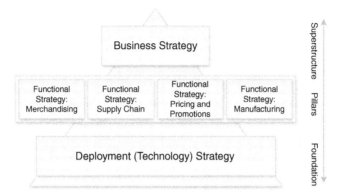

FIGURE 8.2 Bottom-Up View of Business, Functional, and Deployment Strategies

advantages required to achieve the corporate goals. This view clearly reinforces the top-down view but also establishes the *nature* of each of these strategies. Extending the architectural paradigm, if the firm was a building, then one could say that the technology forms the foundation, the functional strategies form the load-bearing structure or the pillars, and the business strategy forms the shiny superstructure of this building. The analogy goes further, just like the super-structure makes the building viable but depends on the pillars to provide the structural rigidity and the foundation for stability; the business strategy makes the corporation viable, but depends on the functional strategy for process capability and technology as the underlying infrastructure. This is represented in Figure 8.2.

With these conceptual visualizations and the arguments presented earlier, it is clear that unless the three strategies are designed together to support and leverage each other, there really is no hope for supply chain nirvana!

WHAT IS SUPPLY CHAIN NIRVANA?

This seems like a logical question for a chapter with this title. Nirvana typically denotes a state of simultaneous stability and dynamic equilibrium which is at peace with oneself and the world. It also denotes a complete awareness of self and the world outside. In the context of supply chain, it typifies a supply chain that is similarly stable, but also in dynamic equilibrium as it reacts to the changes within and outside the firm, and a supply chain that is fully aware of these changes and its capabilities to react to these changes.

It requires being aware of questions like these. What is the ideal supply chain that the firm needs? What capabilities will this supply chain have? How will these capabilities serve the corporation's strategic needs? How should they decide what capabilities are more important than others? How should they prioritize and sequence the creation of such capabilities? How should they implement them? How does technology play a part in it? What about the business goals? How does the corporate strategy affect the supply chain capabilities and how do supply chain capabilities affect the corporate strategy in turn? How can supply chain enable realization of the business goals? These are not simple questions to answer, because they require a deep understanding of the purpose of the supply chain in the context of firm's business.

In an ideal world, a supply chain should maintain a stable state of flows from demand to supply with optimal labor, optimal resources, optimal inventories, an ability to change course as demand or supply changes, never out of stock, with perfect order fulfillment, and yet providing the industry's best metrics on inventory turnover, costs of operations, return on assets, and so on. This supply chain should not be isolated, but a part of a larger community supply chain that enables it to collaborate, react, realign, and optimize continuously. It will be great for the supply chain to have the ability to run on autopilot and self-correct whenever imbalances are encountered between supply and demand, and resources and work. It may be able to report on itself, point exceptions, raise alerts, and let the users know when they need to intervene and how and what is expected from such intervention. In short the desired result is a perfectly balanced, optimized, and visible supply chain that seldom needs attention and where all partners are always aware of changes happening in real-time, automatically responding to such changes without any constant need to manually intervene and correct their processes.

Even if all of this was possible, should all companies pursue all these capabilities? Since creating these capabilities is expensive, they must be prioritized in the order of the competitive advantages they create. How can a company decide what capabilities are required for them to survive, to compete, and to have an advantage over its peers? How do they determine this and prioritize investments into creating these capabilities? What is the best supply chain strategy for a company and how should it be defined? Since supply chains extend beyond the company's four walls, but still affect their operations, what is the scope of a well-designed supply chain? What kind of collaboration and partnership must exist for creating competitive advantages through supply chain? Can a supply chain as idealized above be possible or even desirable?

What is it that a corporation's supply chain must be able to do for it to become a strategic asset rather than remaining a set of operational processes? Is there such a thing as supply chain nirvana?

The answer is just as philosophic as the question. A corporate supply chain must be able to do all of the above or none of it. It should be agile but also lean, it should be demand-driven but also supply-aware, it should help lower costs but also raise efficiency. The fact is that a lot of the success metrics that we relate with the supply chains are opposites, and so are the demands placed on the supply chains. *That is why there is no right supply chain prescription—it is right for you if it works for you.* In this context there really is no common picture of an ideal supply chain or supply chain nirvana, rather, it is a private affair, a private picture, a personal destination that every company must define and pursue for itself.

DEFINING A SUPPLY CHAIN STRATEGY THAT WORKS

In defining a supply chain strategy that is right for the firm, a firm may draw from the community resources for research, innovation, and solutions, but must define for itself the destination in terms of supply chain capabilities that are aligned with its larger corporate strategy. The reason that every corporation must define its own supply chain strategy is that supply chains have an extremely large footprint, they affect a lot of operational and planning areas in any firm, and can be leveraged in numerous ways to achieve the goals that the firms seeks from its supply chain. The definition of the "right" supply chain varies by the company asking the question. What is right for one corporation may not be so desirable for another.

These differences may not be obvious when the supply chain functions are looked at as aggregates. After all, all supply chains must support common business processes like demand and supply planning, or transportation and warehousing. These business processes also are common across most industries and industry segments. So why should supply chains for these firms be different? Why should there not be one "right" supply chain? The answer lies in the fact that differences in supply chains arise only when one dives into details from the aggregate functional views. Just as Porter mentioned in his research on corporate strategy that the business of a firm may look similar to another's when seen in aggregate, but differences arise when the business is dissected and specifics are magnified, the functions of supply chains also behave in a similar fashion.

Let us review this with an example. The supply chain for a generic retailer, for example, simply has the three basic generic business functions of Buy, Distribute, and Sell. However, when one starts expanding the underlying functions and specific operations, there will hardly be any similarity between any two retailers. As retailers, they do share some similarities, but on a day-to-day operational basis, they are most likely very different from each other. The logic that the Macy's warehouse supervisor follows when confronted with short supplies in the warehouse will be definitely different from the logic followed by a supervisor at a Ross warehouse. These differences arise due to the differences in their business models: after all, Macy's customers expect to see similar assortments in all stores while Ross's customers expect to see unique one-time assortments that may never be repeated. These differences can be a result of explicitly designed capability that can be leveraged as a unique strength and converted into competitive advantage or may simply be the legacy of a historical process constraint that has become a habit.

Therefore, such functional differences become obvious only when the functions are decomposed into their constituent subfunctions, individual processes, tasks, transactions, and parameters. For example, dissecting the "buy" function for a retailer will definitely lead us to the subfunctions of merchandising plans, assortments, sourcing, demand planning, supply planning and purchasing. A casual glance at the assortment at Macy's and Ross will be enough for one to know that while both firms have capabilities developed in the identical business functions mentioned here, they conduct those functions in a very different manner. Ross follows a more opportunistic model for its assortment (which is driven more from the supply side of the equation), while Macy's main assortment is fixed (though seasonal) and lends itself to long-term planning driven from the demand side of the equation. Therefore, while both the retailers will have to develop capabilities in the identical business functions of merchandising, assortment planning, sourcing, demand planning, supply planning, and purchasing, the similarities simply end there. Their criteria for measuring the effectiveness of their business functions will be different, their expectations from these functions will be different, and the critical importance of these business functions to each of them will also be different for these retailers.

Therefore, while the major functions supported by a supply chain remain the same across corporations and even across industries, their individual processes differ. These differences in processes become obvious at different levels of granularity and they may have different origins as well. Some of these differences arise simply because firms have always done business in a certain way and history becomes a habit, while other differences may exist by design to provide the firm with explicit process advantages.

Consider a simple example: While everyone uses a purchase order to buy materials and merchandise from their vendors, rarely will two firms process their purchase orders in exactly the same manner. They may have different approval processes, different requirements for the vendor acknowledgement, different compliance expectations, and different cost-allocation procedures when the invoices come due. The demand forecasting parameters, inventory planning algorithms, replenishment policies, and product allocation process when supplies are low, shipment creation, shipment track and trace—almost every process will have nuances that are specific to a corporation. That is why the solution providers have such a tough time building applications that can be uniformly adopted across the wide spectrum of their customers. That is also the reason why, in spite of having thousands of configuration options that change the behavior of commercial-off-the-shelf (COTS) applications, there is rarely an implementation that has no customization done at all!

To sum it up, it is this *specificity* of the individual processes of a firm that collectively defines the supply chain that is right for them. It also defines their state of supply chain *nirvana*, which is bound to be different from anyone else's. These *specificities* may exist by deliberate design or may have evolved because they worked in the past or may exist simply because of the firm's specific history.

When companies follow an explicit process for planning their business strategy and building business capabilities, the *specificity* is a result of deliberate design and action. In this case, these *specificities* exist because they were created to support functional capabilities sought by the firm and because they provide a specific, tangible, competitive advantage to the firm within the context of that function.

Numerous processes exist throughout the supply chain function providing companies with the opportunities to do something that is uniquely valuable in their situation and cannot be easily replicated even when the competition might catch up with the general concept. But these opportunities are visible only to those firms that are fully aware of their own business strategy and who wish to pursue this unabashedly in their pursuit to create competitive advantages. The following three principles emerge for creating an effective supply chain strategy:

WAL-MART: **COMPETITIVE ADVANTAGE THROUGH SPECIFICITY**

Wal-Mart's process to allocate supplies from their cross-docking facilities using the latest known demand in stores is a functional capability that has proved to be a distinct competitive advantage for Wal-Mart. It allows them to reduce their inventory and distribution costs and reduces the replenishment lead-time for their stores. But diving deeper into the capability, the *specificities* of the process arise in algorithms used for allocation when the supplies are more or less than required. Which stores should get more, who should go without, who must deal with excess inventory on the store floor? The actual logic involved in this process is what makes it *specific* to Wal-Mart, even when others would undoubtedly replicate roughly similar cross-docking capabilities over time. The *specificity* also arises due to Wal-Mart's unique combination of business systems such as demand forecasting and inventory planning that support this cross-docking capability. This unique combination of business systems and their capabilities is another source of competitive advantage for Wal-Mart that is hard to replicate, since these business systems are so unique to the firm. It is this *specificity* in the processes that makes it unique and extends the life of the competitive advantage for Wal-Mart. Therefore, when *specificity* is the result of deliberate thinking and design, it adds to the strategy's value by enabling it to create, sustain, or extend a unique competitive advantage.

1. Be aware of the functional capabilities needed by the business strategies.
2. Design the *specificities* that must be built into the processes to create competitive advantages.
3. Deploy the solutions to enable the processes aligned with the technology strategy to make them sustainable.

Therefore an effective supply chain strategy must focus on aligning the business and supply chain strategies, designing the differentiators to build advantage, and pursuing a coherent technology strategy to support them— this is what we have termed *supply chain nirvana*. This approach produces optimal results for capital investments and explicitly works toward achieving corporate goals. Contrast this approach with the popular course that many firms follow in the hope that improved supply chain efficiencies will bring the

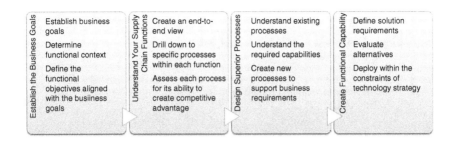

FIGURE 8.3 Overview of Steps in Creating an Effective Supply Chain Strategy

benefits they seek, without explicitly defining those benefits or designing their processes to achieve them. Without first understanding what is important to the firm's business, a successful supply chain design cannot be created to develop competitive advantages to help the firm achieve its business and financial goals. Creating and realizing the results of such understanding is the objective of the supply chain strategy and, to build one, firms must do the following.

Establish (the Business Goals)

This is the logical first step (see Figure 8.3). Chapter 3 makes a case that supply chain strategy must follow the business strategy. Unless a firm has established a clear business strategy that can be articulated for each business function that must support the business strategy, the functional strategy cannot be shaped.

Defining business goals means identifying what is important to the business. What does the firm want to do to make its business successful and profitable? It means identifying areas that the firm will focus on, to create their clear business identity and to compete in their chosen industry and customer segments. These goals will essentially be a set of statements that drive the firm's business and set the tone for the capabilities they must build.

Business strategy and the business goals set by it help the supply chain design in many ways. They identify the capabilities that the supply chain must build as well as basic principles and constraints for the supply chain design. The Wal-Mart example shows how its business goals drive its supply chain capabilities. However, this does not mean that having the same business goals will always translate into the same capabilities for all firms. The capabilities

WAL-MART'S **SUPPLY CHAIN: CONNECTION WITH THE BUSINESS GOALS**

To get an idea of the business goals, consider the following statements reproduced here from Wal-Mart's annual reports and other published material:

From Wal-Mart's annual report for FY2008: "Wal-Mart is very committed to a disciplined capital efficiency model as we continue to emphasize the Company's return on investment, or ROI, which involves balancing returns and growth," and "In addition to ROI, we remain focused on improving comparable store sales, inventory management and expense leverage. And, our goal of growing operating income faster than sales remains a priority," and " . . . we positioned ourselves as the unbeatable price leader."

Wal-Mart repeats some of these business goals in their annual report for FY2009: "We will maintain our focus on price leadership in every market," and "Our team is very focused on working to improve return on investment (ROI). Our capital efficiency process drives expansion decisions," and "Sustainability is a permanent part of our culture. It helps us remove waste, lower costs and provide savings to our customers."

These are part of the statements that would constitute the business strategy at Wal-Mart. How do these statements drive supply chain design? They do so by defining the goals for their supply chain to meet. The themes in these statements repeat, which is expected because they reflect a business strategy that must be stable so that investments can be made in building capabilities to support them. A volatile business strategy is clearly deficient as a strategy, because it will not be able to provide the stable long-term context for the business functions to evolve.

Now, let us see how some of these statements could have affected the firm's supply chain design. Price leadership is one of the consistent themes in Wal-Mart's strategy. There are several supply chain capabilities that directly contribute to price leadership. A good inventory management capability can reduce inventories throughout the Wal-Mart supply chain. For 2009, Wal-Mart reported an inventory turnover of 8.87 (Cost of Sales/Amount of Inventory). On inventories of $34 billion, every tenth of a percent reduction in inventories is equal to adding $34 million to the operating cash. Between the FY2000 and FY2009, Wal-Mart improved their inventory turns from 6.43 to 8.87, an improvement of over 40 percent (see Figure 8.4), which is roughly equivalent to adding $27 billion to their operating cash flow in 2009.

Creating a good inventory management function requires that the firms build capabilities to plan optimal inventory levels for every location where inventories are stocked, identify the services level for each of these locations, and finally build capabilities to provide inventory visibility across their whole network near or at a real-time basis so that system-wide inventories can be taken into account when manual intervention is required to react to unexpected situations.

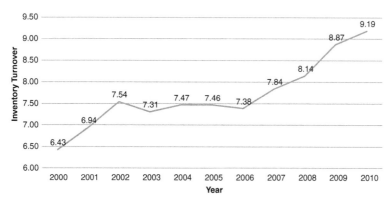

FIGURE 8.4   Wal-Mart's Inventory Turns from FY2000 to FY2010

Source: Data adapted from Wal-Mart's annual reports.

In fact, the capability of optimally managing the inventory helps Wal-Mart in achieving other goals as well: "return on investment" and "growing operating income faster than sales." Any reduction in inventory directly affects the operating cash requirements, making the operations more efficient by reducing the total amount of cash required for the operations.

Other supply chain capabilities that are helping Wal-Mart in achieving their stated goals are transportation and warehousing processes. Distribution costs typically constitute the second-largest cost for retailers, and optimizing the transportation expenses and investing in warehouse process automation can directly reduce this expense. Transport optimization increases trailer utilization and reduces miles driven, creating logistics saving. These transportation capabilities also contribute directly toward the sustainability goals of the firm, since they reduce the total miles traveled. In September 2009, Wal-Mart reported that they had eliminated 90 million miles in 2008 by increasing the

(continued)

(continued)

efficiency of their fleet.[1] This saved Wal-Mart $200 million in transportation costs.

The sustainability goals of Wal-Mart are sure to drive other supply chain capabilities as well, for example, the sourcing practices in which Wal-Mart is working with their suppliers to redesign packaging to reduce waste. This effort directly results in more efficient use of resources in packaging, but it can also increase efficiencies in distribution and stocking, if the new packaging affects the weight and volume characteristics, as well as enables recycling after consumption. It reduces the cost of merchandise and the cost of distribution for Wal-Mart. Additionally, it creates more recycling opportunities for its consumers and contributes toward Wal-Mart's corporate sustainability goals.

Each of the business goals need to be articulated in the context of the targeted business function to create the functional strategy and identify capabilities that must be built. Once the business strategy sets the direction for a business function, more precise and short-term measurable goals can be quantified for annual improvements that can be used for identifying and prioritizing short-term investments and project-phases.

Wal-Mart identifies the following corporate sustainability goals for its Logistics Sustainable Value Network (SVN):

- Achieve a 25 percent increase in fleet efficiency in the United States by October 2008 (2005 Baseline).
- Double fleet efficiency in the United States by 2015 (2005 Baseline).

By identifying logistics in the goals statement, Wal-Mart is also identifying the business function it is planning to leverage in its pursuit of its business goals. Notice that the higher level goals are long-term directives and do not enforce annual targets. However, the metric against which the success will be measured is clearly identified. Wal-Mart also defines how this metric will be calculated. "We calculate our fleet efficiency by dividing the number of miles we travelled by the average fuel efficiency, as measured in miles per gallon. This gives us the amount of fuel we used. We next take the number of cases we delivered during the same time period and divide it by the amount of fuel we used to deliver the cases. The resulting metric is cases shipped per gallon burned."

Clearly identifying and defining the success metric, Wal-Mart provides functional direction for its supply chain that offers several options to build the capabilities that can help the firm achieve the stated goals. For example, it can reduce the miles traveled and/or increase the utilization of the trailers.

These two factors can become the intermediate functional metrics that can be measured in the short term and more precisely to establish the overall progress toward the business goals. (Notice that Wal-Mart could also reach its stated goals by increasing the fuel efficiency of its vehicles, although this is an unlikely capability for Wal-Mart to develop for obvious reasons.)

required depend on the industry, products, and customer segments. For example, a manufacturer having a business goal to reduce the costs can do so in many ways.

■ It can achieve lower costs by inventing a new manufacturing process with a lower unit cost of production.
■ It can achieve its goal by finding a way to increase the asset utilization through better scheduling of its factories or by changing its tooling to achieve quicker set-up changes between batches.
■ It may reduce costs through a product redesign with cheaper parts or through simplification of the manufacturing process. It may mean finding cheaper sources of supplies that reduce the total landed cost or extending the existing supply contracts to hedge against rising prices of raw materials.
■ Or, the manufacturer may adopt a combination of the options presented here for achieving the cost reduction goals.

The options available for achieving a specific goal may drive the firm to develop capabilities in one or several different business functions. The choice depends on many factors, including its organizational strengths, available skills, extent and sustainability of the advantage created, and factors such as the cost, time, and effort required to do so. These criteria determine which business functions will be most suitable to create capabilities to support the strategic goals of the firm.

Even when the obvious choice to achieve the goals is to create supply chain capabilities, several options may exist due to the large scope of supply chain processes in the enterprise. Identifying the best options for investment requires a good understanding of the supply chain functions and individual evaluation of available alternatives for their ability to create competitive advantages.

But, no matter what type of industry, product, and customer segment a corporation chooses to compete in, the firm must identify their business goals to create effective supply chains. Only this alignment provides the basis for a successful design of supply chains that can create competitive advantages for the firm, rather than simply supporting their tactical operations. Establishing clear business goals helps in defining the objectives of the supply chain function in the enterprise. These objectives drive the process design and help evaluate the solutions to support the supply chain processes.

Understand (Your Supply Chain Functions)

The next step toward designing and deploying an effective supply chain is to understand the supply chain functions in the specific context of the firm's business. While the supply chain functions may look alike at a higher level, the differences appear when we drill down to the individual processes. These processes differ from firm to firm and are what makes their supply chains different. Understanding these processes allows us to assess them with respect to their ability to create competitive advantages and also helps to identify opportunities to expand, improve, create, or enhance existing processes to create required capabilities in pursuit of the competitive advantages. They also serve another important purpose: that of determining their relationships with each other and creating an end-to-end view of the firm's supply chain. Both of these aspects are important constituents of this step.

Understanding a function does not mean a casual listing of the functions in the business process or a vague understanding of how and where they are used. The purpose of understanding the supply chain functions is to clearly understand the *utility* of that function toward enabling the firm's business. Understanding must lead to the ability to analyze, evaluate, assess, and relate this function to the other business functions that collectively enable the business of the firm. That should be the basic spirit of this step.

This means that the firm clearly establishes what the function contributes toward conducting the firm's business. For every function, ask the following questions:

■ Is the function required? Can the firm carry on its business without this functional capability? What activities will be at peril if this function is made unavailable?

- Why is this function required? Is it required due to a regulatory mandate? Is this required simply to conduct business transactions? Is this required to make the transactions more efficient by automating or error-proofing it?
- What level of competence does the firm have in this function? Is it at par with the competition?
- What is the relationship of this function with the others? What other functions will be disaffected if this function is disrupted? What other functions must be available for this function to work smoothly?
- Does the function directly affect any of the business strategy goals? Can this function be enhanced to directly affect any of the business strategy goals?
- Does this function belong to a core competency of the business? Does the firm have an advantage by controlling this function closely? Can the firm get an advantage by enhancing this function?

Table 8.1 shows this analysis for demand forecasting. The analysis assumes that the firm is in the business of manufacturing and distributing nonalcoholic beverage that are sold through the standard retail channel. The firm has contracts with major retail chains and directly manages their products

TABLE 8.1 Functional Analysis for Demand Forecasting to Establish the Value of the Business Function for the Firm

Understanding Demand Forecasting for a Beverage Manufacturer and Distributor	
Is the function required? Can the firm carry on its business without this functional capability? What activities will be at peril if this function was made unavailable?	Yes, the function supports the outbound product shipments from the warehouse. Since the firm's business is based on keeping store shelves stocked in advance of actual retail demand, it is necessary that firm forecasts demand for scheduling shipments as well as for manufacturing. The outbound ship schedule will be at peril if demand forecast is not available.
Why is this function required? Is it required due to a regulatory mandate? Is this required simply to conduct business transactions? Is this required to make the transactions more efficient by automating or error-proofing it?	This is basic business requirement. Using statistical forecasting makes this less subjective to the user whims, skills, or experience. Automation of this function allows us to efficiently forecast demand for all the product-location-time combinations that we need.

(continued)

TABLE 8.1 *(Continued)*

Understanding Demand Forecasting for a Beverage Manufacturer and Distributor	
What level of competence does the firm have in this function? Is it at par with the competition?	This is at par with the competition.
What is the relationship of this function with the others? What other functions will get disaffected if this function was disrupted? What other functions must be available for this function to work smoothly?	Warehouse shipment schedule and production schedules will be affected if there is disruption to this function. The integrated feed of retailers' point-of-sale (POS) data on our products is vital to this function.
Does the function directly affect any of the business strategy goals? Can this function be enhanced to directly affect any of the business strategy goals?	It directly affects the business goal of not losing a sale due to stock-out. It can also be leveraged for enhanced brand image by being always available to the consumer.
Does this function belong to a core competency of the business? Does the firm have an advantage by controlling this function closely? Can the firm get an advantage by enhancing this function?	Yes, the firm must closely control this function as it directly relates to sales data which is sensitive information. Higher forecast accuracy and close collaboration with the retailers can provide competitive advantage, because most other manufacturers lag in these capabilities. The advantage can be further enhanced with real-time collaboration with the retailers' POS feeds, because that can drive down the inventory in warehouses without affecting service levels.

on the retailers' shelves in the stores. Therefore, the company is directly responsible for maintaining the products in stock and loses sales when they are out. For such a company, demand forecasting as a function will be an important business function as this capability directly affects their ability to keep their products in stock and therefore, manage their revenues positively.

The functional landscape of the business that identifies all the major business functions can be leveraged in understanding the supply chain functions as well as their relationships with other critical business functions. This knowledge is necessary for creating assessment scorecards for each of the functions evaluated. The actual deliverable from this step can be more or less elaborate than what is shown in Table 8.1 and the selected functions may also be more or less granular than depicted. The purpose is to create an objective picture of a firm's functional capabilities and identify those that are directly aligned with the firm's business strategy. As long as this objective is met, the granularity of the analysis does not quite matter.

The second but equally important objective in this analysis is to gather an end-to-end view of the enterprise supply chain, its relationship with other critical business functions, and their mutual impact on each other. Optimizing a single function in isolation is never a good idea and unless the impact of such a change can be evaluated on the whole enterprise as a system, such individual changes are likely to prove questionable. For example, consider the obvious case of sourcing decisions isolated from the rest of the supply chain: When the sourcing department decides to save costs by contracting for cheaper materials, it may look like a great idea; after all, there could be nothing wrong with saving some costs upfront starting with the raw materials. But this decision may affect the transportation costs, if this cheaper source of materials is located on another continent. It will also affect the supply lead time, thus constraining flexibility of the manufacturing or distribution operations, and may affect the manufacturing costs if the cheaper materials introduce any additional processing requirements or if they affect the quality of manufactured products. All these factors affect the total cost of this decision and, unless evaluated together, it does not become clear how this decision affects the corporation as a whole. However, such decision making in isolation and without considering their impact across the supply chain happens more frequently than one would imagine.

A real-world example is provided by Shoshanah Cohen and Joseph Roussel in their book on *Strategic Supply Chain Management*. Avon declined to label their bottles themselves for a long time, viewing this as additional cost and complexity. However, after developing an end-to-end supply chain visibility, Avon saw the opportunity in postponing the creation of its final product by placing the labels in the desired target language. It successfully deployed an idea that had been pushed out earlier, after understanding that this allowed them to postpone the production of final finished goods and better align their supplies to the end-demand without tremendously increasing their inventory.

Design (Superior Processes)

Earlier in this chapter, we discussed the process *specificity* that makes individual supply chains different from each other. We also discussed how these

PROCESS **DESIGN AND COMPETITIVE ADVANTAGE**

Consider Comcast's process for their customer service phone lines. As soon as the customer connects, an automated system directs them to enter account identification information and collects information on the type of help they would need. However, Comcast does not have the ability to pass on this information to their customer service representative (CSR) systematically. As a result, when the CSR comes online and requests the exact same information again from the customer, there is an immediate gap between the customer's expectation and the actual process. This not only causes process delays, but also creates customer dissatisfaction and distrust in Comcast's ability to address the customer concern. Of course, it makes the CSR's job harder as they must contend with explaining why they need to request the same information that the customer has already supplied. A simple but badly designed process creates additional costs of longer call-times, job-satisfaction issues for their people in CSR roles, customer distrust, and a general feeling of corporate insincerity. While the fix is simple, it will likely take Comcast time to address this issue, simply because the process was not correctly designed before deploying the technology solution enabling the process. Can this process, properly redesigned, create any competitive advantage for Comcast? To an extent, it will, because simple as it is, the capabilities of their competitors are no better and therefore, even simple changes like this can provide competitive advantages sustainable for some time.

process differences come into being. One of the origins of such differences is by design: when processes are designed to be better than those of the competitors, they have the potential of creating competitive advantages for the firm. Therefore, this step involves reviewing the core supply chain processes and redesigning them with an explicit intent of maintaining or creating competitive advantage.

Within the supply chain function also, there are several processes that can be evaluated and redesigned for creating cost savings or enhancing customer experience, thereby creating competitive advantages.

The scope of supply chain functions cover planning and execution processes and, therefore, reviewing, evaluating, and redesigning any of these processes can create competitive differentiators.

THE **BULLWHIP EFFECT**

When Procter & Gamble (P&G) pulls the point-of-sale (POS) data for their products from Wal-Mart, it helps them understand the end demand of their products better. Having a direct view of the end-consumer demand not only helps P&G in managing their production and distribution operations better, it also helps them to ensure that Wal-Mart shelves are always well-stocked with their products. But it also helps Wal-Mart by saving it the expense of creating forecasts and managing replenishment of these products. Does this create any competitive advantages for P&G? It most definitely does, because not many manufacturers have been able to create similar collaborative relationships with large retailers. It helps them in reducing the "bullwhip" effect that comes into play when more tiers are added between the end-consumer demand and the source of supply. The bullwhip effect causes plan volatility, resource leveling and asset utilization issues, and inventory mismatches resulting in stock-outs or obsolescence. By designing and deploying a superior process, P&G avoids or substantially reduces the results of the bullwhip effect on their supply chain.

Better planning processes such as the one discussed for P&G ensure that the plans are optimal, feasible, and stable. Better planning processes reduce plan-volatility, allow for better scheduling of available resources, increase asset utilization, and create feasible schedules for execution through constraint-based optimization. Planning processes may not seem to directly result in savings or differentiation; however, they control operations that directly affect costs and flexibility. The financial impact of P&G's planning processes may not be precisely measurable; however, there is little doubt that better plans help stabilize operations and enhance operational efficiencies for them. A below-par inventory planning process, for example, will almost always create higher costs related to stock-outs and obsolescence, even though it may be difficult to pinpoint the exact savings created by avoiding stock-outs and obsolescence by deploying a better inventory optimization process, because it is hard to predict which stock-outs were averted through better inventory planning. Of course, such savings can be measured in approximate ways by establishing a baseline and comparing the *before* and *after* numbers. The ability to measure the financial impact due to better designed processes depends on the nature of the process itself. For example, some planning processes such as purchase planning are quite capable of calculating exact dollar savings as a result of bid optimization, contract optimization, and so on.

Execution processes that support operations for purchasing, manufacturing, warehousing, and logistics also afford opportunities for creating competitive advantages. These processes can reduce operational costs through automation that enhances efficiency or improve aspects of customer experience by enabling flexible operations that can quickly react to changing demand or specific customer requests. Most of the time, the impact of improving these processes is most visible and can be directly calculated in the reduced cost of merchandise, manufacturing resources, set-up change time, handling costs, and shipping costs. For example, adopting a better process for building shipments for the inbound orders from the suppliers to the distribution centers, a firm can reduce the total miles traveled by selecting better routes and increase the trailer utilization by building better loads. Both of these will result in lower distribution costs for the firm, which can be passed on to its customers. Similarly, a better process for handling freight invoices and claims can also result in direct measurable savings.

Defining which process is *better* than the other depends on the context and specific expectations of the firm, because there is no *right* answer across the board for any process. While some generalizations can be made, the *right* process can only be designed in the context of the larger function. Several factors affect the process design: what happens before a specific process, what kind of information is available, what are the constraints, what is the objective, what metrics will measure the process effectiveness, what is the next process, and what are the information expectations of the next step. In general, while designing a process, look for improvements as follows:

- **Shorten.** Can the process be shortened? Critically evaluate the steps to see if all steps are adding value toward meeting the process objectives. If not, can they be removed?
- **Integrate.** Can the process be integrated as part of another process? A larger integrated process may be easier to manage, enable, and optimize. Look at the processes before and after the one in question and evaluate if they truly need to be independent or can be combined with each other for better flow. This is generally true when processes need optimization and an integrated process can typically be optimized better because it offers visibility into constraints across all its steps.
- **Automate.** Are any parts of the process so well defined that they can be automated? If a process contains a decision-logic that is well defined and

can be modeled through an algorithm, try to automate the process. This will not only make it more efficient, but also more objective.

■ **Error-proof.** Are there parts of the process that depend on user inputs? Can these inputs be error-proofed so that the user cannot provide invalid inputs by mistake?

■ **Visible.** Is the process transparent to the user? Can the output of an automated process be verified? Will making the process visible enhance the user's confidence and increase overall efficiency? A lot of optimization-based products typically operate as black-boxes, leaving the users wondering how the results were computed. While it may not be possible or even desirable to open up all such processes, opening up the parts of the process that allow quick assessment or validation of the results or a quick sanity check provides users with the confidence to quickly release the results and therefore enhances overall efficiencies.

In designing superior processes, remember that the processes evolve in their capabilities from conducting the basic business transaction, to bringing a firm up to par with the industry standard, to creating real competitive advantage. Not all processes will be able to evolve to the last stage; however, most processes can be made superior through simplification that reduces costs and increases efficiency, while some can be redesigned to create capabilities that are unique, inimitable in the short run, and create distinct advantages for the firm, and that is the objective of this step.

The Japanese concept of *kaizen* would be relevant to mention in this discussion on process. *Kaizen* is a philosophy advocating the need for continuous improvement in the business processes. This is true for the process design, which is not an end in itself, but rather a continuous process of review and enhancements in functional capabilities that create and maintain the competitive lead.

Implement (the Solution)

Of course, no process, however well designed, can start to create results until deployed. That brings us to this last step in deploying the supply chain strategy. Deployment of a process is likely the most important of these steps, because this is where the process capability is actually created. How a process is deployed determines its usage, efficiency, and its ability to create any competitive advantages designed into the process. To be effective, the deployment must fit into the natural flow of the user's workday. It should be integrated with other relevant processes and must provide the context before and after the specific process for which the user is responsible. No process is stand-alone, and not having the right context can make it inefficient and of questionable value.

For example, consider a user who fulfills the role of inventory analyst at a retailer. As an inventory analyst, the user is responsible for reviewing the output of the inventory planning function, which will typically consist of proposed inventory levels expressed as days of supply, days of demand, or absolute quantities. The inventory analyst is expected to analyze the results and quickly spot any exceptions to make manual overrides, with the objective of reducing future stock-out situations while simultaneously keeping the inventories within budgeted targets. A well-designed process supporting this role will require many capabilities to be developed beyond the obvious ability to plan inventory. It will require the ability to model supply chain network, forecast demand, compute the optimal inventory levels to provide the desired service levels, plan replenishment orders, and project the demand and supply picture into the future, so that the inventory analyst can complete his job. Notice the number of processes that must be enabled and work together to support the role of inventory analyst. The minimal interaction requirements for supporting the inventory analyst will be to provide a static report on the projected demand and supply picture and let the user review and analyze the data. However, an effective process will not only provide the projected data on demand and supply, but also allow the user to dynamically and interactively manipulate the data to define and spot exception, to drill down and conduct a root-cause analysis, to identify the root of the problem when inventory exceptions occur, and, finally, a way to resolve those exceptions or recommend and delegate actions designed to address those situations. Inventory exceptions can occur due to several reasons, such as demand volatility, supply volatility, constrained distribution capacity, constrained sourcing budgets, lack of supply contracts, and so on. Therefore, an ideal deployment of the process must be integrated with the demand forecast, planned promotions, planned replenishments, sourcing contracts, budgets, and any other data that may help to determine the root cause of an inventory exception. The extended and integrated processes help the inventory analyst to get the right context before recommending a course of action to resolve a problem. The deployed process must also enable a friendly user interface for interacting with the underlying systems so that it is easy for the inventory analyst to access the required information; relate it to the task at hand; compare it with past trends and targets; analyze, create, and compare alternative scenarios to evaluate the impact of her decisions; and, finally, resolve or provide the recommended action through delegation. This requires that the process is not only functionally rich but is also exposed through a highly usable interface to interact with the user.

That brings us to the following two principles of implementation best-practice:

1. **Integration.** As very few enterprise processes are independent, therefore, a good implementation must provide integration with other related functions. Such integration enhances process efficiency through automation, provides a fuller context for the information within the targeted process, enhances process visibility, and supports error-proofing through data and process integrity.

2. **Usability.** The second aspect of a good implementation is usability. Since most supply chain processes are data intensive, the usability of the implemented solution enormously affects the quality of a process and its ability to produce competitive advantages. Usability itself has many dimensions, from on-screen user interaction with the ability to effectively manipulate and analyze data to the ability to define and spot exceptions and trends to scenario creation and evaluation, and extends to the system's ability to effectively support on-the-fly computations, graphical representation of complex information, model scenarios, and manage large amounts of data in a manner that supports the user in a scalable and responsive fashion.

To the preceding list, one may like to add the information-access and audit functions, but these are primarily important to the enterprise from the governance point of view and do not directly add toward enhancing the enabled function's ability to create competitive advantages.

While the four steps presented here to define an effective supply chain strategy appear to be simple enough, they serve well to align the supply chain strategy with the business and deployment strategies. In spite of their simplicity, it is quite uncommon to find firms that follow the rigorous discipline of such an alignment; rather, most companies follow the easier, short-sighted approach that emphasizes crisis management and spends little effort on building process infrastructure that will support long-lasting competitive advantage. The result is a hodge-podge of supply chain processes that are not designed to create any specific advantages, nor aligned with the strategic objectives of the business. While such processes may support day-to-day supply chain operations, they do not necessarily create any competitive advantages or provide capabilities that can drive efficiencies in planning, operations, collaboration, or visibility. When processes are developed without any explicit thought to align them with the required business capabilities, without understanding how they relate to other processes, and without designing specific differentiators to create advantages, then such processes are typically not integrated or optimized, nor are they capable of helping the firm to achieve its stated business goals beyond the execution of routine tasks.

WHAT CAN A WELL-ALIGNED SUPPLY CHAIN STRATEGY DO FOR YOU?

The next logical question would be: what can a well-aligned supply chain strategy do for you? How does a firm benefit from an explicit effort to align their business strategy with the supply chain strategy and enable the capabilities through a technology strategy that, in turn, is aligned with the functional strategies? There are several benefits that such a strategic alignment brings to an organization. Some of them are direct and they affect the firm's financial performance. The impact of such measures can be calculated relatively easily. Others are more subtle and affect the culture and organizational efficiency, but their impact may be harder to measure.

When supply chain strategies are aligned with the business strategy, they create more than the simple return on investment (ROI) that typically drives the capital investment initiatives. They impact the business in ways that may simply be unimaginable in the past. They may create brand new options for the business strategies, thus creating new opportunities for growth and innovation. They also impact the organization by creating a visible synergy that invigorates the people and inspires them to be part of the organizational success story. After all, success begets success and people like to share the glory!

There are several ways that a strategically aligned supply chain will impact an organization (see Figure 8.5).

Business Impacts

When supply chain strategy is aligned with the business strategy, it makes the business strategy more efficient, because the firm's supply chain is specifically designed to support their business model and create the competitive

FIGURE 8.5 What Can Supply Chain Strategy Do for You?

advantages sought by the business strategy. It is no longer a matter of pursuing unclear goals using some theoretical best practices, rather it is a supply chain being explicitly designed and deployed to pursue well-stated and articulated business objectives. *In fact, best practices are normally just not good enough to create any genuine competitive advantages at all, but just enough to bring the firm up to parity with the best in the industry, because they are based on what has been done in an industry, not what can be potentially done.* (See the example of Cemex in the following pages to understand more about the best in industry and the potential for improvement beyond that.) Creating advantages means going beyond what has been done, which means thinking beyond the best practices. It requires an obvious effort to understand the business objectives, interpret them from the capability point of view to define an effective supply chain that would not only support the business operations, but will actively lead the corporation by creating competitive advantages and capabilities. As all resource and capital investments are made explicitly to create those supply chain capabilities, they directly help the firm achieve its business objectives with the most optimal investments and in the shortest possible time. The following are the business impacts of a supply chain strategy well aligned with the firm's corporate strategy:

- **Alignment of the goals.** A well-aligned supply chain strategy directly supports the business strategy, directly helping the firm to achieve its corporate objectives.
- **Capital investment prioritization.** A well-aligned supply chain strategy helps in establishing a transparent and effective method for determining the priority of capital investments in the supply chain initiatives. The initiatives that are aligned with the strategy and enable supply chain capabilities to create competitive advantages get higher priority than others. As the strategy also provides a long-term road map, it has constraints by design to ensure that all supply chain capabilities are complementary to each other and do not create islands of processes that cannot be extended or integrated as business objectives evolve or new opportunities become available.
- **New business opportunities.** As new supply chain capabilities are enabled, the business strategy can start leveraging such capabilities to benefit from opportunities that may become available as a result of the new capabilities. For example, a transportation management system that may originally have been driven to lower shipping costs can open new opportunities for better collaboration with the customers by sharing the in-transit information of their orders in real-time. This can provide the firm with a distinct differentiator, allowing them to pursue a new customer niche.

The new business opportunities created through supply chain capabilities can immensely change the structure, scale, and nature of business itself. This is due simply to the fact that supply chains extend throughout the whole value chain of the firm, affecting almost everything in turn and, if pursued in earnest, will lead to capabilities that open brand-new business opportunities for firms willing to expand their horizons. There are a couple of hidden lessons in this statement: (1) that the competitive advantages can come from any part of the value chain or supply chain, and (2) that any of these advantages, once created, can be replicated in other areas or used to drive differentiators in ways that may not be visible before the advantage is established.

Financial Impacts

The financial impacts of the supply chain help firms target and achieve the financial goals of the corporation through more efficient use of capital

CEMEX: **LEVERAGING CAPABILITIES TO CREATE NEW BUSINESS MODELS**

Cemex is an example of a company that reinvented itself, not once but twice, in the 1990s and later. Cemex was a local cement producer in Mexico that completely transformed itself from a small local player to become one of the largest suppliers of building materials in the world. While there is a lot more to the story of this transformation, we will analyze it from the point of view of the supply chain capabilities of the firm. In 1985, Cemex decided to divest noncore assets and focus on the cement value chain, most likely in reaction to the consolidation in the cement industry and its vulnerable position due to its small size. It needed to find the differentiators that would allow it to grow and compete in a new world when the Mexican economy was opened to foreign competition in the early 1990s. Cemex did this through *process differentiation*: in a series of process initiatives that were initiated by Lorenzo Zambrano, the company not only solved some of its immediate problems, but actually created new businesses based on the new capabilities.

When Zambrano took over Cemex as CEO, most of its manufacturing plants worked in silos, there was no information exchange, no standard processes, no metrics, and no way to do any of that. He started with investing in technology that would allow plants to upload sales, production, and energy data into a centralized system accessible to executives at the head office. This was followed up by more investments in enhancing the systems for manufacturing and distribution. Cemex's distribution initiative, named Dynamic Synchronization of Operations, outfitted their concrete-mixing trucks with GPS units and allowed Cemex to cut down the time for ready-mix concrete delivery to commercial sites from three hours (then the industry standard) to twenty minutes, in spite of Mexico's traffic gridlock, poor communication network, and often incorrect paperwork. Prior to this initiative, Cemex's customer service representatives could not promise delivery time with any real conviction, which meant missed deliveries, high customer dissatisfaction, last-minute changes to orders, and volatile demand. Cemex installed their own satellite-based links to connect all their plants to a corporate portal to establish reliable connectivity, invested heavily in technology to create capabilities for collaboration, operational measurements, manufacturing and distribution logistics, and eventually a business-to-business (B2B) portal for accepting and fulfilling orders.

(continued)

(continued)

While Cemex originally created these capabilities to resolve the problems of inefficiency and poor customer satisfaction, once available, they opened new business opportunities for Cemex which would not have existed, if Cemex had not embarked upon their business strategy of creating advantages through process differentiation and aligned their supply chain strategy to that objective. Creating these capabilities enabled Cemex from simply selling "commodities" to selling "solutions," which is a huge transformation for a mature industry like cement. Of course, it also takes an innovative mind-set to go beyond the conventional wisdom to evolve from the role of a cement manufacturer to a construction enabler. As Cemex's CEO told Stanford, "We understand our real business is helping our customers complete their construction projects." That change in the mind-set and the newly built supply chain capabilities enabled Cemex to start collaborating at an unprecedented scale with its distributors, in turn creating a deep distribution network for itself and a dependable product and service reputation for its distributors. The effort resulted in the creation of Construrama, which is a portal that allows Cemex, its distributors, and its customers to share information with each other on demand, supply, and distribution in near-real time. It provides access to technology to the distributors that they would not have been able to afford, on-demand visibility to Cemex, and a highly satisfying experience to its customers. In turn, Cemex enjoys a unique competitive advantage, strong brand loyalty, higher market penetration, and increased sales. Within a year of its launch, Construrama became the largest construction materials chain in Latin America. Until then, Cemex primarily supplied to commercial sites or distributors only and had very poor visibility into the end-demand. The capabilities opened the door to a brand-new business model by allowing Cemex to service smaller, individual customers in far-flung areas and create a strong brand for its products.

In addition, these capabilities also enable Cemex to reduce costs and charge a premium price for its services, driving higher-than-average profitability in the mature building materials industry.

initiatives while simultaneously building the supply chain capabilities that the firm seeks. Supply chain capabilities reduce direct costs affecting both the cost of sales and return on assets positively, and also reduce the operating cash required to run the business operations.

From the financial point of view, supply chain processes can be largely divided into two categories:

1. First are the processes that help increase efficiency of deployed capital: that either reduce the amount of inventory in the supply chain or reduce the replenishment lead-time. Examples of such capabilities are demand forecasting, inventory optimization, replenishment planning, collaborative supply planning, network design, route and shipment optimization, and so on. These processes reduce the cash that is otherwise required to maintain nonoptimal levels of buffers for inventories either in stock or in transit. These planning capabilities optimize the inventory in the system, affecting the cash flow positively, and go well with situations in which a business must reduce the cost of working capital or dependence on debt for working capital. It is worthwhile to remember that all supply chains need inventory and time buffers to hedge against the naturally occurring variance in demand and supply. However, advanced mathematical models and best-in-class processes together can reduce these buffers and the associated costs substantially while maintaining the supply chain's ability to effectively service demand.

2. Then there are other supply chain processes that directly reduce the cost of operations through automating or optimizing the process. Examples of such processes are transportation optimization that reduces the total miles traveled, increase the vehicle/container utilization rates, or shift loads to more efficient modes of transport, thus pushing down the cost of transportation. Warehousing capabilities that allow labor planning and scheduling, dynamic task assignment, and order-fulfillment planning can reduce the cost of direct labor in the warehousing operations. Automation of transactions for verification of invoices and payments to suppliers and carriers can reduce the administrative overheads. Similar automation can be achieved for purchasing, expediting, receipts, and shipping transactions, each one adding to the cost savings. Bid optimization during sourcing, contract negotiations using spend analysis and projected demand to leverage volume buying, and reverse auctions are examples of other supply chain capabilities that can reduce direct spend. Direct labor in manufacturing can be reduced through better planning, scheduling, and sequencing. Manufacturing models such as Dell's that allow just-in-time deliveries to the manufacturing plants with vendor-managed inventories can also save work-in-progress inventory costs, as well as affect the days-payable favorably.

Therefore, the financial impact of a well-aligned supply chain strategy is huge and typically falls in the following two categories, reflecting the same financial point of view on supply chain process just discussed:

1. **Direct cost reduction.** Some of the supply chain processes reduce the cost of direct labor and direct material and positively impact the profitability of the corporation by reducing the cost of sales. The reduction in cost of sales results in higher operating profit, sometimes also called gross profit. A higher operating profit drives higher margin and a better return on assets.

2. **Working capital reduction.** Other supply chain processes reduce the required working capital while maintaining the same level of service through more efficient use of deployed capital. This is achieved by optimal deployment of inventories and labor throughout the supply chain. The reduction in working capital required to run daily operations improves the asset turnover of the corporation, resulting in a better return on assets. Of course, the need for lower working capital also reduces the cost of borrowing such money, further reducing the expenses needed to run the company.

WAL-MART: **PRICE LEADERSHIP STRATEGY**

Consider the data from Wal-Mart: Wal-Mart has always followed the price leadership strategy since its inception. To support this business strategy, Wal-Mart consistently built supply chain capabilities that were fully aligned with its business strategy of being the price leader. In fact, Wal-Mart pioneered many of the supply chain capabilities in the retail industry. The consistency of their strategy and persistent focus on delivering it through their supply chain capabilities not only helped Wal-Mart to survive their competition, such as Kmart, but also to effectively create the largest-ever retailer in the world. Figure 8.6 shows the sales and inventory data for Wal-Mart from 2000 through 2010. The inventories to support rising sales increase in synchronization with each other until 2006, where the rate of growth in inventories clearly slows down, in spite of the continual rise in sales. This means that for every incremental point growth in inventory, their sales rose more than a point. Between 2008 and 2009, the inventory curve has a negative slope, which means that Wal-Mart managed to grow their sales while simultaneously reducing their inventories for the next two consecutive years of 2009 and 2010.

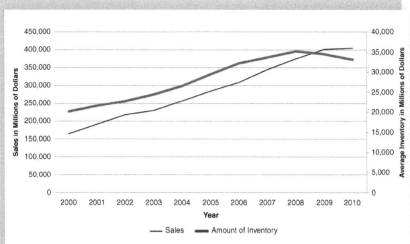

FIGURE 8.6 Sales and Inventory Chart for Wal-Mart

Source: Data adapted from Wal-Mart's annual reports.

The gross margins for Wal-Mart also show a consistent upward trend over the same period. Figure 8.7 shows that Wal-Mart's gross margins rose from 21.4 percent to 24.8 percent. The gross margins directly reflect Wal-Mart's ability to reduce its cost of sales and their supply chain initiatives supporting their business strategy.

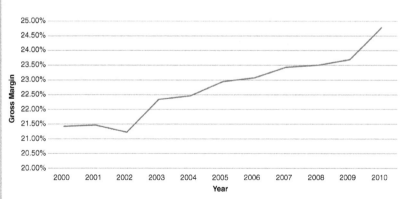

FIGURE 8.7 Gross Margin Chart for Wal-Mart

Source: Data adapted from Wal-Mart's annual reports.

Organizational Impacts

An alignment of business and supply chain strategies also impacts the organization. There are several benefits that arise from such an alignment. In fact, the organizational impacts arise as much from the discipline of strategic planning as from aligning the functional planning to business strategy. A well-established business strategy needs constant evaluation, feedback, and validation to be relevant as the market changes and emerges. This means that the firm must explicitly scour the external environment for changes (those that have happened and those that are potentially predicted to happen) and assess its own capabilities to evaluate its own competitive advantages. Such an assessment forces the firm to revalidate the objectives of its business strategy. Further, aligning their supply chain strategy with the objectives of the business strategy forces the firm to look for capabilities that are quickly becoming commonplace and will soon lose their ability to provide sustained competitive advantage. In turn, such an assessment creates an opportunity to evaluate other potential processes which must be enhanced to create and retain the competitive advantage otherwise being lost due to widespread adoption. A well-established process for strategic planning invigorates the organization by providing its people with the opportunity to be innovative and contribute actively toward the firm's future success. It impacts the organization in the following ways:

- **Reduced friction.** A clearly established and articulated business strategy sets visible goals for the business leaders to achieve. It helps competing teams work together toward the shared corporate objectives established by the business strategy. Since the capital investments are directed based on the investment's ability to create capabilities aligned with the business strategy, it creates a transparent environment where teams can work together without political considerations in making decisions. The environment fosters a team culture that thrives to achieve the common corporate goals rather than a culture promoting one-upmanship and individual trailblazers.
- **Shared vision.** When firms establish and share a clearly defined business strategy, it creates a shared vision and a common goal to achieve. It makes it easier for the functional teams to assess their own processes, identify the gaps, and define how their capabilities must evolve to support and enhance the business strategy. In the absence of a business

strategy, the functional capabilities of a firm have no clear path of evolution. This creates a vacuum that is typically filled in by "best-practice" processes that firms try to emulate from the industry. While these are generally accepted generic process guidelines, there are two problems with the so-called "best-practice" processes. First, they may not be "best" in the specific situation that the firm operates to achieve their corporate objectives. Second, these processes are generic and while they are good starting points and have the potential to bring the firm at up to par with the completion, they rarely suffice to create competitive advantages. This is due to the simple fact that these processes already exist and are well accepted in the industry and expected by the customers. Remember that to create advantages the process must be designed with a specific goal in mind and it is such "specificity" that makes them unique and creates the advantages for the firm adopting them. Creating this *specificity* requires a clear objective that the process must achieve for the *firm*. This creates an opportunity to innovate and the innovation creates the advantage that becomes unique to that firm even when their processes are based on the larger industry best practice. When teams share and understand a common vision created through the business strategy, it provides them with the objectives to drive the process design to create enough "specificity" in deploying a capability to create the competitive advantage.

▪ **Preemptive outlook.** Since the strategies are naturally forward-looking, a corporate culture based on strategic planning allows firms to create an environment where the corporate leaders develop a preemptive outlook toward solving business problems rather than reacting to resolve issues after they become problems. The process of establishing a business strategy requires a diligent effort to evaluate the industry, environment, and competition, and assess the firm's strengths and weaknesses in this context. Aligning the supply chain strategy to the business strategy, once again, forces the firm's leaders to assess the competitive landscape from the point of view of their supply chain capabilities. When these planning exercises are conducted diligently and regularly, the firm's executive team develops a preemptive thinking as second nature. This also establishes a continuous cycle of assessing the firm's competitive placement within the industry and its capability to remain there. This not only creates short-term advantages, but actually provides the firm with a continued platform for success.

Though the organizational impacts of strategy alignment may be harder to measure, they positively affect the culture by reducing friction and supporting collaborative team work. In a pioneering work relating the corporate culture to the financial performance, Kotter and Heskett[2] analyze the results of a large number of firms and present a positive correlation between the two. They analyzed the results of 207 American companies over an 11-year period to report that "firms with cultures that emphasized all the key managerial constituencies (customers, stockholders, and employees) and leadership from managers at all levels outperformed firms that did not have those cultural traits by a huge margin. Over an 11-year period, the former increased revenues by an average of 682 percent versus 166 percent for the latter . . . and improved their net incomes by 756 percent versus 1 percent."

Finally, how does a firm know that they have achieved supply chain *nirvana*? Is it a point in the journey or the journey itself? The answer to the question is simple: no competitive advantage is forever, competitive advantages erode over time; therefore, to be in a state of supply chain *nirvana*, the corporation must always be in motion. It is a vibrant, not a static, state. It is a state of continuous evolution. To be in this state requires that the corporation is continuously assessing (its environment), analyzing (its advantages), evaluating (options), and evolving! It is a state of flux and requires diligent effort and a conviction to be the leader, to innovate, to win. Others have called it adaptability, but no matter how one may name it, the fact is that markets are ever-changing phenomena and corporations need supply chains that continuously adapt to these changes to maintain the competitive advantages.

HOW TO GET THERE

Let us see what it takes for a corporation to get there. While most of the firms provide lip service to strategic planning, few are sincere about it. It shows. Very few companies have adopted strategic planning as a core discipline of corporate management and undoubtedly, these are also the firms that are the leaders in their industry segments. They have defined and elaborated their business strategies and deployed business models that have strictly evolved to achieve the objectives of their business strategy. Southwest Airlines following a *cost*-based business strategy, Dell following a *differentiation* strategy, Wal-Mart following a *cost* strategy, P&G following a *focus* strategy, and 3M with their *differentiation* strategy are all examples of very visible corporations

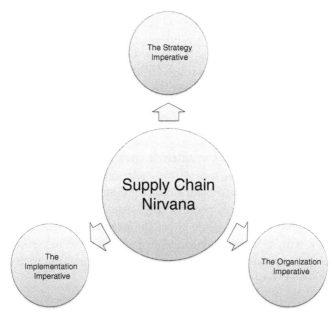

FIGURE 8.8 The Supply-Chain Nirvana

successfully adopting their functional capabilities to closely support the business strategy. Supply chain capabilities were only part of their success story, but these capabilities were designed to achieve the goals established by their business strategy and leveraged to create the differentiators sought. Dell, Wal-Mart, and P&G remain well-known examples because their supply chains are key to their success and were designed specifically to support their professed business strategies.

How did these corporations get there? The subject likely deserves a book-length discussion, but the following three ingredients, as shown in Figure 8.8, are crucial when it comes to achieving supply chain *nirvana*.

The Strategy Imperative

The first most important aspect is the strategy imperative: Does the corporation have a robust strategic planning culture supported by equally vigorous processes to support the strategy planning exercises? In the current Wall Street culture with the imminent focus always on the closest quarter, it is easy to lose focus of the long-term objectives of the business and the business strategies needed to achieve them. That is not only myopic, but it can be potentially disastrous. Strategic planning exercises provide the corporation with the process, tools, and opportunity to assess the changing environment and its potential effect on their business. It also provides them with processes to develop long-term road maps for implementing business strategies, prioritize such investments, and evolve such road maps as the situation demands. The following practices can help establish a potent strategic planning process:

- Monitor the changes in the external environment including economic, regulatory, technology, competitive, and demographic changes. All of these changes can create opportunities or destroy the existing advantages the firm has through its superior supply chain. Assess the changes for their potential effect on the business and the need for changing the business strategy. If such changes in business strategy are desirable, then make sure that the functional strategies are assessed for changes to their capability development road maps.

HEWLETT-PACKARD: ASSESSMENT OF THE EXTERNAL ENVIRONMENT

When the printer technology was still in its infancy in the 1980s, Hewlett-Packard (HP) started their product development and manufacturing facilities for the inkjet printer in the United States. As demand grew across the world, the main manufacturing facility for the inkjet printers was moved to Singapore. However, by the mid-1990s, when the inkjet printer technology had matured, HP simply outsourced the manufacturing of their inkjet printers. Each of these business decisions was based on their assessment of the external environment and its potential effect on their operations, and the changes in HP's business strategy for their inkjet printers triggered changes in the supply chain strategy and deployment as well. Also notice that these were preemptive actions taken in advance of the trends actually coming to pass with the objective to maintain the competitive advantages of the firm in that market. The continuous monitoring and assessment of the environment and corresponding changes to their business and supply chain strategies ensure HP's continued leadership in the target industry segment.

The example of HP also emphasizes the importance of making the changes to the business strategy first so that the supply chain and other functional strategies can leverage those decisions to realign themselves with the business strategy. Many firms do not understand the importance of establishing the business strategy *before* developing or assessing their functional capabilities and the lack of such understanding can only lead to redundant and conflicting capabilities and misdirected investments into efforts that don't directly contribute to moving the firm toward its business objectives.

▪ When it comes to strategic planning, take the larger view of the supply chain. Remember that the supply chains continue beyond the organizational boundaries. Identify partners that are critical to the success of the firm and its supply chain and consider their interests and incentives while developing the capabilities road map. While the internal supply chain costs can be controlled relatively easily, the total cost of the products depends on the total cost of the larger supply chain and directly affects the competitiveness of the firm. The same can be said about the supply chain agility and its ability to quickly react to changes in demand and supplies. Both of these factors affect the competitiveness of the business and, therefore, must be part of the strategic planning discussions. Such a view enables stronger partner relationships and promotes a collaborative environment where all partners share the objectives of the supply chain.

DELL: **THE EXTENDED SUPPLY CHAIN VIEW**

Dell's legendary *cash-to-cash cycle* numbers are achieved in part through an active and collaborative approach with its vendors. Dell shares the demand data with its vendors and requires them to maintain inventories in Dell's factory warehouses for the production of the computers. The inventory is owned by the vendor until it is picked up and sent directly to the production floor. Within a few hours of the inventory changing hands, the finished products are shipped to the end customer. In an assemble-to-order scenario like Dell's, this lowers the cost basis, which in turn allows Dell to compete on price. However, this is not a one-sided play. In return for stocking the inventory, Dell shares the demand with its vendors and guarantees to provide a certain

(continued)

(continued)

percentage of its business to every vendor in the program. The price and payment terms are negotiated on the projected volumes and the guaranteed uptake; and demand sharing provides transparency and trust among all the participants. It is the vendor's responsibility to maintain adequate levels of inventory to supply the production floor requirements or lose the fulfillment order, which creates an incentive to maintain good service levels. As most parts are interchangeable and can be supplied by multiple vendors, Dell practically gets guaranteed supplies for its raw materials, vendors get a relatively stable picture of demand along with a guaranteed share of Dell's business, and everybody comes out a winner. By pushing the ownership of the inventory till the last possible minute, Dell effectively extends the days-payable-outstanding (DPO) parameter of the cash-to-cash equation that finally leads to their negative cash-to-cash cycles. A negative cash-to-cash cycle means that Dell's supply chain does not require any working cash at all!

The example from Dell shows how the extended supply chain view can provide opportunities for reducing costs, increasing agility, and providing a collaborative environment where the risks and rewards are shared to create common incentives. Toyota works with its vendors and logistics partners in a fashion quite similar to Dell's, in which the factory warehouse is maintained by a third-party logistics provider to maintain the just-in-time supplies to the production floor while simultaneously managing the inbound raw material receipts to the factory warehouse. The production lines share real-time information with the logistics provider to enable the replenishment of the correct components to the floor just in time. If a production line hits a snag and stops, the delay is communicated immediately, to affect changes to the deliveries from the warehouse. This avoids inventory and work-in-progress build-up on the floor, promotes an efficient working environment, and reduces rework, scrap, and defective finished products.

Finally, active demand collaboration reduces the bullwhip effect in the supply chain. As end-customer demand fluctuates, the changes are shared without delay with all the partners and the whole supply chain is enabled to respond to minimize the impact of changes.

▪ As part of the strategic planning, identify supply chain risks and prepare contingency plans. Some of these contingency plans will affect the required functional capabilities that can take time to build. Therefore, such capabilities must be recognized in advance and must be built in as part of the supply chain processes rather than created during an actual emergency. As an example, consider supply disruptions that can happen due to several reasons, including natural disasters, terrorism, security threats, piracy, supplier's financial collapse, and infrastructure or process failure. While the supply disruptions can be effectively minimized by developing backup supply sources in geographically distributed regions, such alternate sources must be developed in advance and relationships must be maintained with these suppliers before they can be leveraged in a real supply disruption. As development of such sources takes time and effort, the strategic planning exercise provides an opportunity to identify significant supply risks and develop alternate sources for them.

The supply chain risks are not limited to supply disruptions alone. Other areas of the supply chain to watch for risks are costs, compliance, demand volatility, product quality, social branding, and technology. Cost overruns can arise from freight, merchandise, compliance, and operations and adversely affect the efficiencies. Compliance issues in supply chains are generally a result of international trade and the inability to fully grasp the regulatory requirements, but they can result in fines and the suspension of a business license in extreme cases. Demand volatility can result in lost sales or inventory obsolescence and can be a result of any of the several reasons including weather, economy, inaccurate forecasts, and other social or political disruptions. Poor product quality can result in recalls and liabilities. Branding issues can result from off-shore labor practices, intellectual property thefts, even controversial acts by foreign governments in which the firm has substantial business presence: all of which may require alternate sourcing, changes in manufacturing and labor practices, the relocation of facilities, and so on. Technology failure is another significant area of supply chain risks: a data center disaster can lead to devastating consequences by affecting the business critical systems that allow the managers to control and drive replenishments and operations. It can even affect business continuity if the scope and timing of the disaster is substantial.

Strategic planning exercises provide an opportunity to detect and understand such risks. They also provide for creating contingency plans and processes that can be executed if such a disaster were to actually happen. Without such preparations, most firms are highly vulnerable to supply chains risks that can prove to be fatal.

- Take the long-term view of the corporation's needs and have a consistent business strategy. While it may be tempting for top executives to change their teams and undo work done by their predecessors, unless there is a compelling business reason to do so this typically leads to the waste of corporate resources, a demoralized organization, and a lack of pride and ownership in the firm's stated direction among the managers, leading to unnecessary delays in building the capabilities needed by the firm.
- Finally, a well-orchestrated strategic planning process provides managers with an objective way to plan and prioritize the evolution of their functional capabilities to support the firm's business. As most firms have a limited amount of capital available for such investments, it is important that the allocation of this capital is based on sound planning and an objective assessment of the needs and expected returns through the invested capital.

All capital investment proposals for building capabilities should be evaluated to determine if the proposed function is core to the firm's business, required for regulatory reasons, or required for competitive reasons. Core functional capabilities are those without which the business cannot exist; an example of such a capability for retailers will be the ability to accept credit card payments. Core capabilities must exist for a

THE **IMPORTANCE OF LONG-TERM STRATEGY**

Among the many reasons leading up to Kmart's failure in 2002, one was the lack of a long-term strategy based on a proven business model. While Kmart started with the same low-cost premise as Wal-Mart, they digressed from their stated strategy several times during their long history: among these digressions were the introduction of private label merchandise, unnecessary store format changes, growth through acquisitions (Borders and Sports Authority, among others), and their tentative foray into the grocery business. Most of these initiatives were rolled back by Kmart's successive leaders, eventually threatening the firm's existence when it filed for bankruptcy in January 2002.

business to exist, and all businesses develop these capabilities simply in order to come into existence and survive during the initial years. The second group of capabilities that must be created are the regulatory requirements that a firm must comply with; for example, all public companies must publish their financial statements using generally accepted accounting practices (GAAP). These capabilities also must be built immediately because they can threaten the existence of the firm. Then there are capabilities that firms develop to be up to par with their peers in the industry segment; for example, consider the ability of a bank to provide online banking to their customers. Such capabilities ensure that the firm is competitive within the industry segment. Finally, firms develop capabilities that exceed the generally acceptable levels of functional competence and create competitive advantages for them. While the first three simply ensure survival, it is the last group of functional capabilities that truly allows firms to grow profitably.

The strategic planning process must enable an assessment of proposed capital projects in all aspects presented here. For the capabilities that will potentially create competitive advantage, it must also consider questions presented in Chapter 3 to ensure that the advantages created are aligned with the business strategy and will truly help achieve the firm's objectives.

LACK **OF CONSISTENT DIRECTION**

Quoting from the book *Kmart's Ten Deadly Sins*, "Few projects begun under one CIO were ever continued or completed under the next, requiring that work be stopped and restarted with each changing of the guard."[3] Once again, lack of having a consistent and articulated business strategy and therefore a missing functional strategy must have added to the chaos in evolving information technology as an enabler. In absence of a long-term strategy, it would be easy for the new incoming CIO to disregard the work already done and restart the project. Surely, this does not bode well for the capital investments in building business capabilities which typically take years to build and leverage, or for the morale of the team involved as they live through the volatile results of executive decisions made without an obvious reason to change direction.

The Organizational Imperative

Organizational structure is the second-most important step in achieving supply chain nirvana. The scope of supply chain functions and hence their contribution to the financial fate of any company is immense. Unfortunately, the organizational structures in most companies have not kept pace with the influence of the supply chain functions. Supply chain processes single-handedly control the largest number of components contributing toward the cost of goods sold (COGS) for most manufacturing and retail firms. COGS is alternately called cost of sales, cost of products, cost of products sold, or something similar. But, what is important is what constitutes the cost of sales. The following examples taken from the annual reports of some of the public companies present a good overview of the cost of sales:

- **Procter & Gamble (P&G), FY2009.** "Cost of products sold is primarily comprised of direct materials and supplies consumed in the manufacture of product, as well as manufacturing labor, depreciation expense and direct overhead expense necessary to acquire and convert the purchased materials and supplies into finished product. Cost of products sold also includes the cost to distribute products to customers, inbound freight costs, internal transfer costs, warehousing costs and other shipping and handling activity."
- **Wal-Mart, FY2009.** "Cost of sales includes actual product cost, the cost of transportation to the Company's warehouses, stores and clubs from suppliers, the cost of transportation from the Company's warehouses to the stores and clubs and the cost of warehousing for our Sam's Club segment."
- **Target, FY2009.** "Total cost of products sold including Freight expenses associated with moving merchandise from our vendors to our distribution centers and our retail stores, and among our distribution and retail facilities; Vendor income that is not reimbursement of specific, incremental and identifiable costs; Inventory shrink, Markdowns, Outbound shipping and handling expenses associated with sales to our guests, Terms cash discount, Distribution center costs, including compensation and benefits costs."

Now consider this: typically, almost all the components of COGS fall within the scope of supply chain processes (see Table 8.2). It also makes the largest part of company's costs, being 50 percent of 2009 sales for P&G, 76 percent for

TABLE 8.2 Most of the Components of the Cost of Sales Are Managed through Supply Chain Processes

Cost Component of COGS	Supply Chain Process Managing the Cost Component
Direct Materials and Supplies, Cost of Raw Materials and Inputs (for manufacturers), or Merchandise (for retailers), etc.	Forecasting, Replenishment, Inventory Management, Sourcing, Purchasing
Direct Labor, Cost of Transformation (production, manufacturing, processing, etc.), Depreciation, Direct Manufacturing Overheads, etc.	Production Planning, Factory Planning, Resource Planning, Inventory (WIP) Management
Cost of Freight (all inbound, outbound, and intrafacility transfers of material)	Transportation Management
Cost of Warehousing, Inventory Shrink, Obsolescence, Mark-downs, Handling, Inventory Carrying	Warehouse Management, Labor Management, Inventory Management (finished goods or merchandise)

Wal-Mart, and 70 percent of sales at Target for FY2009. Following are some of most common expenses included in the COGS and the supply chain process that can potentially optimize it.

However, very few companies have an executive dedicated to their supply chains. An AMR report[4] based on an industry-wide survey of 90 organizations states that only 38 percent of respondents identified a chief supply chain officer (CSCO) or equivalent executive vice president as their highest ranking official. Furthermore, of the 38 percent that stated they had a CSCO or equivalent, only 33 percent of them report directly to the CEO. This means only about 12.5 percent of the organizations they surveyed have a CSCO that reports directly to the CEO. Unfortunately, these results are not atypical.

Firms that are serious about creating and maintaining competitive advantages through their supply chains must establish an executive-level leadership for the evolution of their supply chain capabilities. Only then, can they start to truly leverage the supply chain initiatives toward achieving their business goals. Creating an organization headed by a C-level executive creates the credibility, organizational imperative, and the financial clout that supply chain transformations need due to their cross-functional and expansive scope (see Figure 8.9).

Such an individual would ideally have a cross-functional experience in business and technology, as well as across all supply chain functions from

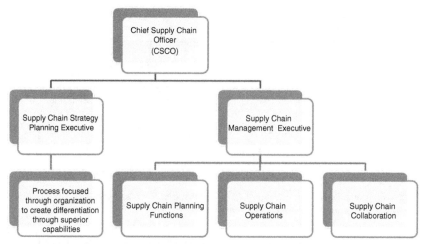

FIGURE 8.9 A Proposed Supply-Chain Organization with Integrated Operations

planning and optimization to execution and operations. A wide exposure across business and technology ensures that the executive not only appreciates the business imperatives, but is also familiar with the nuances of underlying technology and processes. Cross-functional experience within supply chain processes ensures that the individual is capable of creating an integrated supply chain vision and, therefore, deploying processes with enough differentiators to create competitive advantages for the firm. This is the chief supply chain officer (CSCO) role.

The CSCO should be ideally supported by two more senior leaders responsible for supply chain strategy and management respectively. The first position enables the organization to proactively plan, design, and deploy their supply chain capabilities rather than having them evolve organically as the business grows, while the second remains firmly in control of day-to-day supply chain activities ranging from planning through operations. As both of these positions report into the CSCO, it becomes easier to ensure alignment between the supply chain strategy and management, which is the key to successful evolution of the supply chains.

The supply chain strategy organization is responsible for continuous assessment of the supply chain practices within the firm, emerging functional needs, best industry practices, evaluation of solutions, vendors and technology, strategic supply chain planning, prioritization, capital investments, returns on capital investments, deployment and measurements of success metrics toward their ability to create promised competitive advantages. In short, the focus of this organization is the process and the ability to create differentiation through superior processes.

The supply chain management organization is responsible for day-to-day management of the supply chain functions to run the business. This organization is ideally organized by planning, execution, and collaboration functions all reporting to a single supply chain leader. An integrated reporting structure for planning and execution functions fosters internal collaboration and allows the firms to measure their efficiency metrics across functions rather than defining them by functional silos.

Supply chain nirvana is primarily a state of enhanced alignment between the business and supply chain strategies. Achieving this enhanced alignment requires an organization that mimics this collaborative aspect and may require explicit reorganization to achieve the common organizational goals.

The Implementation Imperative

While having the right strategy and the organization facilitate good supply chain design, it is the implementation of a process or solution that finally creates the planned capability. It is the implementation phase where all the strategies come together and manifest themselves through well-designed, well-engineered processes: either in perfect harmony, complementing and sustaining each other, or in eternal duress in conflict with each other and held together only through organizational diktat and technical wizardry. The implementation imperative for achieving supply chain nirvana is not very different from an efficiently run project execution that is completely aligned with the long-term strategy, derives from it, and feeds back to it, thereby mutually sustaining each other.

As more and more processes are enabled through technology, the implementation imperative becomes mostly concerned with the project management aspects of implementing the solution enabling the supply chain processes. It is a reflection of the discipline that the firm exhorts on its capital investments in their journey to create the supply chain capabilities. While the larger enterprises have brought such discipline and focus to the technology investments by adopting the concepts of enterprise architecture (EA), information technology infrastructure library (ITIL), and service management, most companies don't have any established methodology to control and measure the efficiency of such investments, even though the basic principles, as follow, are quite simple:

- Follow the strategic road map for development of functional capabilities. Make sure that all capital projects are aligned with the designed evolution of the supply chain capabilities. Also understand that the strategic road map for any functional area is not a static document, but is itself an evolving artifact that is revised in response to the changes in business strategy, existing capabilities, and environmental changes. Aligning the capital projects with such a higher-level plan ensures that the supply chain is designed rather than an accidental mutation of the one-time needs of the firm. There will always be business and process needs that must be addressed urgently and will digress from the planned evolution, but as long as these are identified as such and a transition path back to the road map is identifiable, such requests can be accommodated harmlessly.
- Develop a governance process for project reviews at predetermined stages of the execution. This ensures that solutions deliver what is expected of them and are still relevant to the business. Most companies create a gate process that validates the capital projects at several stages such as conceptualization, business requirements, solution design, solution development, validation, and implementation. Such reviews force the project teams to ensure the basic alignment of solution to the business requirements and its continued relevance in an evolving function.
- Identify the metrics that will be used to determine the success of new business capability. This is by far the most overlooked aspect of capital investments that create the functional capabilities for firms. Unless there are proven returns through improved costs, customer satisfaction, revenues, cycle times, or other measurable parameters, the extent of any competitive advantage created through a capability becomes questionable. By establishing success criteria in advance, the firms create a transparent environment for continued strategic investments into functions that deliver the most advantages. The metrics used in the success criteria can be calculated for a time before a capability is created, changed, or enhanced and compared with the values for the same metrics after the successful implementation of the new process or solution. An organization-wide process for consistently measuring the success of the capital projects eventually leads to an objective prioritization process and more efficient use of capital toward building functional capabilities. Wal-Mart provides a good example of the metric definition and target setting that was covered earlier in the section titled Establish (the Business Goals).
- *Remember that the technology simply enables business processes; it cannot replace or overcome their deficiencies.* Therefore, it is imperative to have a

business strategy and a functional strategy in place before selecting a technology-based solution to enable the business capabilities. If the selected solution is not custom-built, desist from unnecessary customization of the packaged solutions since it leads to higher costs of implementation, longer lead time before the system becomes productive, and ultimately higher maintenance costs during its useful life cycle. It may even prevent technology upgrades as the business needs to change, thus keeping the firm from innovating and growing as the industry around it evolves.

■ Since technology is typically the enabler for the processes, this phase also concerns itself greatly with the assessment, selection, deployment, or enhancement of technology as part of the implementation. This is where the technology strategy connects together with the business and functional strategies to create solutions that are well designed and deployed in a sustainable, cost-effective, and flexible fashion so that they can change and evolve in response to the changing supply chain needs of the firm. It is a good idea at this time to refresh the scope and objectives of the technology strategy covered in Chapter 4.

KMARTIZATION

In the book *Kmart's Ten Deadly Sins*,[5] Turner quotes *Computerworld's* Laberis, who points out, "The belief persists in some quarters that IT somehow can overcome failings in marketing, sales, or other key strategic and operational areas, when, in fact, it can't." In another chapter of her book, she continues, "On the flip side, sometimes Kmart goes overboard with customizing—modifying programs when modification may not have been necessary. Apparently, such was the case with its warehouse management system. . . . Kmart took it through its Kmartization process, which caused problems down the line . . . . Kmart has a culture of 'we're big, we're proprietary, we're different from everybody else,' so they had this huge group of programmers working on modifying the code. The result was that 95 percent of the customization was pointless because all the things were already being done in the system, albeit in a different way." Both of these depict the situations pointed out by the preceding principle—treat technology strictly as an enabler, but respect the fact that building and maintaining unnecessary customization in packaged technology solutions is expensive and inefficient. Be open to discussing changes in business processes to leverage the best practices designed into the solution by the solution provider.

Remember that not a single one of the preceding imperatives in and of itself leads to successful supply chain design and deployment, but together they create an environment of inquiry, innovation, and objectivity that leads to a well-designed supply chain function that supports the business and allows it to grow to its fullest potential.

KEEPING IT ALL TOGETHER

Supply chain *nirvana* is not a static state. It is a continuously evolving, but sustainable state of enhanced alignment of the supply chain capabilities with the objectives of the business strategy. As the business environment changes and the business strategy evolves, it changes the required supply chain capabilities and the expectations of the business from its supply chain. Since such change is frequent, therefore, the state of supply chain *nirvana* is an ever-evolving journey. The keywords in the state of supply chain nirvana are *alignment* and *sustainability*.

For example, consider the existing environment, which is heavily charged with the environmental impact of economic activity. A lot of this impact is a direct result of the existing activities in the corporate supply chains. While the social and regulatory expectations are still evolving to constrain the impact of such activity on the environment by controlling the greenhouse gas (GHG) emissions, carbon-dioxide (CO_2) gas emissions, and other potentially harmful industrial discharges into the natural environment, some companies have taken the lead and have started redesigning their supply chains proactively. This is a perfect example of how firms in the state of supply chain *nirvana* not only react to the changes, but proactively seek to change their business strategies and redesign their supply chains to support the new objectives of the business and build advantages. It is not uncommon for the leading corporations today to release their annual sustainability reports outlining their efforts, investments, and results for creating a safer environment through green and sustainable business practices. Most of these sustainability reports also mention metrics showing the total carbon footprint of the firm's activities. Some of the metrics that are calculated and presented in these reports, such as amount of solid waste generated or fresh water used were unthinkable just a few years ago; neither was there a perceived need to monitor these metrics, nor did the firms have any processes enabling such measurement, if one was required.

WAL-MART: **THREE CORE GOALS FOR SUSTAINABILITY**

Wal-Mart, the world's largest retailer, set up three core goals in October 2005: to be supplied 100 percent by renewable energy; to create zero waste; and to sell products that sustain our resources and the environment. As part of these efforts, Wal-Mart measures and reports their greenhouse-gas (GHG) footprint, CO_2 emissions, fleet efficiency, fuel efficiency, packaging, weight of plastic bag waste, solid waste, and several other environmental factors, most of which would not exist without this initiative.

While retailers can use GHG footprint and CO_2 emissions to measure the sustainability of their activities, other companies are pioneering different types of environmental reporting, such as those in the mining industry who track and report their water and energy usage.

What is left unsaid in these reports is that these initiatives affect their supply chains, which must evolve and change in response to the evolving business strategy of these firms. A large number of these metrics will require new processes to be established or existing processes to be enhanced for

VEDANTA: **ENERGY AND WATER CONSERVATION**

Vedanta, a global metals and mining company also releases annual sustainability reports. In their 2009 report,[6] the company states that "Conservation of natural resources is a fundamental tenet. We are conscious, and are taking concrete steps with set targets at each of our businesses to use fewer resources. Our performance on energy and water conservation has been promising and even beyond targets in some instances, which are detailed in the report. This will continue to be a key area of focus in the coming years too." They also report metrics such as water consumption, energy consumption, and industrial residue recycling.

capturing the required data and then improve upon them through a better process. These improved processes may be based on better efficiency, alternate processes, alternate sourcing, collaboration with partners, better product or packaging designs, better materials, recycling, and so on. Most, if not all, of these improvements will affect their supply chains and will require the supply chain processes to continuously align with the business strategy and deliver on the new objectives.

That brings us back to the two keywords: *alignment* and *sustainability*.

We establish throughout this book the need for the alignment between business and supply chain strategies. In fact, that is the basic tenet of this book: without such an alignment, there is no supply chain nirvana. Given that, let us focus on the strategy of *sustainability* and its role in keeping it all together.

This sentiment underlines the concept of *sustainability*. No strategy is going to work, deliver results, or attract consistent capital investments unless it is

WAL-MART: **EMERGING SUSTAINABILITY PRACTICES**

Wal-Mart's 2009 Global Sustainability Report Executive Summary[7] includes these words from its CEO, Mike Duke.

I believe we're on our way to achieving our goal of making sustainability sustainable at Wal-Mart. We've said many times before that our Company would remain committed to sustainability during the good times and the tough times. There's no question that the tough times are here. And there's no question that almost every company, including Wal-Mart, is looking to reduce costs. But what you'll see in this Report is that we're not scaling back or even just staying the course in sustainability. We're expanding our efforts around the world. . . . The fact is sustainability at Wal-Mart isn't a stand-alone issue that's separate from or unrelated to our business. It's not an abstract or philanthropic program. We don't even see it as corporate social responsibility. Sustainability is built into our business. It's completely aligned with our model, our mission and our culture. Simply put, sustainability is built into our business because it's so good for our business. Sustainability helps us deliver on our

Every Day Low Price business model. Using more renewable energy, reducing waste and selling sustainable products helps us take costs out of the system. This year, for instance, we surpassed our goal of achieving 25 percent greater fleet efficiency. The savings from this and other sustainability initiatives translate into lower costs and low prices for our customers.

sustainable for the business. Any supply chain strategy must ensure that the benefits it delivers to the business are the benefits that the business wants from its supply chain, whether such benefits are financial, social, or regulatory in nature. Unless this is true, the supply chain strategy cannot reach a state of *nirvana*.

How does a company ensure that alignment of its strategies and its sustainability efforts continue to enjoy the blissful state of mutual benefit? How does it keep it all together? It all finally goes back to the three imperatives presented in earlier section on How to Get There. A vigorous process for strategic planning through a dynamic organization leadership and a focused implementation team will ensure that the supply chain strategy is closely aligned with the business; it evolves with the business needs, and creates the capabilities that are most relevant and efficient for creating the competitive differentiators that the firm is looking for. These imperatives together create the environment for continuous assessment of the firm's needs, competition, best practices, and regulation, and identifies capability gaps that have the best potential to preempt, bring up to par, and lead by creating competitive advantages through supply chain processes.

Therefore, a dynamic, energetic, innovative supply chain organization with well-established strategic planning processes and a focused and knowledgeable implementation team is the key to keeping it all together. Once achieved, the state of supply chain nirvana needs to be sustained through active, vigorous, and relevant action. That alone leads to a state of sustained supply chain nirvana, the goal of all supply chain pioneers.

An Overview of the Scope of the Supply Chain in Modern Corporations

THIS APPENDIX PRESENTS AN overview of the functional scope of the supply chain in modern corporations. Historically, supply chains were synonymous with logistics operations and primarily focused on transportation and warehousing operations. However, most practitioners today take an extended view of the supply chain and view it as managing all of their demand and supply activities from their suppliers to their customers. This view includes the planning, execution, as well as the collaboration activities required to support an end-to-end demand and supply management.

I like to divide the scope of the supply chain primarily into its core and extended functions:

- **Core supply chain functions.** The core functions of the supply chain relate to activities that are limited to within the four walls of the corporation. These are the processes that are typically covered within what is called the *supply chain management (SCM) space.*

    Examples of these functions are demand planning, supply planning, manufacturing, warehousing, transportation, supply chain visibility, and supply chain network optimization. These functions differ from those in the extended supply chain in that they are typically managed completely within the four walls of the corporations. While partner collaboration is desirable for these operations, it is not critical to their central intent. The data required for these functions is usually generated within the corporation and available without any constraints or privacy concerns. The changes to this data are governed by corporate policies and are therefore predictable.

While these functions generate data and transactions that can enable collaboration with partners, such partnering is typically beyond the scope of conventional or core SCM processes.

▪ **Extended Supply Chain Functions.** The extended functions of the supply chain extend the processes at either end of the corporate supply chain, and create the extended supply chains representing the partners and enabling collaborative processes where such processes are relevant.

On the supply end, *supplier relationship management (SRM)* complements the SCM core processes. The SRM processes add capabilities such as bidding, bid analysis and awards, strategic sourcing, collaboration, supplier performance management, supplier compliance, and supplier scorecarding. Most of the SRM processes are quite relevant to the core-SCM discussion because they control the supply risks in a supply chain. While the SRM processes do not directly affect the routine supply operations, they affect the supply risks by controlling the upstream process of bidding and sourcing, the operational processes of sharing replenishment and supply data, and the downstream processes of supplier compliance and scorecarding. Together with the core-SCM processes of replenishment planning and purchasing, the SRM processes complete the picture of the supply management functions.

On the demand end, *customer relationship management* (CRM) complements the SCM core processes. The CRM processes add the capability for quote and opportunity management, customer order and fulfillment management, returns and exchanges, customer collaboration, customer segmentation, profiling, and other customer analytics such as lifetime value and demographics, market-basket analysis, and so on. CRM processes may further support marketing functions such as pricing, promotions, targeted marketing campaigns, and customer support functions through call centers. Different industries need different types of CRM functions depending on their target customer, channels, type of merchandise, and maturity. CRM processes cover a large functional landscape and are typically beyond the scope of the core-SCM processes, although they affect each other and require substantial amount of coordination.

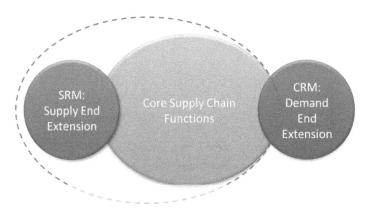

FIGURE B.1   Core and Extended Supply Chain Functions

Figure B.1 shows this relationship between the core and extended supply chain functions.

Another way to think of the functional scope of supply chains is to divide it into functions that support planning, execution, and collaboration respectively (see Figure B.2). This is simply a logical distinction for aiding the understanding, because these distinctions fade in the context of business processes that may extend from one to another for creating effective capabilities.

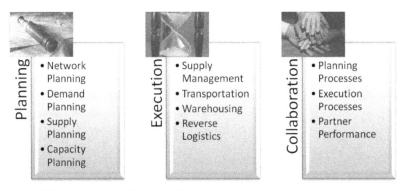

FIGURE B.2   Overview of Supply Chain Landscape

SUPPLY CHAIN PLANNING

Supply chain planning typically consists of functions that produce a relatively longer-term picture for future operations (see Figure B.3). These processes are designed to provide decision-support tools for supply chain managers. They typically have a longer planning horizon, and are modeled at an abstract level and at a higher granularity than the physical assets of a supply chain. The planning processes provide the ability to create multiple scenarios and evaluate them for specific metrics to determine the optimal plans. They are often modeled using complex mathematical models and solved for optimizing one of the overriding objectives. The output of these planning processes is adopted by the execution processes for action.

For example, consider the process of inventory planning. This process typically determines inventory stocking levels, ordering frequency, and order quantities at all locations that need inventory. A typical inventory planning process may be modeled at warehouse or store level, and needs demand and supply information in weekly or monthly buckets as the main input. Based on the user-defined target service level, this process can generate multiple scenarios for inventory deployment for minimizing inventory costs. Finally,

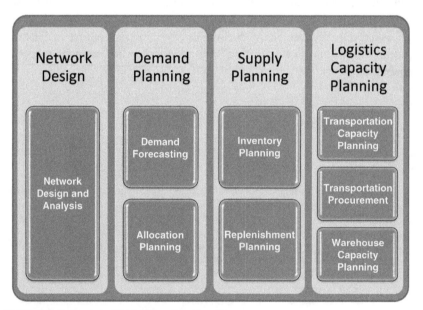

FIGURE B.3 Supply Chain Planning Functions

the output of the inventory planning process is adopted as an input to the replenishment planning process that provides the purchase suggestions for execution.

Supply chain planning functions include the network planning, demand planning, supply planning, and logistics planning processes. These are the processes that are generally used as a decision-support system rather than for supporting immediate execution. The output of these processes typically gets adopted by the execution functions as input decision parameters. For example, the projected replenishment needs computed by the replenishment planning process will drive the purchase orders created and managed as part of the replenishment execution functions. This relationship allows the operations of an enterprise to be aligned with its plans, making sure that the immediate actions help achieve the longer-term objectives of the organization.

The network planning processes help in establishing the network of nodes and flow-paths that models the physical supply chain for optimal cost or flow performance. Demand planning processes help in determining the projected demand that the enterprise should plan to address. Supply planning identifies the sources of supply to address the identified demand and establishes how this demand will be fulfilled, either through purchases or manufacturing. Logistics planning processes look at the projected logistics capacity requirements to support the demand and supply projections, and help the organization evaluate the existing routes and facilities and their capacities.

Most of the planning processes require a clear business strategy, clean historical data, and a good understanding of the modeling and solution constraints. As these processes generally do not have an immediate impact but help in aligning the operations with the long-term goals of the corporation, they may appear to have a low effort-to-value ratio. However, underestimating their value in providing cost and operational efficiencies is a mistake.

SUPPLY CHAIN EXECUTION

Supply chain execution typically consists of functions with a relatively short horizon and support immediate execution of daily operations (see Figure B.4). These processes are designed to create an execution schedule for the target business function such as shipping to stores, or production schedules for a factory. They typically have a short execution horizon, and are modeled to closely reflect the physical assets of a supply chain. In creating the best feasible plan of execution, they may create multiple scenarios, though these

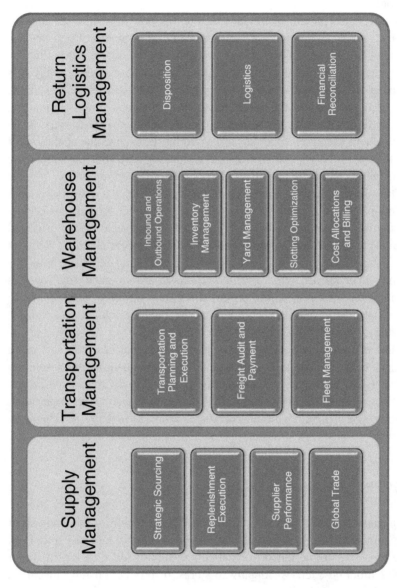

FIGURE B.4 Supply Chain Execution Functions

scenarios typically remain internal to the system. They can also leverage complex mathematical models or simple rules to create feasible execution schedules. Depending on the process, optimization may or may not be an overriding factor for execution processes. The output of these execution processes are activities that may create transactions for the host/enterprise resource planning (ERP) systems.

As an example of a supply chain execution process, let us consider inbound operations at a warehouse. These operations are typically planned for the next few days. They are planned based on the inbound purchase orders or advance shipment notices (ASN). The output of the inbound planning process for a warehouse typically is the schedule of receiving and disposition activities for the warehouse. The process needs to model the warehouse assets to the lowest possible granularity, reflecting the physical assets like dock doors, forklifts, receiving associates, zones, aisles, and locations for creating a feasible execution schedule. The process may internally use a set of decision rules to schedule receiving and for determining the disposition for the inbound inventory. Once executed, the process generates the inventory transactions that are sent to the host/ERP system.

A contrasting example of a supply chain execution process will be shipment planning for the inbound orders. This process also models all the relevant physical assets such as lanes, routes, transportation equipment, and modes, but typically leverages complex mathematical models to create the shipping plans. The overriding objective of this solution is to create a shipment plan that minimizes transportation cost and transports all the orders as required for meet the expected delivery schedules. The output of this process creates shipments that are executed by the carriers, suppliers, and receiving location (warehouse) associates. Once these shipments are executed, it may create carrier transactions for payments that are then integrated back into the resident host/ERP system for settlement.

As shown in Figure B.4, supply chain execution covers the following processes: supply management (ordering, manufacturing), transportation, warehousing, and reverse logistics execution.

The supply management functions help in procurement of materials and capacity that will be required to fulfill the immediate demand. For a retailer, this may be the management of merchandise purchase orders, while for a manufacturer this may consist of procuring the raw materials and establishing a production planning schedule that allows the manufacturer to fill the demand. Transportation and warehousing functions help in managing the flow and stocking of materials required to keep the business running smoothly. These two functions are very critical to a retailer's total supply chain costs, and are important for retailers as well as manufacturers to run their operations smoothly. Reverse logistics functions provide the ability to return merchandise to vendors, such returns being the result of customer returns, bad quality, vendor buybacks, and other similar reasons.

The vendor-facing functions of sourcing and purchasing straddle both the planning as well as the execution processes; these are shown together under the supply chain execution functions in Figure B.4.

These processes help in running day-to-day operations of a company, and are frequently based on the results of the supply chain planning processes. Such adoption from a planning process is highly desirable. It has two distinct benefits: It ensures that the supply chain operations are aligned with the plans, and it guarantees a feasible plan of execution if the higher-level planning was conducted with properly modeled constraints. As a result, the operational plans can be executed with minimal changes.

The focus of the supply chain execution functions is immediate; they create transactions as they execute the plans, and help in managing the operations smoothly. The output from the supply chain execution processes is very often integrated into the resident enterprise resource planning (ERP) system of a company as these transactions affect inventory, financials, and other aspects that the ERP systems need to know about.

SUPPLY CHAIN COLLABORATION

Supply chain collaboration covers the supply chain processes that can be best achieved through collaboration with the partners (see Figure B.5). Though active partnership is not a prerequisite for these processes, it can create huge process efficiencies if available. Examples of such processes are demand collaboration and supply collaboration. Active demand collaboration with the suppliers allows the whole supply chain to react quickly to any demand changes and maximize its ability to optimally fulfill this demand.

The scope of supply chains extends through the organization from the demand end to the supply end. However, the core supply chain functions primarily relate to the demand and supply management processes directly controlled by the enterprise. CRM extends the demand end of supply chains and provides processes for influencing demand by managing customers, prices, and marketing strategies. On the supply end, SRM processes extend the supply

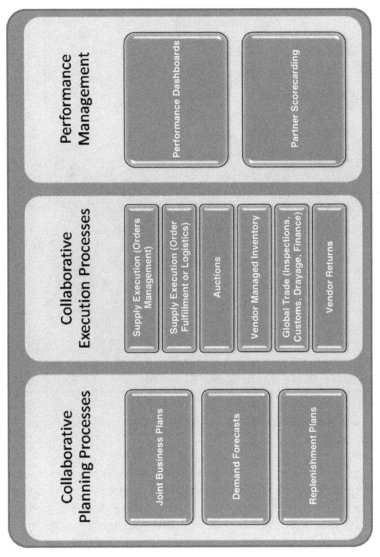

FIGURE B.5 Supply Chain Collaboration Functions

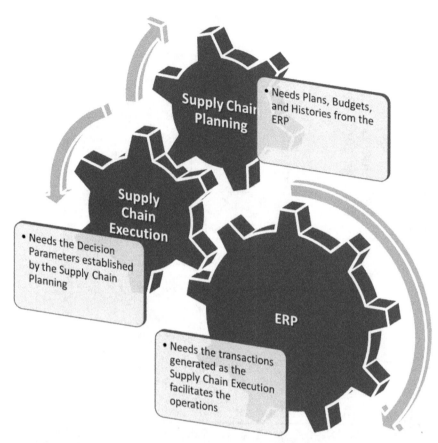

FIGURE B.6 Supply Chain Functions and ERP Systems

chains by managing sourcing and suppliers to ensure reliable sources for fulfilling the demand.

The core supply chain functions themselves can be viewed as planning functions or execution functions. The planning functions project a longer-term view of enterprise plans, allow what-if analysis, and provide the impact of these plans on corporate financial/operational metrics. These planning processes primarily serve as decision-support tools for managers. Examples of the supply chain planning functions are network planning, demand planning, and supply planning. The execution functions provide the schedule of daily operations, and help the enterprise execute the selected supply chain plans through purchasing, manufacturing, distributing, and sales operations. Examples of the supply chain execution functions are transportation and warehousing operations.

Even so, the supply chain planning and execution processes need to be tightly integrated with each other as well as with the resident ERP systems. The supply chain planning processes typically need the transaction histories, budgets, and financial plan data from the ERP system to establish the decision parameters. The supply chain execution functions adopt these decision parameters and help carry out the operations. These operations generate transactions that become part of ERP transaction life cycles. This relationship between the supply chain functions and the ERP systems is shown in Figure B.6.

Finally, supply chain collaboration processes enable sharing the planning and execution process data with the supply chain partners with the intention of enhancing the responsiveness and flexibility of the supply chain. Examples of collaborative processes are demand and supply collaboration with the suppliers or carrier portal to monitor and track shipments.

The Supply Chain and Corporate Financial Performance

UPPLY CHAINS ENABLE A very large spectrum of corporate planning and operational processes. In enabling these processes, they use various assets owned by the firm as well as material, labor, and capital. Effectively designed supply chains optimize the use of such assets and the consumption of material, labor, and capital to support the firm's business needs. As supply chains use several corporate resources, they affect corporate financials in several ways and optimized supply chain processes directly reflect on the financial results of the firm.

In their March/April 2010 issue, Supply Chain Management Review (SCMR) reported results of a survey on the relationship between supply chain excellence and financial results. The survey was conducted by Michigan State University and the authors analyzed the financials of top supply chain companies and their nearest competitors using data from 2004 to 2007. For example, the survey considers Wal-Mart as one of the top supply chain companies with Sears Holdings as the competitor (comparable company). The top supply chain companies in the survey were picked from various sources, like the AMR's Top 25 Supply Chains, Michigan State's SCM rankings, and other similar sources. The analysis presents some of the most convincing data till now, connecting supply chain excellence to the financials of the company.

Here is the summary: the companies that are considered to have excellent supply chain capabilities beat their nearest competition in the following financial metrics:

- They had 50 percent higher net margins.
- They had 20 percent lower operating and SG&A (sales, general, & administration) expenses.
- They had 30 percent less working capital expenses/sales.
- They had twice the ROA (return on assets), and twice the returns on their stock prices.

COST OF SALES

How does supply chain excellence produce these results? Because effectively designed supply chain capabilities can reduce costs all around. Let us start with the *cost of sales*. The cost of sales appears on the income statement right below the revenues. The difference between the revenues and the cost of sales is the gross profit. Therefore, the cost of sales directly determines the gross profit of a firm, and that is directly responsible for the firm's bottom line.

Cost of sales has aliases. It may be called cost of goods sold, cost of products, cost of products sold, or something else similar in connotation. That is not important. What is important is what constitutes the cost of sales. Here are some explanations from some of the recent annual reports from these well-known firms:

- From P&G's annual report 2009: "Cost of products sold is primarily comprised of direct materials and supplies consumed in the manufacture of product, as well as manufacturing labor, depreciation expense and direct overhead expense necessary to acquire and convert the purchased materials and supplies into finished product. Cost of products sold also includes the cost to distribute products to customers, inbound freight costs, internal transfer costs, warehousing costs and other shipping and handling activity."
- From Wal-Mart's annual report 2009: "Cost of sales includes actual product cost, the cost of transportation to the Company's warehouses, stores and clubs from suppliers, the cost of transportation from the Company's warehouses to the stores and clubs and the cost of warehousing for our Sam's Club segment."

▪ From Target's annual report 2009: "Total cost of products sold including Freight expenses associated with moving merchandise from our vendors to our distribution centers and our retail stores, and among our distribution and retail facilities; Vendor income that is not reimbursement of specific, incremental and identifiable costs; Inventory shrink, Markdowns, Outbound shipping and handling expenses associated with sales to our guests, Terms cash discount, Distribution center costs, including compensation and benefits costs."

Here is why the supply chain capabilities are important to control cost of sales: typically, almost all the components of cost of goods sold (COGS) fall within the scope of supply chain processes. COGS also makes the largest part of a company's costs. For example, the COGS compares to 50 percent of 2009 sales for P&G, 76 percent for Wal-Mart, and 70 percent of sales at Target for FY2009. Therefore, if one had to start looking at reducing costs, COGS fits the bill nicely. This is the largest pie piece of expense in an organization and even a small reduction in this will naturally generate a large impact on the firm's bottom line. Table C.1 shows some of most common expenses included in the COGS and the supply chain process that can potentially optimize it.

As Table C.1 shows, the major components that constitute the cost of sales are the cost of merchandise or raw materials, cost of distribution, cost of manufacturing, and the cost of labor. The supply chain capabilities that can help reduce these costs are as follows:

▪ The cost of materials, whether raw materials or merchandise, can be reduced through strategic sourcing, bid optimization, and supplier contracts-based optimization. Good demand and supply management practices also help in reducing the cost of materials by reducing obsolescence. Obsolete inventory typically results in merchandise clearance and write-offs, both of which increase the total costs of materials.

▪ Distribution costs primarily consist of warehousing and transportation. Supply chain processes that can help reduce these costs are network planning, warehouse management, and transportation management. The warehousing management capabilities reduce the warehousing costs through better use of space, better inventory management in the warehouse, automation, and optimized labor scheduling. Network planning can reduce the cost of distribution through optimal positioning of the distribution centers with respect to the suppliers and stores. Transportation management capabilities help reduce the distribution costs by

TABLE C.1 Components of Cost of Sales and Supply Chain Processes That Help Manage Them

Cost Component of COGS	Supply Chain Process Managing the Cost Component	Financial Metrics Affected
Direct Materials and Supplies, Cost of Raw Materials and Inputs (for manufacturers), or Merchandise (for retailers), etc.	Forecasting, Replenishment, Inventory Management (raw materials), Sourcing, Purchasing	Gross Margin, EBITDA, Inventory, Inventory Turnover, Current Assets, Working Capital, Return on Assets.
Direct Labor, Cost of Transformation (production, manufacturing, processing, etc.), Depreciation, Direct Manufacturing Overheads, etc.	Production Planning, Factory Planning, Resource Planning, Inventory (work-in-progress) Management	Gross Margin, EBITDA, Working Capital, Return on Capital Employed.
Cost of Freight (all inbound, outbound, and intra-facility transfers of material)	Transportation Management	Gross Margin, EBITDA, Working Capital.
Cost of Warehousing, Inventory Shrink, Obsolescence, Mark-downs, Handling, Inventory Carrying	Warehouse Management, Labor Management, Inventory Management (finished goods or merchandise)	Gross Margin, EBITDA, Working Capital.

optimizing shipments that reduce the total miles driven and enhance the container and trailer volume utilization. Better fleet management capabilities can increase the efficiency of the fleet and freight invoice automation can reduce the expenses related to validating and paying for freight.

■ Manufacturing costs can be reduced through better scheduling and factory planning processes. Supply chain optimization solutions that allow modeling of the demand, available inventory, available resources, operations, and sequencing constraints are typically used to produce feasible manufacturing schedules that can optimize the usage of assets and resources to produce manufacturing schedules that drive most profitable product-mix for the given demand or maximize the demand fulfillment for given orders. Increasing the asset utilization reduces the need for investing in capital assets, thus reducing long-term debt used to finance capital investments. In turn, it positively impacts return on capital employed by reducing the total current liabilities.

▪ Major labor costs for the retailers occur in warehouses and the stores, and for manufacturers, they occur in the factories. Warehouse management processes can help directly reduce the labor costs in the warehouses, by better labor planning, scheduling, and task tracking. Better demand forecasting in the stores helps in streamlining the labor plans in the stores. Manufacturing labor costs are minimized through better scheduling and factory planning capabilities that can model the material and asset constraints to produce feasible labor plans.

Any reduction in the cost of sales directly translates into increased margins assuming the other factors remain constant.

INVENTORY

As supply chain practitioners, we appreciate the significance of inventory in maintaining the supply chain flows and the service levels. Let us review the importance of inventory toward the corporate financials. Inventory is one of the components directly reported on the corporate balance sheets. It appears under the current assets and gets consolidated in the total assets of a company. Good inventory planning practices can significantly lower the inventory in the supply chain without having an adverse effect on the supply chain's ability to fulfill demand. This is typically achieved by deploying inventory optimization solutions that allow the firms to model their entire network, and the demand and supply at each node along the network with the targeted service levels for all the flows. Good demand forecasting capability forms the foundation of an effective inventory optimization function.

Reducing inventory reduces the current assets of a firm. A drop in the current assets reduces the total asset basis that translates into higher returns on assets, and it reduces the working capital (which is the difference between the current assets and current liabilities), which means lower interest expense on borrowings that are typically used to finance the working capital. Managing inventories through an efficient supply chain can produce all kinds of interesting financial rewards; consider, for example, the case of Wal-Mart. In the year ending January 31, 2010, Wal-Mart reported current assets of $48.3 billion and current liabilities of $55.5 billion. Since working capital is

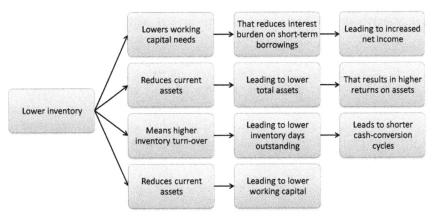

FIGURE C.1   Effects of Reducing Inventory on the Corporate Financials

calculated as current assets minus the current liabilities, this means that Wal-Mart has operations that produce more cash than they need to run these operations!

Inventories affect a few other financial numbers as well (see Figure C.1):

- It affects the return on assets (ROA). The ROA measures the profitability of a firm relative to the assets it uses to generate the profits. It is calculated as net-income divided by the total assets of a firm. When the inventories are reduced, the total assets of the firm are reduced, thus increasing the return on its total assets. This is also supported by the SCMR's survey mentioned earlier in this appendix.
- Inventory also affects the cash-conversion cycle of a firm. The cash-conversion cycle is a measurement of the time that the firm takes to convert its investments into return, generally measured in days as the sum of inventory days (days inventory outstanding) and days receivables (or days sales outstanding) minus days payables (or days payable outstanding). Reducing inventory reduces the days inventory outstanding— keeping the other two terms constant, any reduction in inventory will naturally result in shortening the cash-conversion cycle.
- Since maintaining inventory in the supply chain costs capital, any reduction in the inventory levels reduces the need for working capital. Need for less working capital reduces the interest expenses of a firm. The interest reduction translates into higher net profit, because the interest is deducted from the earnings before interest, taxes, depreciation, and

amortization (EBITDA) to calculate net profit. Lower working capital requirements also lead to lower short-term debt. Lower debt levels improve a firm's debt-ratio as well debt-to-equity-ratio.

▪ Reducing inventories increases the inventory turnover of a firm. Inventory turnover measures the number of times the company is able to sell and replace its inventory over a period. It is calculated as cost of goods sold divided by average inventory valued at cost. When compared to the peers within an industry, a higher inventory turnover ratio represents strong sales and effective inventory planning and replenishment functions.

There are several supply chain processes that affect inventory and help reduce total inventory in the supply chain while maintaining the fulfillment or service levels to replenish the stores.

Better demand forecasting, inventory planning, and replenishment planning processes together help in reducing inventory in the system. Good demand and supply planning practices with the help of the correct tools have been shown to dramatically reduce inventories. Any reduction in inventory directly reduces the current assets and positively impacts the returns on assets.

Supply chain network optimization can also help reduce inventory levels by optimizing a network that is most efficient for replenishing the stores. This is a one-time benefit, and as the supply chain network consisting of stores, warehouses, and suppliers continues to grow, the supply network must be reevaluated to keep pace with the changes. However, frequent changes to the supply chain network are impractical due to heavy capital costs and long lead-times required to set up distribution centers.

WORKING CAPITAL

Corporations need money for running their day-to-day operations. The funds required for the operations increase the capital requirements of the company and increase the cost of capital. Reducing the working capital required for running operations reduces the total capital requirements as well as the cost of finance. Reduced operating expenses are another direct result of a well-designed and implemented supply chain. Note that we are using the terms *working capital* in the context of capital required to fund day-to-day operations of a firm. This is different from the working capital as reported on the balance sheet, which is typically a snap shot in time calculated as the difference between current assets and the current liabilities of a corporation.

Earlier in this Appendix, we presented how supply chains can become an effective tool to reduce the cost of goods sold as well as the inventories. Another direct benefit of reducing the cost of goods sold and reducing the inventory required to maintain the sales is reduced need of working capital to run the operations of the corporations. Reducing the working capital enhances the capital efficiency of a firm by reducing the funds required as well as the interest burden to finance the extra funds.

Working capital reductions through effective supply chain processes result from the following:

- The cost reductions in the cost of goods sold components reduce the total capital required to run the operations of the firm effectively. This cost reduction directly translates in reduced need of the funds and the reduced cost of financing those funds.
- Lower inventory levels to maintain the given level of sales increase the inventory turns of the firm. Lower inventory levels also result in lower capital required to maintain these inventory levels. As the inventory turns go up, the days in inventory go down affecting the cash conversion cycle positively. A shorter cash-conversion cycle means lower operating capital requirements.
- Other supply chain processes like sourcing and purchasing can be leveraged to affect the days payable positively. An increase in the days-payable-outstanding (DPO) also results in faster cash conversion cycles consequently reducing the operating capital requirements.

As reduced capital requirements for operations primarily affect the cost of financing and therefore the interest burden on a firm, these reductions directly impact the operating expenses that are shown in the income statement. Lower operating expenses result in higher operating and net income.

TUNE YOUR SUPPLY CHAIN FOR FINANCIAL PERFORMANCE

For another view of the broad relationship between various financial measures and the corresponding supply chain capabilities that can directly impact these results, see Figure C.2, which shows the *levers* controlled by

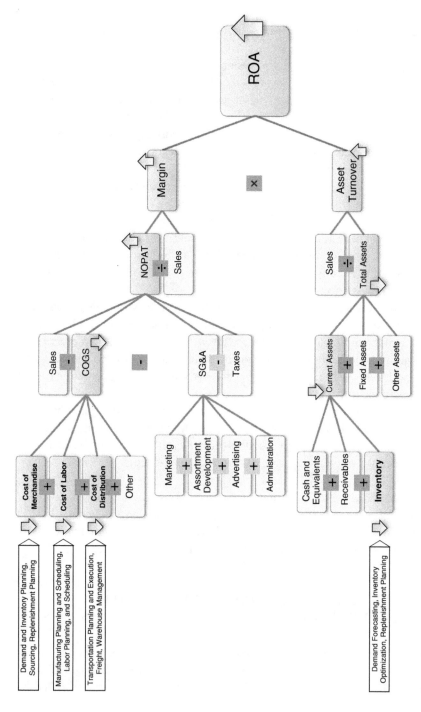

FIGURE C.2 Relationship between Operational Processes Managed by Supply Chain Functions and the Corporate Results

the supply chain processes and their impact on corporate financial as they get consolidated into the financial performance metrics. This figure presents a different point of view for understanding the financial impact of the supply chain capabilities of a firm. From this point of view, a practitioner can think of the supply chain processes as those reducing the cost of sales (in the top half) and others that increase the asset turnover (the bottom half). The supply chain processes in the first category directly help reduce costs, while those in the second category increase the productivity of the assets by increasing the efficiency of the firm's operations.

Starting from the left, for example, consider the costs of merchandise, labor, and distribution. Improved supply chain processes can impact each of these cost areas, which in turn affect the cost of sales that increases the margin, eventually affecting the bottom-line. Alternately, if one were to reduce inventories, they would affect the current assets and in turn, increase the return on assets. The figure presents a cheat-sheet for supply chain managers, showing what processes in the supply chain should be tuned to directly affect a selected financial metric.

Really, it is that simple.

Notes

INTRODUCTION

1. Charles W. L. Hill and Gareth R. Jones, *Strategic Management Theory* (New York: Houghton Mifflin Company, 2006), 160, 164, 174.

CHAPTER 1

1. Kenneth Andrews, *Concepts of Corporate Strategy* (New York: McGraw-Hill/ Irwin, 1994), 89–102.
2. Kenneth E. Stone, "Competing with the Mass Merchandisers" (paper presented at the Small Business Forum, University of Wisconsin-Extension Small Business Development Center, Spring 1991).
3. David J. Collis and Cynthia A. Montgomery, "Competing on Resources: Strategy in the 1990s," *Harvard Business Review* (July–Aug. 1995).

CHAPTER 2

1. IBM (Information Systems Division, Entry Systems Business), "Personal Computer Announced by IBM," Press Release, August 12, 1982, www.03.ibm .com/ibm/history/documents/pdf/pcpress.pdf (accessed March 16, 2010).

CHAPTER 3

1. Brad Tuttle, "Small Airlines Fly under the Radar," CNN, May 1, 2009, www .cnn.com/2009/TRAVEL/business.travel/04/09/upstart.airlines/index.html (accessed June 10, 2009).
2. Computer Associates International, Inc., Fundinguniverse.com, www.funding universe.com/company-histories/Computer-Associates-International-Inc-

Company-History.html (accessed April 12, 2010); Computer Associates corporate Web site, "About Us—History," www.ca.com/us/about/content.aspx? cid=120941 (accessed April 10, 2010).

3. J. B. Barney, "Firm Resources and Sustained Competitive Advantage," *Journal of Management* 17, no. 1 (1991): 99–120.

4. "Chevron Announces First Oil from Tahiti Field in Gulf of Mexico," Chevron Press Release, May 6, 2009, www.chevron.com/news/press/release/? id=2009-05-06 (accessed March 23, 2010).

5. George Stalk, Philip Evans, and Lawrence E. Shulman, "Competing on Capabilities: The New Rules of Corporate Strategy," *Harvard Business Review* (March–April 1992).

6. David J. Collis and Cynthia A. Montgomery, "Creating Corporate Advantage," *Harvard Business Review* (May–June 1998).

7. Charles W. L. Hill and Gareth R. Jones, *Essentials of Strategic Management* (Mason, OH: South-Western, 2008), 80.

8. John Kotter and James Heskett, *Corporate Culture and Performance* (New York: Free Press, 1992), 11.

9. Michael Porter, *Competitive Advantage: Creating and Sustaining Superior Performance* (New York: Free Press, 1985), 33–61.

10. "Investor Fact Sheet," Toyota corporate Web site, www.toyota.com/about/ our_business/investor_relations/Factsheet_FY09.pdf (accessed June 18, 2010).

11. "Forbes 2000 List," *Forbes.com*, www.forbes.com/lists/results.jhtml?pass ListId=18&passYear=2004&passListType=Company&searchParameter1= unset&searchParameter2=unset&resultsStart=1&resultsHowMany=100& resultsSortProperties=%2Bnumberfield1%2C%2Bstringfield2&resultsSort CategoryName=rank&passKeyword=&category1=category&category2= category&fromColumnClick=true (accessed June 18, 2010).

12. Kendra Marr, "Toyota Passes General Motors as World's Largest Carmaker," *Washington Post*, January 22, 2009, www.washingtonpost.com/wp-dyn/ content/article/2009/01/21/AR2009012101216.html (accessed June 18, 2010).

13. "Auto Sales," *Wall Street Journal*, June 2, 2010, http://online.wsj.com/mdc/ public/page/2_3022-autosales.html (accessed June 18, 2010).

CHAPTER 5

1. Martin Christopher, Helen Peck, and Denis A. Towill, "A Taxonomy for Selecting Global Supply Chain Strategies" (research paper, Cranfield University, UK and Cardiff University, UK, 2000).

2. Keith Bradsher, "China Tightens Grip on Rare Minerals," *New York Times,* September 1, 2009, www.nytimes.com/2009/09/01/business/global/01minerals.html (accessed May 25, 2010).

CHAPTER 6

1. Chana R. Schoenberger, "How Kmart Blew It," *Forbes.com* (January 18, 2002), www.forbes.com/2002/01/18/0118kmart_print.html (accessed May 7, 2010).

CHAPTER 7

1. Mark Schultz, "Architecture Principles: Creating the Foundation for Robust Architecture," IBM Developerworks (2007), www.ibm.com/developerworks/library/ar-archprinc/ (accessed September 29, 2009).
2. The Open Group, "Architecture Principles," TOGAF, www.opengroup.org/architecture/togaf9-doc/arch/chap23.html (accessed May 12, 2010).
3. Marcia Layton Turner, *Kmart's 10 Deadly Sins: How Incompetence Tainted an American Icon* (Hoboken, NJ: John Wiley & Sons, Inc., 2003), 36.
4. Marcia Layton Turner, *Kmart's 10 Deadly Sins: How Incompetence Tainted an American Icon* (Hoboken, NJ: John Wiley & Sons, Inc., 2003), 124.
5. Marcia Layton Turner, *Kmart's 10 Deadly Sins: How Incompetence Tainted an American Icon* (Hoboken, NJ: John Wiley & Sons, Inc., 2003), 130, 149.
6. Marcia Layton Turner, *Kmart's 10 Deadly Sins: How Incompetence Tainted an American Icon* (Hoboken, NJ: John Wiley & Sons, Inc., 2003), 127.

CHAPTER 8

1. Wal-Mart, "Sustainable Logistics Fact Sheet," www.walmartstores.com/download/2314.pdf (accessed October 13, 2009).
2. John P. Kotter, and James L. Heskett, *Corporate Culture and Performance* (New York: Free Press, 1992), 11.
3. Marcia Layton Turner, *Kmart's 10 Deadly Sins: How Incompetence Tainted an American Icon* (Hoboken, NJ: John Wiley & Sons, Inc., 2003), 137.
4. David Aquino, "Driving Supply Chain Transformation through the Chief Supply Chain Officer," *AMR Research* (March 4, 2009).
5. Marcia Layton Turner, *Kmart's 10 Deadly Sins: How Incompetence Tainted an American Icon* (Hoboken, NJ: John Wiley & Sons, Inc., 2003), 141, 157.

6. Vedanta Resources PLC, "Sustainable Development Report 2008," www. vedantaresources.com/uploads/vedantasustainabledevelopmentreport2008. pdf (accessed January 15, 2010).

7. Wal-Mart, "2009 Global Sustainability Report Executive Summary," www. walmartstores.com/download/3835.pdf (accessed August 18, 2010).

Bibliography

Andrews, Kenneth. *The Concept of Corporate Strategy*. New York: Dow Jones-Irwin, 1972.

Cohen, Shoshanah, and Joseph Roussel. *Strategic Supply Chain Management: The 5 Disciplines for Top Performance*. New York: McGraw-Hill, 2005.

David, Fred R. *Strategic Management: Concepts*. Upper Saddle River, NJ: Prentice-Hall, 1999.

Hamel, Gary. *Leading the Revolution: How to Thrive in Turbulent Times by Making Innovation a Way of Life*. Cambridge, MA: Harvard Business Press, 2002.

Harvard Business Review on Corporate Strategy. Cambridge, MA: Harvard Business School Press, 1999.

Hill, Charles W. L., and Gareth R. Jones. *Strategic Management Theory: An Integrated Approach*. New York: Houghton Mifflin, 2007.

Hrebiniak, Lawrence G. *Making Strategy Work: Leading Effective Execution and Change*. Philadelphia, PA: Wharton School Publishing, 2009.

Kotter, John P., and James L. Heskett. *Corporate Culture and Performance*. New York: Free Press, 1992.

Porter, Michael E. *Competitive Advantage: Creating and Sustaining Superior Performance*. New York: Free Press, 1985.

Ross, Jeanne W., Peter Weill, and David C. Robertson, *Enterprise Architecture as Strategy: Creating a Foundation for Business Execution*. Cambridge, MA: Harvard Business School Press, 2006.

Sehgal, Vivek. *Enterprise Supply Chain Management: Integrating Best-in-Class Processes*. Hoboken, NJ: John Wiley & Sons, 2009.

Turner, Marcia Layton. *Kmart's 10 Deadly Sins*. Hoboken, NJ: John Wiley & Sons, 2003.

About the Author

Vivek Sehgal is Senior Director of Research at Manhattan Associates, the world's foremost supply chain solutions company, with over 1,200 customers, including 17 of AMR's Top 50 supply chains, and 43 of the top 100 retailers. Prior to working with Manhattan Associates, Sehgal worked for Fortune 20 companies such as The Home Depot and General Electric in various leadership roles in their supply chain technology groups. At Manhattan Associates, he works with clients and internal development teams to define new optimization opportunities in supply chain solutions. He holds a masters degree in Industrial Engineering. His blog is available at www.supplychainmusings.com.

Index